# THE CROPLAND CRISIS

Myth or Reality?

# THE CROPLAND CRISIS

## Myth or Reality?

*Pierre R. Crosson*, editor

Published for Resources for the Future
By The Johns Hopkins University Press
Baltimore and London

Published for Resources for the Future
By The Johns Hopkins University Press, Baltimore, Maryland 21218

**Library of Congress Cataloging in Publication Data**
Main entry under title:

The Cropland crisis.

  Includes index.
  1. Land capability for agriculture—United
States—Congresses.   2. Soils—United States—Congresses. 3. Agriculture—United States—Congresses.
4. Land use, Rural—United States—Congresses.
5. Produce trade—United States—Congresses.
6. Agriculture and state—United States—Congresses.
I. Crosson, Pierre R.
S599.A1C76        333.76'0973        81-48246
ISBN 0-8018-2816-3                    AACR2
ISBN 0-8018-2817-1 (pbk.)

This book was prepared in RFF's Renewable Resources Division, Kenneth D. Frederick, director, and funded by the Rockefeller Foundation. It was edited by Ruth Haas and designed by Elsa Williams. Pierre R. Crosson is a senior fellow at Resources for the Future.

# Contributors

Martin E. Abel, *Schnittker Associates*

Bruce R. Beattie, *Department of Agricultural Economics, Montana State University*

Norman Berg, *Soil Conservation Service, U.S. Department of Agriculture*

Robert Boxley, *National Agricultural Lands Study*

Michael Brewer, *National Agricultural Lands Study*

Daniel W. Bromley, *Department of Agricultural Economics, University of Wisconsin*

Sterling Brubaker, *Resources for the Future*

Emery N. Castle, *Resources for the Future*

Marion Clawson, *Resources for the Future*

Pierre R. Crosson, *Resources for the Future*

Kenneth D. Frederick, *Resources for the Future*

Earl O. Heady, *Department of Economics, Iowa State University*

Robert G. Healy, *The Conservation Foundation*

Leroy Quance, *Economics, Statistics and Cooperatives Service, U.S. Department of Agriculture*

Vernon W. Ruttan, *Department of Agricultural and Applied Economics, University of Minnesota*

Earl R. Swanson, *Department of Agricultural Economics, University of Illinois*

# Contents

# 3
# Growth in Demand for U.S. Crop and Animal Production by 2005   *Martin E. Abel*   63

# 4
# The Potential Supply of Cropland
*Michael Brewer and Robert Boxley*   93

# 5
# Irrigation and the Adequacy of Agricultural Land   *Kenneth D. Frederick*   117

# Tables

# Foreword

Agricultural development has been one of the nation's great success stories in recent decades. Total crop production increased 97 percent between 1950 and 1981 with a 3 percent increase in cropland and a 63 percent reduction in labor use. Indeed, farmers were so productive that U.S. agricultural policy over most of this period was dominated by the issue of farm surpluses.

By the late 1970s, however, there was growing concern over the adequacy of our land base to meet future food, fiber, and energy needs. Both supply and demand factors contributed to this concern. Declining rates of productivity growth, irreversible losses of farmland to nonagricultural uses, erosion, and rising input costs (especially energy-intensive inputs such as fertilizers) were seen as long-term threats to the capacity of U.S. farmers to meet future increases in demand without sharply increasing prices. The 1970s brought an unprecedented rise in foreign demand for U.S. agricultural output and the prospect of much larger future levels of agricultural exports. Moreover, the rising costs and diminishing stock of fossil fuels raised the possibility that a growing portion of the output from U.S. farmlands might be diverted to produce liquid fuels or to substitute for the petroleum and natural gas liquid feedstocks used in the chemical industry.

To help sort out the magnitude and implications of these factors, Resources for the Future organized a conference of interested academic, government, industry, and foundation people to consider the issues surrounding the adequacy of agricultural land in the United States. The conference, "The Adequacy of Agricultural Land—

Future Problems and Policy Alternatives," was held on June 19–20, 1980 in Washington, D.C. with financial support from the Rockefeller Foundation. It was centered on six papers which examined the growth in demand for crop and animal production, technological change as it bears on the demand for agricultural land, the potential supply of cropland, the role of irrigation and its implications for the supply of and demand for agricultural land, the implications that prospective supply and demand conditions will have for the long-run economic and environmental costs of farming, and policy issues and alternatives. These papers and the comments of discussants comprise the contents of this book.

The agricultural lands conference and the resulting publication complement a variety of other work that is under way at Resources for the Future. A research program on resource and environmental issues associated with expanding agricultural production was initiated about seven years ago under the direction of Pierre Crosson. The program's first publication, *The World Food Situation: Resource and Environmental Issues in the Developing Countries and the United States,* by Crosson and Frederick, is a reconnaissance of the resource and environmental factors likely to affect food production to the end of the century. Subsequent research products, which are in various stages of RFF's publication process, include book-length manuscripts on the resource and environmental impacts of agricultural trends in the United States and a study of the past and future growth of irrigation in the seventeen western states. Related research currently under way includes an exploratory study of productivity losses caused by erosion damage in the United States, a study of the criteria for land use planning and control, and a reexamination of the federal lands which will look at recent trends and present uses and consider alternative use, management, and ownership patterns. In addition, RFF has just initiated a food and agricultural policy program under the direction of Kenneth Farrell.

Financial support for these research efforts has come from the Rockefeller Foundation, which funded some of RFF's early research on resource and environmental issues of agricultural expansion as well as the agricultural lands conference; the Richard King Mellon Foundation, which provided a generous grant for land use research; the Andrew W. Mellon Foundation, which is funding the erosion research; the Ford Foundation, which underwrote some of the early agriculture research and has provided a start-up grant for the agricultural policy program; and the Environmental Protection Agency's Environmental Research Laboratory in Athens, Georgia, which has supported the research on resource and environmental problems of agriculture in the United States. The support of all these institutions is gratefully acknowledged.

December 1981                                 Kenneth D. Frederick
                                              Director
                                              Renewable Resources Division

# Preface

Approximately three decades ago, Nobel Laureate Theodore W. Schultz published an article in the *Economic Journal* entitled, "The Declining Economic Importance of Agricultural Land."[1] He introduced his article by noting that Ricardo had assigned a major role in economics to agricultural land. Schultz acknowledged that, given the circumstances that prevailed at the time of Ricardo, this was most appropriate, but he also noted that R. F. Harrod's influential work in 1948 entitled *Toward a Dynamic Economics* said (quoting Harrod), "I propose to discard the law of diminishing returns from the land as a primary detriment in a progressive economy—I discard it only because in our particular context it appears that its influence may be quantitatively unimportant."

In his article, Schultz attempted to test empirically whether diminishing returns to land could be set aside safely in the contemporary scene. To do this he attempted to assess the validity of two propositions:

1. A declining proportion of the aggregate inputs of the community is required to produce (or to acquire) farm products.
2. Of the inputs employed to produce farm products, the proportion represented by land is not an increasing one, despite the

*This preface is based on introductory remarks made in opening the RFF conference on The Adequacy of Agricultural Land, June 19, 1980.

[1] T. W. Schultz, "The Declining Economic Importance of Agricultural Land," *Economic Journal*, December 1951, pp. 725–740.

recombination of inputs in farming to use less human effort relative to other inputs, including land.

Schultz relied mainly upon U.S. data in assessing the validity of the two propositions. He concluded that the empirical evidence supported the two propositions, but he closed his article with the words:

> We realize land is not for food alone. It is important for other purposes in the community and the economy, purposes which we have neglected throughout this study. The conclusion, however, is firm; the economic developments that have characterized Western communities since Ricardo's time have resulted in empirical production possibilities and in a community choice which has relaxed the niggardliness of nature. As a consequence of these developments, agricultural land has been declining markedly in its importance. Will it continue to do so? Existing circumstances in the United States indicate a strong affirmative answer. Nor is the end in sight. But can existing high food drain communities realize a similar development? As yet we do not know (p. 740).

Despite the fact that almost three decades ago T. W. Schultz thought that agricultural land would decline even more in economic performance, it is my distinct impression that people generally now hold a contrary view. The loss of agricultural land to nonagricultural uses receives considerable press coverage; politicians make speeches about it and pass laws which have the stated objective of discouraging it. It is deplored by government officials, and a National Agricultural Lands Study was conducted within the federal establishment and published in early 1981. A principal conclusion was that preservation of agricultural land is a major national concern. When public hearings were held throughout Oregon a few years ago on land use, concern was expressed about the preservation of agricultural land in every part of the state and in rural and urban areas alike. Since 1950, about the time of Schultz's article, the price of agricultural land has risen much more rapidly than the consumer price index and this seems to provide substance to the concern.

Why is this? People collectively usually do not worry about possible shortages and certainly do not typically take actions to prevent them before they develop. Perhaps the possibility of insufficient or high-priced food is the explanation. However, more than land is required for food production and it is not clear why it should receive such special treatment. Perhaps it is a desire to maintain flexibility—a desire to protect ourselves against uncertainty. Or possibly it is because we want to have some activity near our urban areas that does not entail a highly dense population.

The conference on which this book is based was organized to provide an understanding of the contribution of agricultural land to agricultural production now and in the foreseeable future. Even though Schultz has not been refuted to this time, it does not follow that his thesis will forever be supported by events, and the conference was designed to provide information on the future role of agricultural land in our society. Pierre Crosson, a senior fellow in the Renewable Resources Division at Resources for the Future, with funds provided by the Rockefeller Foundation, organized and managed the conference and edited this volume. I believe a thoughtful reading will demonstrate that he succeeded in adding significantly to our understanding of this complex subject. We find here a systematic treatment of the domestic and international demands for agricultural products, consideration of probable trends in agricultural land use, and development of the possibilities of technical change, as well as discussion of policy measures and issues.

The results tend to be contrary to prevailing popular opinion. Yet, as Crosson notes in chapter 1, part of the difference between the conference results and prevailing opinion may be because of a difference in objectives—the conference reported on here was concerned primarily with the contribution of land to agricultural production while many people, quite properly, have other reasons for keeping land in agricultural use. Yet public policy will not be well served if these other objectives are justified on the basis of inadequate information about the relation of land availability to agricultural output.

December 1981                                        Emery N. Castle

# Acknowledgments

The conference at which the papers in this volume were presented was made possible by a generous grant from the Rockefeller Foundation, for which we are most appreciative.

Thanks go also to those who contributed papers and comments (their names are in the list of contributors) and to the approximately seventy-five people who attended the conference. The latter represented agricultural and forestry interests; conservationists; federal, state, and local governments; foundations; and academia. Their probing questions and comments on issues raised in the papers and by the discussants contributed much to the lively exchanges which marked the conference.

A number of people at RFF, in addition to those who gave papers, made valuable contributions to the conference. The able editorial hand of Ruth Haas is unseen but present throughout this volume. She could rightly be listed as co-editor. Elsa Williams designed and oversaw the production of the attractive brochure which was used to advertise the conference. And Maybelle Frashure took responsibility for managing the typing of the manuscript as well as for much of the logistics.

December 1981                                     Pierre R. Crosson

# 1

# The Long-Term Adequacy of Agricultural Land in the United States

*Pierre R. Crosson*

## Introduction

Will the United States have enough agricultural land to meet rising demands for food and fiber over the next two to three decades and beyond? This question, or some closely related variant of it, was the subject of five major conferences held between November 1979 and July 1980. It was addressed in an important study by the U.S. Department of Agriculture (USDA) and was the principal focus of another interagency study by the federal government, spearheaded by the USDA and the Council on Environmental Quality.[1]

Three events appear to have triggered this renewed concern with an old topic: (1) a rapid increase in U.S. grain and soybean exports since the early 1970s, which expanded cropland by 50–60 million acres; (2) an apparent reduction in growth of crop yields over the

[1]The conferences were that of Resources for the Future, June 1980, at which the papers in this volume were presented; the National Conference on Soil Conservation Policies, November 1979, sponsored by the Soil Conservation Society of America, in cooperation with the National Association of Conservation Districts and the U.S. Department of Agriculture; Conference on the Farm and the City, April 1980, sponsored by the American Assembly; Conference on Rural Conservation, June 1980, sponsored jointly by the National Association of Conservation Districts and the National Trust for Historic Preservation; Conference on the Future of American Agriculture as a Strategic Resource, July 1980, sponsored by the Conservation Foundation. The studies are by the U.S. Department of Agriculture, *RCA Appraisal 1980*, Review Draft, Part II (no date), and the *National Agricultural Lands Study, Final Report*, U.S. Department of Agriculture and Council on Environmental Quality, 1981.

I am grateful for helpful comments from Bruce Beattie, Ruth Haas, Earl Heady, Robert Healy, Lawrence Libby, Paul Portney, Philip Raup, and Neil Sampson.

1

same period; (3) a report by the USDA that losses of agricultural land
to nonagricultural uses accelerated in 1967–75 compared with the
preceding decade.[2] Taken together, these events seem to portend
steeply rising pressure on the nation's supply of agricultural land,
calling into question our ability to meet rising foreign demands for
food and fiber, if not domestic demands.

While the question of the adequacy of agricultural land is much
discussed, there is no consensus. Views range from the apocalyptic
["The 1980s may be known as the decade the earth ran out of earth,"
according to one of the speakers at a conference sponsored jointly
by the National Association of Conservation Districts (NACD) and the
National Trust for Historic Preservation (NTHP)] to the notion that
the current loss of agricultural land to nonagricultural uses is a matter
of national concern that calls for action at the federal level (the
National Agricultural Lands Study), to the position that while one
should not be complacent about the agricultural land issue, it is not a
matter of pressing national concern. Among contributors at the RFF
conference, the prevailing view, as reflected in the papers in this
volume, was closer to the last of those described than to either of the
other two.

None of the conference papers presents a consensus on the adequacy of agricultural land, and I do not attempt one here. My own
view, based on the analysis in chapter 6, is that the real economic costs
of agricultural land are likely to rise and that, joined with rising real
costs of energy, fertilizer, and water, and relatively slow growth in
productivity, the result would be rising real costs of agricultural production. Moreover, the conversion to crops of much land now in
pasture, forest, and range could cause a substantial increase in erosion. With the economic costs of production and the social costs of
erosion both rising, an increase in concern about the adequacy of
agricultural land is likely. However, I do not have the same sense of
urgency about the issue as that expressed in the National Agricultural
Lands Study or at the NACD/NTHP conference. For reasons discussed later, the judgment about rising economic and social costs is
subject to high uncertainty. Moreover, the problem, if it develops, will
emerge gradually enough to permit corrective action before there
is a crisis.

[2]R. Dideriksen, A. R. Hidlebaugh, and K. O. Schmude, *Potential Cropland Study*, U.S.
Department of Agriculture, Soil Conservation Service (Washington, D.C., 1977).

Why is it so difficult to reach consensus about the adequacy of agricultural land? There appear to be two principal reasons. One is that the discussants are concerned with different aspects of adequacy without clearly recognizing this. They seem to be addressing the same question, but in fact they are not. The second reason is that even when the discussants agree on a definition of adequacy, they differ in how they read the evidence over the long term. By defining the question more precisely, it should be possible to improve the focus of the discussion and eliminate some of the differences in conclusions. Where the latter reflect differing readings of the evidence, however, equally competent and disinterested people may still come to different conclusions.

## Framing the Question

Most of the discussion of the adequacy of agricultural land seems to focus on the question of whether the United States will have enough land to meet rising demands for food and fiber. This way of framing the question implicitly, if not explicitly, treats land as a factor of production. It is an essential factor of course, but not the only one. Indeed, in the United States other factors together contribute about three times as much as land to total agricultural production. This being the case, the "adequacy" of land cannot be determined independently of the cost and productivity of the land relative to the costs and productivities of other factors. If pressure on the supply of land makes it increasingly scarce, causing its price to rise relative to those of other productive factors, or if the productivity of the land declines (e.g., because of erosion), then farmers will have an incentive to substitute other factors for land in production. This will restrain the increases in the price of land and offset at least some of the decline in productivity that otherwise would occur.

On the other hand, if pressure on the supply of land rises rapidly or if possibilities for substituting other factors for land are narrowly constrained, a rise in the price of land or a decline in its productivity could result in a significant increase in the cost of agricultural production. In this case, those concerned about agricultural land would most likely agree that there was indeed a problem of adequacy, although they still might differ as to its seriousness.

If the discussion were framed in the context of the costs of production to the nation, and land was considered only one among many factors of production, there still could be differences but that element sometimes giving the discussion the character of a "dialogue of the deaf" would be absent, or at least much less prominent. This element is present in large part because some of those ostensibly concerned with the adequacy of land as a factor of agricultural production are really concerned about it as a source of amenity values, such as open spaces.[3] Preservation of agricultural land also preserves rural life styles, an objective important to many, not excluding urban dwellers. The Jeffersonian concept of the yeoman farmer as the backbone of a democratic society and best guarantee against government tyranny has by no means been swept away by the urbanization of American life. It is significant that some of the most vigorous public agitation about preservation of agricultural land and the most ambitious policies to achieve it are in states which contribute relatively little to the nation's agricultural production capacity, for example, New York, New Jersey, Maryland, and Oregon. Among major pro-ducing areas—California, the Cornbelt, the Plains states, and the Mississippi Delta—only California has adopted measures that have the sweep or force of those undertaken in these states.

If the concern with the adequacy of agricultural land is really a concern for amenity values, even the strongest arguments that land preservation is unnecessary to maintain productive capacity will not be persuasive. Amenity values and production values are not the same, and demonstrations that one set of values can be preserved will be irrelevant if the real concern is with the other, and it appears threatened.

If much of the concern about agricultural land is really over amenity values rather than productive capacity, why is the discussion typically cast in terms of capacity? Why are the amenity and capacity issues not treated separately, as they should be? One cannot be sure, but two reasons come to mind. One is muddled thinking, a simple failure to recognize that agricultural land provides both commodity and amenity values, but not in fixed proportions. The other reason is that

[3]Some who argue for preservation of agricultural land to protect productive capacity do so to cloak purely private interests (e.g., some farmers in metropolitan areas who seek to have their land taxed at its value in agriculture rather than at its value in urban uses). While this interest is significant, concern with the public interest clearly is of major importance in any discussion of the adequacy of agricultural land. This concern is the subject of this essay.

maintenance of capacity is more likely to enlist political support than maintenance of amenity values. This is likely to be particularly compelling if the objective is to shape national policies for agricultural land preservation. Threats to our ability to feed ourselves and meet our felt obligations to a hungry world are more likely to mobilize a political response to preserve agricultural land than threats to the pleasures of a Sunday afternoon drive through the countryside.

Even when there is no confusion between the amenity and capacity issues, there is often a failure to recognize that when the focus is on capacity the issue is the *economic* availability of land, not its physical availability. After the USDA's Conservation Needs Inventory of 1967 (CNI) revealed that there were 264 million acres of land in forest, range, and pasture with the physical capability of being used for cropland, that figure frequently was cited as evidence that losses of cropland to nonagricultural uses posed no threat to long-run productive capacity.[4] Such "evidence" proves nothing, however, in the absence of information about the economic and environmental costs of converting the land to crops.[5]

The failure to reckon the availability of agricultural land by the economic and environmental costs of bringing it into production is part of a more general failure to recognize that for useful discussion of resource management decisions, capacity must be defined in economic, not physical terms. In virtually every conceivable circumstance, output of any particular commodity or of any sector of the economy can be increased at some cost; the longer the time horizon, the greater the increase in output for a given cost increase. Situations in which no additional output is possible because of absolute physical limits to the availability of one or more resources are so rare as to be of little practical importance. Where they occur, they can most appro-

---

[4]The USDA's National Resources Inventory (NRI) of 1977, an update of the CNI, found only 127 million acres with high-to-medium potential for conversion to cropland. The discrepancy between this and the CNI's 264 million acres cannot be explained by conversion of land to crops between 1967 and 1977, and in fact no explanation is given in the NRI. Some of the difference, however, probably reflects the fact that the NRI takes account of costs of converting the land to crops, although the costs are not specified in detail. Brewer and Boxley and Crosson discuss the NRI estimates of potential cropland. See also Robert Healy's discussion of Brewer and Boxley's paper.

[5]Environmental costs here mean those resulting directly from agricultural production, making them analogous to economic production costs: erosion, fertilizer and pesticide pollution, and soil and water salinity resulting from irrigation. So defined, environmental costs do not include loss of amenity values.

priately be treated for analytical purposes as polar cases of the economic definition of capacity where marginal costs of production become infinite.

It is clear that the country's ability to increase production of food and fiber will not be constrained by physical limits to the amount of land that can be turned to agricultural production, but such a statement is irrelevant to judging whether our supply of agricultural land will be adequate. The sooner such statements are eliminated from the discussion of adequacy, the sooner it can focus on the relevant issues: the economic and environmental costs of meeting demands on the land.

Acceptance of the economic concept of the capacity of agricultural land carries a cost of its own, however. It means that judgments about adequacy are likely to be ambiguous. Clearly, if demands on the land can be met with no increase in economic and environmental costs, all could agree that the supply of land is adequate. But if these costs rise, judgments become more difficult. Any increase in cost is less favorable than no increase, but few would argue that any increase demonstrates that the supply of land is inadequate. How much must costs increase before serious questions of adequacy would arise? There is no clear answer to this question, but that is true for any resource. Rising costs raise questions of resource adequacy when they begin to disrupt achievement of widely held social goals, such as improving the standard of living. The escalating prices of art may be distressing to museum managers and other collectors, but they cause no concern among governments or the publics they represent. A 10 percent increase in the price of food, however, is quite another matter.

We thus can expect no unambiguous answer to the question of the adequacy of agricultural land. However, it will help clarify discussion of the issue if the question is defined properly.

**Reading the Evidence**

Even where distinctions between capacity and amenity issues are properly made, and people agree on how to frame the question of adequacy, they still may arrive at sharply different answers because they read the evidence differently.

When the issue is capacity, opinions depend upon judgments about three future events: (1) the prospective growth of demand for food and fiber; (2) the prospective growth of per-acre yields; and (3) the supply of land, where supply is defined as the amount of land that can be brought into production at specified economic and environmental costs. The faster the expected increase in demand, the slower the expected increase in yields, and the more inelastic the supply of land, the more likely the perception of a shortage.

This point is vividly illustrated by the contrasting projections of production growth in the National Agricultural Lands Study (NALS) and by Martin Abel in this volume (chapter 3). The key difference between the two sets of projections is in exports. The NALS projects an annual growth of 4.5 to 6.5 percent in total agricultural exports between 1980 and 2000. Abel's projection of grain and soybean exports to 2005 implies an annual growth of 2.3 percent between that year and 1980. Since most of the growth in exports will be in grains and soybeans, Abel's projections for these commodities imply less than 2.3 percent growth in total agricultural exports. Both the NALS and Abel assume constant real prices.

This difference in growth of export demand is the main reason for the difference between the NALS conclusion that the adequacy of agricultural land is now a crucial national concern and my own—which is that it is not. (My assumptions about trends in yields are not essentially different from those of the NALS. I am somewhat more optimistic about the supply of cropland, but this difference is small compared with the difference in export projections.) If I believed that exports were likely to grow as fast as projected by the NALS, I would share their view that the country faces a serious shortage of agricultural land.

Similar differences may—in fact, do—arise in interpreting the evidence on trends in crop yields,[6] and information about the economic and environmental costs of bringing more land under crops is so meager that widely differing estimates are equally plausible.

## Key Areas of Uncertainty

My relatively optimistic conclusion about the capacity issue was derived from analysis of the growth of demand for grains and soybeans (chapter 3), of trends in technology and yields (chapter 2), and

[6]There is the suggestion of such a difference in the chapters by Heady and Crosson in this volume.

of the potential supply of cropland (chapters 4 and 5). The conclusions in each chapter represent the authors' best judgments of what
the future will look like, but all of them recognize that the future is
uncertain and their conclusions perhaps wrong. Consequently, tentativeness pervades each of the discussions.

In the balance of this section I deal with the key uncertainties as I
perceive them. I suspect the authors of the rest of the chapters in this
volume would share my perceptions in most respects, but they are not
responsible for the views I express here.

*Growth of U.S. Exports*

Both Abel and Heady make it clear that foreign demand is the
dynamic element in the growth of total demand for U.S. agricultural
production. Because the income elasticity of domestic demand for
food and fiber is low, the growth of per capita income adds little to the
growth of domestic demand; neither does domestic population
growth. Foreign demand, however, has increased rapidly since the
early 1970s, reflecting both population and income growth abroad
and the strong competitive position of the United States in world
markets for grains and soybeans.

Virtually all observers expect continued growth in world income,
but the sharp increase in energy prices since 1973 and the prospect for
continued increases make predictions about future growth rates uncertain. The easy confidence of the 1950s and 1960s in this regard no
longer holds.

Recent declines in population fertility in the developing countries
add to the uncertainty about the increases in demand. If these declines
portend a slower growth in LDC population than anyone thought
likely only a few years ago, the contribution of population growth to
demand for U.S. food exports would be less than expected. On the
other hand, slower population growth in the LDCs might make it
possible for these countries to achieve faster increases in per capita
income, stimulating more rapid growth in demand. The relationship
between growth in population and per capita income is not well
understood, however, so it is unclear what net effect slower population growth in the LDCs would have on growth in demand for food.

Food production and demand are more interdependent in the
LDCs than in the developed countries because a much higher proportion of LDC income originates in agriculture. If the increase in food

production lags, the growth of income and hence of demand for food will also be restrained. A healthy rate of growth in LDC food production, however, is quite consistent with a sustained rise in food imports, at least for several decades. Because per capita income is low, the income elasticity of demand for food is relatively high. Per capita income growth of 3.0 to 3.5 percent annually, combined with a population growth of some 2 percent, could easily result in a 3.5 percent annual growth in food demand. Hence, even if food production were to increase 3 percent annually—a healthy rate—food imports would rise.

Leaders of the People's Republic of China (PRC) and the Soviet Union would deny any similarity between their policies, but for foreign observers the food policies of both countries have much in common: opaqueness and resulting uncertainty about future food imports. There is evidence that both countries have decided to upgrade the diets of their people and are prepared to increase imports substantially to achieve this, if necessary. The main thrust of food policy in both countries, however, is to increase domestic production, imports being viewed as a last resort when domestic production falls short. In the Soviet Union this has happened often enough in recent years to produce wide fluctuations in grain imports. Chinese production either is less variable or we see less evidence of it.

In both countries it is not easy for outsiders to discern the long-term prospects for growth in food production or the implications that food policies have for imports. One can create plausible scenarios in which both countries would import many tens of millions of tons of grains and soybeans by the first decade of the next century. Other scenarios with imports no greater than the averages of recent years are equally plausible. Everything depends not only on productive performance in each country but also on attitudes toward being dependent on external sources for food. Inevitably, there is high uncertainty surrounding prediction of both factors.

Grain imports by the European Community were stable for many years, but recently they have begun to decline and grain exports to increase. This pattern reflects the stimulus given to EC grain production by the Community's policy of high price supports. There is evidence, however, that the high cost of the policy is beginning to build pressure to modify it, reducing the spread between world and Community grain prices. A significant move in this direction could result in marked expansion of Community grain imports as lower internal prices stimulate domestic demand and restrain domestic supply by forcing out marginal producers. A change in the Community's grain price policy thus could significantly boost world trade in grain. Whether such a change will occur, or when, and its magnitude are all highly uncertain. Agricultural interests within the Community continue to wield much influence, particularly in France and Germany, and national security interests also are perceived to be involved. Part of the argument for protection of Community food producers is to assure a minimum supply in the event imports are cut off, for whatever reason.

Japan emerged in the 1970s as a major importer of feedgrains and soybeans, reflecting high and rising incomes of Japanese consumers, a growing preference for meat in their diet, and a negligible domestic capacity to produce feedgrains and soybeans. Still, by the end of the 1970s, per capita meat consumption in Japan was only a small fraction of what it is in the United States. If Japanese per capita consumption were to approach the U.S. level over the next several decades, world trade in feedgrains and soybeans would grow significantly faster than if Japanese consumption remained at present levels or increased only moderately. Which is the more likely outcome? There is no basis for confident prediction, which adds yet more uncertainty to judgments about trends in the world food trade.

Finally, the future competitive position of the United States in world food markets is uncertain. As indicated earlier, Abel's projections of production probably would entail rising real costs, reflecting the failure of agricultural productivity to keep up with the rise in real prices of farm inputs, including land. Aside from the uncertainty about trends in productivity, which is dealt with later, it is not clear that higher production costs would necessarily erode the U.S. position in world agricultural markets. Much of the projected increase in costs is owed to the expected rise in real prices of energy and fertilizer and increased scarcity of water for irrigation. If these conditions occur in the United States, they are likely to prevail in other countries as well. If they do, the U.S. position would not be weakened unless productivity growth in other countries exceeded that of the United States.

There is evidence that in the LDCs the marginal productivity of fertilizer is higher than in the United States, which suggests that these countries could absorb rising fertilizer prices more readily than U.S. farmers. The evidence is not conclusive, however, and in any case many LDC farmers may not have easy access to fertilizer even if its productivity is high. Import controls, for example, may be imposed to protect a balance of payments imperiled by rising energy and fertilizer prices. In short, rising real costs of food production in the United States have uncertain implications for U.S. food exports.

### Trends in Total Productivity and Yields

There has been much discussion of total productivity and crop yield trends in recent years, and much concern that growth of both was slowing, or even plateauing, as Earl Heady expresses it. The evidence indicates that both total productivity and crop yields grew at slower percentage rates from 1972 to 1979 than from 1950 to 1972. Crop yields also grew more slowly in absolute annual amount after 1972, but total productivity growth, so measured, increased slightly.

The evidence for yields is unequivocal in showing slower growth after 1972, although, as Heady notes, there is no convincing indication that yields have plateaued. He argues further that yields and total productivity in the 1970s were so affected by fluctuations in the weather as to obscure trend behavior. His conclusion is that there is not enough information yet to determine confidently whether the behavior of yields and total productivity in the 1970s marks the beginning of new trends or is only a temporary deviation from the trends established in the two decades or so ending in the early 1970s.

Heady's conclusion implies great uncertainty about the growth of the demand for cropland. As noted in the preceding section, if the growth of productivity does not keep pace with input prices, costs of production will rise, perhaps restricting the growth of production. Other things remaining the same, this also would restrict the growth of demand for cropland.

Uncertainty about yield growth, however, has the most dramatic impact on projections of the demand for cropland. In chapter 6 I projected yields of grains and soybeans to grow 1.2 percent annually 1977–79 to 2005 and concluded that with this yield growth farmers would demand 292 million acres of land to meet Abel's projected production of grains and soybeans in 2005. This would be 62 million acres more than they used to produce these crops in 1977–79.

The 1.2 percent figure is my best judgment about the prospective growth of grain and soybean yields, but given the present uncertainty about yield trends, plausible cases can be made for both higher and lower projections. If grain and soybean yields grow at 2.0 percent annually instead of 1.2 percent, farmers would demand only 237 million acres for these crops in 2005, 55 million acres less than with 1.2 percent growth and only 7 million acres more than in 1977–79. Two percent growth of grain and soybean yields evidently implies significantly less pressure on the agricultural land base than 1.2 percent growth.

If grain and soybean yields grow 1.0 percent annually, however, farmers would demand 310 million acres for grains and soybeans in 2005, 80 million acres more than in 1977–79. If I had projected a 1.0 percent growth of grain and soybean yields, I would have concluded that accommodation of Abel's production projection would entail economic costs of land in 2005 significantly higher than at present and significantly higher than with 1.2 percent yield growth. I would view this outcome as raising a more serious question about the adequacy of agricultural land than is suggested by 1.2 percent growth of yields.

Judgments about the adequacy of agricultural land thus are powerfully influenced by what one thinks about trends in crop yields. Given the present uncertainty about these trends, equally plausible arguments can be made for any figure within the 1.0 to 2.0 percent range. Until a consensus can be formed around a figure in a more narrow range, knowledgeable people will continue to differ sharply in their judgments about adequacy.

It probably will take several years at a minimum for such a consensus to form. Additional years of yield experience are needed, especially years not strongly affected by weather. The sharp weather-induced drop in yields in 1980 will not help to clarify yield trends. More information is also needed about the relationship of agricultural research to increases in yield and total productivity. In particular, we need to know more about the public and private decision processes leading to investments in research, about the yield and productivity increases that can be expected per unit of research effort, and about the length of time between investments in research and observable results at the farm level. As Vernon Ruttan points out in his comment on Heady's chapter, we do not know enough about these matters to make confident statements about future trends in yields and productivity. There appears to be no early resolution of the present uncertainty about these trends.

*The Supply of Cropland*

The principal uncertainties about the supply of cropland concern the economic and environmental costs of converting land now in pasture, forest, and range to crops and the amount of present and potential cropland likely to be converted to nonagricultural uses.[7] The USDA's National Resources Inventory (NRI) of 1977 showed 127 million acres of land with medium-to-high potential for conversion to cropland. The Potential Cropland Study, done by the USDA in 1975, showed 111 million acres with medium-to-high conversion potential, and the Conservation Needs Inventory of 1967 showed 264 million acres with physical characteristics necessary for conversion (i.e., land in capability classes I–III).

The most recent estimates, those of the NRI, are for land that could be converted to crops under price and yield conditions prevailing in 1976. The usefulness of this information is limited in several ways. The estimates were compiled by observing whether land of comparable class in the vicinity had been converted to crops in 1976. That is, if plots A and B were in comparable land classes and in the same vicinity and plot A had been converted to crops in 1976, then it was assumed that plot B also was convertible. In his comment on Brewer and Boxley, Robert Healy points out that additional information about plots A and B is necessary before B can be counted as convertible. The owner of B may be more deeply committed to noncrop uses of his land than the owner of plot A. Indeed, it is legitimate to ask if plot B were convertible to crops under price and yield conditions prevailing in 1976, why was it not converted?

The NRI estimate of potential cropland also is of limited usefulness because there is no certainty that future price and yield conditions will duplicate those of 1976. The NRI estimate in effect gives a point on the supply curve of cropland when what is really needed is the curve itself. Studies of conversion potential in the Mississippi delta and Iowa develop supply curves for those areas.[8] This work provides useful

---

[7]Kenneth Frederick's chapter deals with the future supply of irrigated land. While that future is by no means perfectly clear, the uncertainty about it is less than for land conversion costs and losses of land to nonagricultural uses. I also believe the uncertainty about irrigation is less consequential for judgments about the adequacy of agricultural land than uncertainty about the other two factors affecting the supply of land.

[8]See the references in table 6-4 in this volume.

insights but says nothing about potential cropland in other areas of the country.

The USDA's land use inventories of 1958, 1967, and 1975 indicated that conversions of rural land to urban and other nonagricultural uses accelerated from 1.9 million acres per year in 1958–67 to 2.9 million acres per year in 1967–75. This apparent increase in the amount of agricultural land converted annually to essentially irreversible non-agricultural uses sparked much of the increased concern about the adequacy of agricultural land.

One's expectations about the future rate of conversion of potential cropland to nonagricultural uses can make a substantial difference in expectations about pressure on the supply of cropland. Drawing on the work of Brewer and Boxley, I assumed that conversion would occur at a rate of 750,000 acres per year from 1977 to 2005, a total of 21 million acres. Many of those most concerned about the future adequacy of agricultural land appear to assume that the 1967–75 conversion rate of 2.9 million acres will continue indefinitely for a total of about 80 million acres from 1977 to 2005. If the NRI's 127 million acres is taken as a rough estimate of potential cropland and increased net demand for cropland is projected at about 50 million acres (as is done in chapter 6), then conversion of 21 million acres to nonagricultural uses implies substantially less pressure on the supply of cropland than conversion of 80 million acres to these uses. I suspect that for many the difference would be decisive in judging whether or not the country faces a problem of adequate agricultural land.

*Environmental Costs*

The principal environmental costs of agricultural production are those resulting from erosion, from salinity produced by irrigation, and from unintended effects of fertilizers and pesticides. In my judgment, erosion is presently and will continue to be the most important of these costs. For this reason, and because of space limitations, I deal only with erosion in chapter 6.

Little is known about these environmental costs at present, and the ability to predict them over several decades is even more limited. The annual costs of cleaning reservoirs and other water bodies of sediment resulting from erosion are known, but we are ignorant of other off-farm costs of erosion, for example, the loss of recreational values because of silt-laden waters. In its work under the Resources Conservation Act (RCA) the USDA calculated the long-run costs of lost productivity caused by erosion and found them to be significant.[9] The USDA is quite aware of the inadequacies of the data on which these estimates are based and regards them as no more than crude first approximations. The fact is that little is known about the parameters defining the relationship between erosion and productivity of the land; and even if the relationship could be specified, the values of the parameters doubtless would vary widely from place to place, depending upon soil type, depth of topsoil, nature of the underlying parent material, climate variables and so on.

The NRI estimates the amount of erosion by state and land class in 1977, although these estimates are based on application of the universal soil loss equation, not on actual measurement of erosion. Nonetheless, they provide a base from which to think about future erosion. That future is quite unpredictable, however, because of uncertainty about the spread of conservation tillage, which reduces erosion by 50 to 90 percent compared with conventional (moldboard plow) tillage. It currently is used on roughly 25 percent of the nation's cropland. Studies done at Iowa State University for RFF (reported in chapter 6) indicate that the future amount of erosion will be significantly affected by the amount and kinds of conservation tillage adopted by American farmers.

The prospective spread of conservation tillage is indeterminate for two reasons. (1) Too little is known about the economics of the technology to be able to confidently predict adoption rates by farmers. (2) Conservation tillage relies more heavily than conventional tillage on herbicides to control weeds. While current evidence suggests that herbicides have relatively minor effects on the environment, the evidence is incomplete. As more information becomes available, controls on the use of herbicides may greatly restrict the spread of conservation tillage.

Thus uncertainty about the environmental costs of erosion and how the amount of erosion may change over the next several decades imparts additional tentativeness to any judgments about the ability of agricultural land to meet anticipated needs.

[9]I counted erosion-induced losses of productivity as environmental costs (chapter 6). In his comment, Earl Swanson observes that these losses perhaps should be counted as economic costs since they show up as reduced yields. To maintain consistency with my original treatment, however, I here count losses of productivity because of erosion as environmental costs.

## The Agricultural Lands Conference

The RFF conference on agricultural lands posed the issue of adequacy in terms of the rising economic and environmental costs of large-scale conversions of pasture, forest, and rangelands to crops and the failure to fully reflect these costs in land use decisions.

The announcement of the conference and the selection of papers made it clear that the conference would address the capacity, not the amenity aspect of the adequacy issue, and that capacity was denoted by economic, not physical limits.

Thus the conference was designed to examine the factors underlying the supply of and demand for agricultural land and associated policy issues. Earl Heady's paper sets the tone of the conference, discussing factors affecting both the demand and supply sides of agricultural land markets, and placing the adequacy issue in the context of the more general discussion of resource adequacy that predates Malthus and has its most recent voice in *The Limits to Growth*. Heady treats two main themes: (1) the role of technology in removing constraints on the supply of land; (2) the crucial role of exports in stimulating derived demand for land. He stresses the extraordinary success of technology, especially since the end of World War II, in providing substitutes for land, particularly cheap fertilizer, energy and water, higher yielding crop varieties, improved management practices, and advances in animal husbandry. While acknowledging that fertilizer, energy, and water will be more expensive in the future than in the past, Heady is optimistic that the agricultural research establishment, taking its cue from these emerging scarcities, will develop new land-saving technologies.

Heady raises two principal issues with respect to exports. In a discussion which is sure to be controversial, he asks why the United States is bound to satisfy the food demands of already well-fed countries if doing so uncomfortably stresses our land resources. Heady does not explore the interventionist implications of this argument or the political firestorm it would provoke. But the argument should arouse the interest of those who believe a prime goal of U.S. agricultural policy should be maximum expansion of exports.

The second key export issue Heady raises concerns responses abroad to emerging price and cost trends in U.S. and world agriculture. Heady argues that should increasing scarcity of land and other resources in the United States push feedgrain prices higher, world demand would shift toward substitution of plant protein, in the form of food grains, for animal protein, thus reducing pressure on U.S. land resources. He also sees rising energy and fertilizer prices in the developing countries as having implications for the demand for land in the United States. If these higher prices slow the growth of food production in those countries, the likely result would be faster growth in demand for U.S. exports and increased pressure on the land. Heady asserts that this indirect effect of higher energy and fertilizer prices may be more important for the demand for land than the direct effect.

Since the growth of agricultural production is a key factor in the growth of demand for agricultural land, Martin Abel was asked to develop projections of the main land-using crops for which demand is likely to increase: feedgrains, wheat, soybeans, and rice. These are presented and discussed in chapter 3. Because the main stimulus to growth is export demand, Abel devotes a major share of his paper to the prospective expansion of world trade in these commodities. U.S. exports are then derived from projections of the U.S. share of world trade.

Abel also gives considerable attention to the growth of domestic demand for corn as a sweetener and as feedstock for ethanol production. The projected growth in demand for corn as a sweetener reflects a recent technological breakthrough which permits production of corn sweetener in crystalline form, making it directly competitive with sugar. Abel believes that ethanol production based on corn could reach 2 to 4 billion gallons per year by 2005, which would absorb 20 to 40 million metric tons of corn. In 1978–79, about 1.5 million metric tons of corn went into ethanol production. While presenting this projection of ethanol demand as his best estimate, Abel notes four reasons why actual demand may fall short of the projection: (1) demand for corn as a feedgrain may force up its price, weakening the competitive position of ethanol; (2) sweet sorghum or sugar cane may prove more efficient as feedstocks for ethanol than corn; (3) by 1985 or 1990, technological breakthroughs may make cellulose a more economically attractive feedstock for ethanol production than corn; (4) by 2005, methanol produced from coal gasification may prove more efficient as a liquid fuel than ethanol.

Abel emphasizes the interdependence of the demand for corn as an ethanol feedstock and as a sweetener and the demand for soybeans as a protein supplement in animal feed. The processes using corn for ethanol and sweetener production leave approximately 630 pounds of residue for every metric ton of corn processed. The protein content of the residue is only about one-half that of an equivalent amount of soybean meal, and the quality of the residue protein is not as good as that in soybean meal because it lacks certain essential amino acids. Nonetheless, with price adjustments for these differences, the residue can compete effectively with soybeans. Consequently, the large-scale expansion of sweetener and ethanol production based on corn could substantially weaken the growth of demand for soybeans. This is reflected in Abel's projections of U.S. soybean production, which are well below what is suggested by the production trend of the past fifteen years or the trend in the prospective growth in demand for protein feed supplements.

Michael Brewer and Robert Boxley (chapter 4) and Kenneth Frederick (chapter 5) deal with issues bearing on the supply of agricultural land. Brewer was director of research for the National Agricultural Lands Study and Boxley was a senior staff economist on the study. Their paper reports major findings of the NALS with respect to the supply of agricultural land. One of these, which is of particular importance for interpreting trends in the supply of agricultural land, is that land use statistics, in the words of Brewer and Boxley, "are fragmentary, incomplete, and often appear conflicting." One of the purposes of the NALS was to overcome some of these difficulties. While Brewer and Boxley report some progress in this regard, they conclude that much remains to be done.

As indicated earlier, data collected by the U.S. Department of Agriculture showed that between 1967 and 1975 an average of 2.9 million acres of agricultural land was converted annually to urban and other irreversible nonagricultural uses. Brewer and Boxley show that only 675,000 acres of cropland were converted annually between 1967 and 1975, the rest of the 2.9 million acres coming from pasture, range, and forest (1,362,000 acres) and a miscellaneous category of "other" rural land (875,00 acres). There was no indication of how much of the land converted from pasture, range, forest, and "other" uses may have had potential for conversion to cropland. However, in a technical paper prepared for the NALS,[10] Boxley reports that USDA analysts, draw-

<hr />

[10]Robert Boxley, "Competing Demands for U.S. Agricultural Land in the Year 2000." Technical Paper IV, prepared by the research staff of the National Agricultural Lands Study (Washington, D.C., January 1981).

ing on the conversion experience between 1967 and 1975, projected a *maximum* annual conversion to nonagricultural uses of 200,000 acres of high and medium potential cropland. Thus it appears that conversion of cropland (675,000 acres) and potential cropland (200,000 acres) may have been less than 1 million acres per year between 1967 and 1975.

Brewer and Boxley consider four hypotheses that might explain the past rate of conversion: (1) the continued shift of nonfarm population to rural areas; (2) the expansion of road building, particularly the interstate highway system, and rights of way for energy facilities (e.g., power lines); (3) sales of unimproved land for subdivision development; (4) growth of surface mining. The discussion of these hypotheses by Brewer and Boxley is inconclusive about future rates of conversion. However, they note that the completion of the interstate highway system would tend to reduce the rate of conversion; and they cite studies suggesting that the total amount of land taken for surface mining in the next couple of decades is not likely to exceed 2 million acres, not all of which would be agricultural land.

Kenneth Frederick analyzes factors bearing on the expansion of irrigation in the seventeen western states, focusing particularly on the effect of rising energy prices and declining water tables on the cost of pumping groundwater and on the increasing competition for water for nonagricultural uses. He concludes that on all counts the real cost of irrigation water is likely to rise enough to drastically slow the future expansion of irrigation in the West relative to growth in the past couple of decades. Frederick considers various water-saving practices and technologies that farmers might adopt but concludes they would not likely offset the rise in water costs. There is some higher level of crop prices that would have this effect, but Frederick thinks it unlikely prices will rise that high. His analysis points to the conclusion that the role of irrigation in extending the supply of land will be weaker in the future than it was in the past.

In chapter 6 I draw on the analyses of supply and demand factors by Heady, Abel, Brewer–Boxley, and Frederick to explore prospective changes in economic and environmental costs of agricultural land. My conclusion, stated earlier, is that the demand for land will grow faster than the supply, resulting in rising real economic costs of land. With rising real prices of nonland inputs, and relatively slow growth in productivity, the implication is that real costs of agricultural production will rise. Based on work done for RFF by the Center for Agricultural and Rural Development at Iowa State University, I also conclude that bringing in the additional land needed to accommodate Abel's projections of production will result in significantly higher erosion costs. For reasons given in chapter 6, I give only cursory attention to other environmental costs of increased production and land use.

In chapter 7, Sterling Brubaker takes the work of the previous six chapters as his point of departure and discusses three sets of policies bearing on the adequacy of agricultural land: those that affect yields; those that might limit demand; and those that would retain land in agriculture. He concludes that to be effective, demand-limiting policies would have to curtail the expansion of exports and that this runs too strongly against the national interest in maintaining high exports to be politically acceptable.

Policies to retain land in agriculture have not been very effective, nor are they likely to be, in Brubaker's judgment. Conversion occurs because the value of the land in nonagricultural uses exceeds its value in agriculture. Typically the excess is so large as to overwhelm policies seeking to prevent conversion. Zoning ordinances, for example, give way under economic pressure; and such practices as public purchase of development rights prove more costly than the community is willing to bear.

This is not to argue that state and local jurisdictions should not seek to guide or even slow the process of land conversion where orderly spatial development and preservation of local amenities are the goals. Brubaker's point is that while policies to retain agricultural land may achieve these goals, they will not contribute significantly to maintenance of national agricultural production capacity.

Brubaker concludes that to achieve that objective, policies stimulating faster growth of crop yields are more consistent with American traditions in agriculture and sufficiently promising to deserve support. He points to recent advances in biological and genetic research as having high potential for improving growth in yield. He acknowledges a lag in transforming this potential to technologies that farmers can use, but argues this is not a major drawback because the agricultural land problem is not now urgent. He makes the point that our obligation to future generations is not a legacy of specific resources, but a capacity to produce. Technological advance is the key to meeting that obligation.

## Summary

The papers that comprise this volume indicate that meeting demands for food and fiber over the next several decades will put sufficient pressure on the nation's land and other agricultural resources to increase the economic and environmental costs of agricultural production. Rising costs of land and mounting erosion will contribute to the increase in production costs. The prospective increase in land and production costs is cause for concern, but it does not now appear to pose a major threat to the national welfare or to those abroad who count on the United States to supply a significant amount of their food and fiber.

This conclusion, however, is not a basis for complacency over the future adequacy of agricultural land. There are major uncertainties about the growth of demand for food and fiber, growth in crop yields, the supply curve of potential cropland, and the environmental costs of expanding supply. Should demand grow faster than projected here, or yields more slowly, or if the supply of potential cropland becomes more inelastic or environmental costs higher, then pressure on the land base would rise much more steeply than now anticipated, and the nation most likely would judge the supply of land to be inadequate. Of course, if on balance these key factors act to reduce pressure on the land, there would be a concomitant change in the perception of its adequacy.

It is fair to say that most conference participants view the future course of technology as it affects crop yields and the environment as decisive in determining whether the nation's supply of agricultural land will be adequate. Earl Heady demonstrates the dramatic impact of technology in reducing pressure on the agricultural land base while generating substantial increases in production over the past fifty years. This record highlights technology as the key variable to be considered in evaluating future adequacy of the land. And it is precisely the present uncertainty about trends in technology which warns against complacency about adequacy. While the record shows that technology can maintain adequacy, it also shows that technology is not a *deus ex machina*.

Whether technology assures adequacy of the land depends upon whether the nation provides timely support for its development. We cannot be certain that this will happen. The prudent course, therefore, is to support development of land-saving technologies but mean-while to be sensitive to the longer term implications of how the land is used. A useful policy perspective is expressed in the closing lines of Sterling Brubaker's chapter: "Having made this bold flirtation with the temptress of technological progress, I suspect that many of us will still want to go home with Prudence as our long-term partner." While this perhaps gives technology less than its due, it properly underscores the virtues of Prudence.

# 2

# The Adequacy of Agricultural Land:
# A Demand–Supply Perspective

*Earl O. Heady*

## Introduction

The capacity of the land to meet the demand for food and other services has been a recurring public concern since the time of Malthus, but the Malthusian principle was anticipated as early as 1589.[1] Three centuries later, Sir William Crookes again posed the specter of food demand exceeding the capacity of the land to supply it. The topic of his 1898 presidential address to the British Association for the Advancement of Science was not that of world population and starvation, as in the case of Malthus, but of food supply for the "bread eaters" of the world, or the developed countries.[2]

After comparing possible additions to the world's wheat-growing area and the likely increase in the number of bread eaters, Crookes estimated that only three decades remained before all available wheat acreage would have to be under cultivation to meet current needs. He was particularly concerned that the easy expansion of U.S. cropland, by 230 percent between 1870 and 1888, was drawing to a close. He emphasized the potential for yield improvements through increased application of fertilizer, particularly nitrogen. His optimism was based, not on existing technologies, but on the commercial potential of fixing atmospheric nitrogen and using it to produce chemical fertilizers—a technology that was still in the future. Proposing the use

[1] J. A. Schumpeter, *History of Economics Analysis,* 9th ed. (New York, Reeves and Turner, 1954).

[2] Sir William Crookes, *The Wheat Problem* (New York, The Knickerbocker Press, 1899).

of this technology at that time was not unlike a list of potential technological breakthroughs proposed by Wittwer.[3] A characteristic of such
lists is that they give no indication of when some of the breakthroughs
will lessen the demand on land.

Following World War II, there again was concern about food and
land supplies. This postwar interest was accented by the creation of
the Food and Agricultural Organization (FAO), which signified recognition of a potentially major problem. Nutrition goals, staggering
projections of population growth, and the information system of FAO
made many more people aware of the potential problem of inadequate agricultural land. Almost simultaneously, Americans and others
were made aware of limits on supplies of natural resources. The
period was a high point in the U.S. public's concern over conservation
of these resources. Vogt suggested that mismanagement of land and
water resources was proceeding at such a rate that even ongoing levels
of food production might be threatened.[4] In addition, birth rates in
the United States increased sharply, while land was being lost through
erosion. So great was the concern that a national effort was undertaken, with each state enlisted to determine the techniques that might
be adopted and the level to which food production could be raised by
1985. However, the potential of new technology was so great that by
the late 1970s these estimates were far surpassed and the United States
could meet its domestic demands with much less land and a much
larger margin for exports.[5]

The rapid development and application of yield-increasing (land-
substituting) technologies during the 1950s and 1960s caused the
land–food scare largely to recede in the United States and other
developed countries. Fertilizers, pesticides, improved plant and
animal varieties, feed additives, and other biological technologies
greatly reduced the amount of land required to produce a given level
and mix of food commodities. Similarly, irrigation water served as a
substitute for land. During several decades of substitution of other
inputs and technology for land, the nation has been able to produce
and export more food while simultaneously converting land to nonfarm uses. These vast technological advances literally substituted for

[3]S. H. Wittwer, "Food Production: Technology and the Resource Base," *Science* vol.
188 (1975) pp. 179–188.
[4]William Vogt, *Road to Survival* (New York, Sloane Associates, 1948).
[5]The Iowa estimates were that the state could produce 85 bushels of corn per acre in
1985. Iowa's average corn yield in 1979 was 127 bushels per acre.

land as the U.S. public paid farmers to remove land from crop production.

The scare returned momentarily on a world basis with crop short-falls on the Indian subcontinent in 1966–67. The nation and world began considering means to gear up for greater production, but the concern was not great enough to cause U.S. idle land programs to be cancelled. With the return of normal weather in the late 1960s, the prospect of world famine faded into the background, only to appear again with the crop shortfalls in Eastern Europe and Africa during the mid-1970s, leading to the UN–FAO World Food Conference in 1974.

The issue of the adequacy of agricultural land remains with us. Meadows and the Club of Rome rediscovered Malthus's exponential relationships and reiterated his conclusions for a broader array of resources.[6] Others, such as Brown[7] and Eckholm,[8] have reminded us that the world's land area is eroding away, as well as being used in greater amounts by the urban sector, thus threatening the ability to produce sufficient food. Recent concerns with desertification have been in the same vein.[9] The concern over loss of land to urban and other nonfarm uses has become more intense as family and government incomes have grown and the demand for land in nonfarm uses has increased accordingly.[10] Over the period 1950–59, the use of land for urban uses increased by 67 percent while that for transportation

[6]Donella Meadows, Dennis L. Meadows, Jørgen Randers, and W. W. Behrens III, *The Limits to Growth*, a report for the Club of Rome's project on the predicament of mankind (New York, Universe Books, 1972), and Mihajlo Mesarovic and Edward Pestal, *Mankind at the Turning Point*, the second report to the Club of Rome (New York, Dutton, 1974) chapter 9.

[7]Lester R. Brown, *The Worldwide Loss of Cropland*, Worldwatch Paper 24 (Washington, D.C., Worldwatch Institute, 1978).

[8]Erik P. Eckholm, *Losing Ground; Environmental Stress and World Food Prospects* (New York, W. W. Norton, 1976).

[9]See Brown, *Worldwide Loss of Cropland*, and S. H. Wittwer, "Increased Crop Yields and Livestock Productivity," in Marilyn Chou, ed., *World Food Prospects and Agricultural Potential* (New York, Praeger, 1977) pp. 66–135.

[10]Concern of the Midwest governors over the use of prime land for urban, transportation, and recreational purposes caused them to commission a study on alternative policies for prime and fragile lands in the North Central Region [Earl O. Heady, "Social and Economic Conditions Surrounding Agriculture in Year 2000," Plenary session paper, Organization for Economic and Cooperative Development, Directors of Agricultural Research, fifth working session, December 1978]. For similar reasons, former Secretary of Agriculture Butz organized a seminar on retention of prime lands in agriculture [U.S. Department of Agriculture, *Perspectives on Prime Lands*, background papers for seminar on retention of prime lands (Washington, D.C., U.S. Department of Agriculture, 1975)].

increased much less—urban and transportation uses combined increased by 39 percent. However, even by 1970, urban use accounted for only 1.5 percent of the U.S. land supply and transportation for only 1.1 percent.

Yield increases and productivity are also part of the concern over agricultural lands, and views on what is actually happening are conflicting. Brown[11] and Horsfall[12] see yield growth curves beginning to flatten; Thompson[13] suggests that the rate of yield increases in the 1955–70 period that resulted from the use of fertilizers will drop and the trend of the next century will parallel the period 1935–55.

Crosson[14] sees slower growth in total agricultural productivity, as does McElney,[15] with any future gains a result of past agricultural research. Ruttan[16] also sees lagging productivity growth resulting from high energy prices and believes it will parallel that of 1895–1955.

Wittwer fluctuates between pessimism and optimism. At one point, he says he considers that crop yields have plateaued.[17] At another point in the same treatise, he states that "far from achieving scientific and biological limits the world has only begun to explore the capabilities of increasing agricultural production." [18] Again he states, "biological limits have not been achieved for productivity of any of the major food crops . . . a comparison of average world yields for every major crop shows a production ratio of three to one, with some records greater by a factor of six." [19] Other conflicts in opinion also prevail, depending on the time period considered. McGuigg[20] and Lin and

[11]Lester R. Brown, "Carrying Capacity—Biological Systems and Human Numbers," in Capon Spring Public Policy Conference: *Key Issues in Population and Food Policy* (Washington, D.C., University Press of America, 1978).

[12]James G. Horsfall, in *Agricultural Production Efficiency* (Washington, D.C., National Academy of Sciences, 1975).

[13]L. M. Thompson, "Climate Change and World Grain Production," unpublished paper for Council on Foreign Relations, Iowa State University, Ames, 1979.

[14]Pierre Crosson, "Agricultural Land Use: A Technological and Energy Perspective," in Max Schnepf, ed., *Farmland, Food, and the Future* (Ankeny, Iowa, Soil Conservation Society of America, 1979).

[15]F. H. Anderson, ed., *Future Report* vol. 14, no. 16 (July 1976).

[16]Vernon W. Ruttan, "Inflation and Productivity," *American Journal of Agricultural Economics* vol. 61, no. 5 (1979) pp. 896–902.

[17]Wittwer, "Increased Crop Yields and Livestock Productivity," p. 4.

[18]Ibid., p. 7.

[19]Ibid., p. 55.

[20]J. D. McGuigg, "Agripower: Food, A Strategic Weapon," unpublished paper, Columbia, Missouri.

Seaver,[21] using mid-1970s data, suppose a plateau. Swanson et al., using later data, do not find a limit.[22]

Most of the recent doubts about the ability of agriculture to sustain its growth rates were based on observations to the mid-1970s. More recent observations on yields and productivity growth give a somewhat different outlook. We review these data in a later section.

While concern over land and food availability is at least five centuries old, the dire projections of the pessimists have not been realized, at least for the developed world. The successful application of science in the development of new agricultural inputs was outside of Malthus's reckoning and imagination. This, together with economic and social forces which have kept the population growth in developed countries far below the biological potential, has resulted in diets at saturation levels, periodic food surpluses, and an abundance of land for transportation, housing, industrial, and recreational purposes.

## Demands for Land

Land is needed for growing food and fiber crops, for' range and cropland to raise livestock, for forestry and recreation, for living space, and finally for transportation corridors and all the many uses that accompany urban developments. However disparate, these demands are all related through the market, and market forces have thus far been the major allocators of land in the United States.

The relative pressures of these demands will depend on such factors as population, per capita incomes, production prices and technologies, the kind of transportation (for example, air transportation requires much less land than railroad or highways), and government policies. These latter affect the demand for land through trade treaties, indirect trade barriers, an occasional embargo, and most important, through supply control programs. Since the late 1930s, the government has increased the demand for land by paying farmers not to

---

[21]K. T. Lin and S. K. Seaver, "Were Crop Yields Random in Recent Years?" *Southern Journal of Agricultural Economics* (December 1978) pp. 139–142.

[22]E. R. Swanson, D. G. Smith, and J. C. Nyanhoric, "Have Corn and Soybeans Reached a Plateau?" *Journal of American Society of Farm Managers and Rural Appraisers* vol. 43 (1979) pp. 7–11. E. R. Swanson, D. G. Smith, and J. C. Nyanhoric, "Influence of Weather and Technology on Corn and Soybean Yield Trends," *Agricultural Meteorology* vol. 20 (1979) pp. 327–342.

plant on it and by acquiring "surplus" grain and dumping it abroad as food aid. Farmers have benefited in capital gains accordingly.

The elasticities of demand for the goods and services of land vary widely. In the case of food, domestic income elasticities are less for staples such as cereals and potatoes and much higher for certain meats and fresh fruits and vegetables. Thus, except for some offsetting variables, as per capita incomes increase, a nation's agricultural land use can be expected to shift toward feed for livestock rather than cereals for human consumption. This trend has not occurred in the United States primarily because of technologies that have allowed more feedgrain and hay to be grown on a smaller area, and an increasing export demand that has made wheat production profitable. In fact, the demand for land for livestock feed has declined greatly in recent decades. However, should the growth of wheat exports slow and the recent sluggish pace of technological change in agriculture continue, growth in domestic per capita income may increase the demand for land to produce feedgrains.

Since the income elasticity of demand for food is much lower than that for other major products and services, the growth of population and per capita income is likely to shift a rising proportion of the nation's land from farm to nonfarm uses. For example, from 1930 to 1975, land used per capita for urban purposes increased from 0.17 acres to 0.25.[23] High postwar incomes and increased use of the automobile allowed the development of suburban housing and the shopping malls that service these areas. In a similar fashion, high elasticities of demand for recreation and improved transportation technologies have produced a relatively large increase in demand for airports and highways and associated land uses.

While these nonfarm demands for land have grown rapidly, they still claim a small proportion of the nation's land area. They alone have not put intense pressure on the demand for land or real prices for food, partly because of their relatively light requirements for land, compared with food production, but especially because land-substituting technologies lessened the agricultural demand for land in the United States over most of the past half century.

If past trends in nonfarm uses of land continue to 2000, urban areas will absorb only about 2 percent of the total U.S. land area, compared

[23]Raleigh Barlowe, "Demands on Agricultural and Forestry Lands to Service Complementary Uses," in Perspectives on Prime Lands (Washington, D.C., U.S. Department of Agriculture, 1975) pp. 105–119.

with 1.5 percent in 1969, while transportation will require only about 1.2 percent, compared with 1.1 percent in 1969.[24] The growing tendency of individuals to live in multiunit buildings, along with higher energy prices, could even slightly curtail urban, transportation, and recreational demand for land that would otherwise be used for agriculture. Also, the slowing population growth rate will dampen demand for residential land. While land also is used for parks, wilderness and wildlife areas, private recreation, power and defense sites, mining and other service purposes, these uses do not pose the possibility of significantly infringing on agricultural land use.

Far more important than nonagricultural demands for land has been growth in U.S. grain exports to the developed and wealthy countries. Nonfarm demands for land will continue to represent only a small proportion of total demand compared with agricultural exports, as will be shown in a later section. The relatively small increments in nonfarm uses could easily be offset by available technologies that substitute for land. However, it is not likely that these technologies could satisfy future export demand without putting great stress on the land base. Rising export demands, therefore, pose a challenge to develop new land-substituting technologies.

## Substitution for Land Through Technology and Capital Goods

New technologies that raise yields per hectare as well as increased use of current high-yielding technologies are substitutes for land. While new and current technologies can substitute for each other, if they are used together they may produce even greater yields. For example, in the Punjab in India, new, short-stemmed wheat varieties were a substitute for land even without irrigation, fertilizer, or pesticides. When the new seed was used in conjunction with these inputs, yields per hectare increased even more. Heady and Auer, in an analysis of nine crops, found that, the weather aside, the effects of variety improvements, fertilizer, and other crop technologies interacted and were important in increasing production in the period immediately after World War II.[25]

[24] Ibid. Frey shows 2.7 percent or 61 million acres used for urban areas, highways, roads, railroads, and airports [H. T. Frey, "Major Uses of Land in the United States: 1974," Economics, Statistics and Cooperatives Service Report 440 (Washington, D.C., U.S. Department of Agriculture, 1979)].

[25] Earl O. Heady and Ludwig Auer, "Imputation of Production to Technologies," *Journal of Farm Economics* vol. 48, no. 3 (1965) pp. 309–322.

Substitutions of technology for land were widespread during 1945–70, when U.S. farmers greatly increased fertilizer use.[26] Of course, with a bundle of technologies such as improved varieties, fertilizers, pesticides, and planting rate, the rate of substitution of the combined input mix for land can be even higher. These biological substitutes have made land a relatively abundant resource at times and, with an inelastic supply and low reservation price for land, have also depressed farm prices and income over a substantial portion of the past fifty years.[27]

The substitution rates will vary by location, climate, and other environmental factors and the state of technology prevailing. Bishay estimated, for typical fertilizer use levels in developing countries, that a ton of fertilizer substituted for 13.9 acres of land in rice production.[28] Treffeisen estimated fertilizer-land substitutions for a number of countries.[29] Some common marginal rates (acres per ton) that he found were 11.3 for wheat in Argentina, 23.6 for wheat in Chile, 53.5 for rice in Peru, 18.8 for corn in Brazil, 17.6 for wheat in India, 25.9 for rice in the Philippines, and 28.9 for rice in Thailand. These quantities are for typical rates of fertilizer use and relate to the unique experimental conditions under which the basic production functions were estimated. However, they do illustrate the high rate at which other inputs substitute for land. To meet world food demand over the next few decades, massive efforts will need to go into developing new biological technologies that substitute for land. The development of mechanical technologies which mainly substitute for labor, except where they speed up field operations and allow multiple cropping and greater annual total production, can be given low priority for developing countries.

[26]The technical aspects of fertilizer-land substitution are illustrated in the appendix.
[27]Earl O. Heady, "Changes in Income Distribution with Reference to Technical Change," *Journal of Farm Economics* vol. 26, no. 3 (1944) pp. 435–447. Earl O. Heady, "Basic Economic and Welfare Aspects of Farm Technological Advance," *Journal of Farm Economics* vol. 31, no. 2 (1949) pp. 293–316.
[28]Fahmi Bishay, "Marginal Rates of Substitution Between Land, Labor and Fertilizer in Relation to Optimum Planning of Resource Combinations," unpublished Ph.D. thesis, Iowa State University, Ames, 1965.
[29]Alan P. Treffeisen, "A Cross Country Comparison of Land-Fertilizer Substitution Rates and Implications in World Food Production," unpublished Ph.D. thesis, Iowa State University, Ames, 1980.

*Realized Substitutions*

Up to 1940, only modest progress was made in developing yield-increasing technologies. Efforts in agricultural research and education in the early part of the century were relatively small and not as scientifically systematic as they have been in recent decades. However, the research knowledge collected during the 1920s and 1930s, combined with the improved economic environment for agriculture at the start of World War II, produced a leap forward after 1940 that has allowed new technology to serve as a mammoth substitute for land for the past thirty-five years.

The historical development of this technology falls into three periods.[30] From 1860 to 1910, production was increased by increasing acreage; between 1910 and 1940, increased yields resulted from improvements in equipment and the beginning of the scientific research that after 1940 introduced the third stage: dramatic improvement in the form of new seed varieties, fertilizers, pesticides, and improved irrigation methods. Further investment and improvement in agricultural research, favorable real prices for fertilizers, chemicals, machinery, and other inputs, as well as improved irrigation and a greater specialization of crop production, allowed yields to continue to increase in the 1970s. Without these substitutes for land, the nation would have had to convert more land to field crops, import grains, or maintain a lower level of meat production.

The importance of these technologies can be seen by comparing some production figures. In 1910, 119.8 million tons of grain were produced in the United States on 192.5 million acres; in 1979, total grain production was 316.2 million tons on 162.1 million acres (table 2-1). Obtaining the 1979 supply of grain at the 1910 yield level would have required 509.9 million acres. In 1979, corn production of 7.6 billion bushels on 69.4 million acres would have required 271.9 million acres at the 1910 yield level. In a similar sense, 1979 hay acreage would have had to increase from 60.9 million acres to 130.0 million and cotton from 13.0 million acres to 40.4 million.

While greater amounts of grain, hay, and cotton have been produced on a reduced land area, the acreage devoted to soybeans and

[30]Yoo-chi Lu, Philip Cline, and Leroy Quance, "Prospects for Productivity Growth in U.S. Agriculture," Economics, Statistics and Cooperatives Service Report 435 (Washington, D.C., U.S. Department of Agriculture, 1979).

**TABLE 2-1.** Acreage and Production of Selected Crops, 1910–79

| Year | Corn acres | Corn production | Wheat acres | Wheat production | Soybean acres | Soybean production | Grain acres | Grain production | Hay acres | Hay production | Cotton acres | Cotton production |
|---|---|---|---|---|---|---|---|---|---|---|---|---|
| 1910 | 102.2 | 2.9 | 45.7 | 0.6 |  |  | 192.5 | 119.8 | 68.3 | 75.2 | 32.4 | 11.0 |
| 1920 | 101.4 | 2.7 | 62.4 | 0.8 |  |  | 217.9 | 130.4 | 73.0 | 91.7 | 35.9 | 13.4 |
| 1930 | 101.4 | 1.7 | 62.7 | 0.9 | 1.1 | 13.9 | 219.5 | 104.0 | 66.4 | 74.3 | 43.3 | 13.9 |
| 1940 | 86.4 | 2.2 | 53.2 | 0.8 | 4.8 | 78.0 | 195.0 | 116.1 | 73.1 | 96.1 | 23.8 | 12.6 |
| 1945 | 88.1 | 2.6 | 65.1 | 1.1 | 10.7 | 192.1 | 193.6 | 139.6 | 77.0 | 108.5 | 17.0 | 9.0 |
| 1950 | 72.3 | 2.8 | 61.6 | 1.0 | 13.8 | 299.2 | 194.8 | 143.7 | 75.2 | 103.8 | 17.8 | 10.0 |
| 1955 | 68.5 | 2.9 | 47.2 | 0.9 | 18.6 | 323.7 | 182.2 | 149.0 | 75.0 | 112.8 | 16.9 | 14.7 |
| 1960 | 71.6 | 3.9 | 51.8 | 1.4 | 23.7 | 555.3 | 179.7 | 196.3 | 67.2 | 118.2 | 15.3 | 14.3 |
| 1965 | 55.4 | 4.1 | 49.6 | 1.3 | 34.4 | 845.6 | 145.7 | 197.5 | 67.5 | 125.6 | 13.6 | 19.9 |
| 1970 | 57.4 | 4.2 | 43.6 | 1.4 | 42.4 | 1,127.1 | 142.8 | 200.6 | 61.5 | 127.0 | 11.2 | 10.2 |
| 1975 | 67.5 | 5.8 | 69.4 | 2.1 | 53.5 | 1,547.4 | 173.9 | 267.2 | 61.3 | 132.2 | 8.9 | 8.3 |
| 1979 | 69.4 | 7.6 | 62.2 | 2.1 | 70.2 | 2,235.9 | 162.1 | 316.2 | 60.9 | 143.0 | 13.0 | 14.5 |

*Note:* Acres are in millions. Corn and wheat production are in billions of bushels, soybeans are in million bushels, grain and hay are in million short tons, and cotton is millions of bales.

*Sources:* U.S. Department of Agriculture, *Agricultural Statistics*, 1936, 1951, 1965, 1979; *Crop Production*, November 1979: U.S. Department of Commerce, Bureau of Census, *U.S. Census of Agriculture*, 1925 (Washington, D.C., Government Printing Office).

grain sorghum has generally increased. Although yields of these crops rose, demand for them increased even faster. Some increase in grain production resulted as land that had been devoted to oats was shifted to higher yielding grains and as fertilizers were substituted for crop rotations to increase productivity. The 1979 oat acreage was less than a fourth of that in 1935. Finally, more timely and improved tillage operations have made some contribution to crop yields.

While their effect is less apparent, improved livestock technologies also serve as a substitute for land. As feeds are transformed into livestock products at greater rates, less land is needed to produce feed. Especially important have been changes in nutritional practices for swine and poultry, which have reduced greatly the amount of grain required to produce a hundred weight of meat. Genetic improvements also have helped increase the rate at which feeds are transformed into meat, milk, and eggs, and there may still be possibilities for further advances in this area. Milk production per cow has more than doubled since 1925 (table 2-2). While total production is about 55 percent greater, the number of cows milked now is about 40 percent

**TABLE 2-2.** Farm Employment, Number of Farms and Milk Cows, Milk Production, and Fertilizer Used, 1925–79

| Year | Total farm employment | Number of farms | Number of milk cows | Milk production per cow | Fertilizer used |
|------|------|------|------|------|------|
| 1925 | 11.4 | 6,372 | 17.6 | 4.5 | 7.3 |
| 1930 | 11.2 | 6,289 | 22.2 | 4.5 | 8.2 |
| 1935 | 11.7 | 6,812 | 24.3 | 4.2 | 6.5 |
| 1940 | 11.7 | 6,097 | 23.7 | 4.6 | 8.7 |
| 1945 | 10.8 | 5,859 | 25.3 | 4.8 | 14.0 |
| 1950 | 9.9 | 5,382 | 22.8 | 5.3 | 20.3 |
| 1955 | 8.4 | 4,782 | 21.2 | 5.8 | 21.4 |
| 1960 | 7.1 | 3,704 | 17.5 | 7.0 | 24.4 |
| 1965 | 5.6 | 3,153 | 15.0 | 8.3 | 30.3 |
| 1970 | 4.5 | 2,949 | 12.0 | 9.7 | 38.3 |
| 1975 | 4.3 | 2,767 | 11.1 | 10.3 | 40.6 |
| 1979 | 3.8 | 2,333 | 10.8 | 11.5 | 51.0 |

*Note:* Employment in millions, farm numbers in thousands, milk cows in million head, milk production per cow in thousand pounds, and fertilizer used in million tons.

*Sources:* U.S. Department of Agriculture, *Agricultural Statistics,* 1936, 1942, 1947, 1951, 1965, 1978 (Washington, D.C., Government Printing Office); *Dairy Situation,* DS-378, 1979; Iowa Crop Reporting Service, *Number of Farms and Land in Farms,* January 1980; U.S. Department of Agriculture, 1980 *Fertilizer Situation,* FS-10, December 1979; *Farm Labor,* LA1(2-80), February 1980 (Washington, D.C.).

less than in 1925. The resultant saving in feed has greatly reduced the dairy-derived demand for land.

Substitution of tractors and other mechanical equipment for labor reduced the farm work force by two-thirds between 1925 and 1979 (table 2-2). This machine technology also served as a substitute for land by releasing land that was used to grow feed for horses and mules.

From 1940 through 1970, the agricultural labor force declined by an average of 1.2 million persons in each five-year period (table 2-2). Since 1970, the rate at which mechanization and other recent technology has substituted for agricultural labor has slowed. A key question is whether the rate at which capital technology is substituted for land will also diminish.

Technological advance may affect agricultural labor and land differently. Economies of scale or cost may still exist as machinery is spread over more space to bring about larger farms and further reduction of labor. In contrast, intensified use of land through the application of more capital per acre does not have economies of scale and indeed at some point, returns to the additional capital decrease or marginal costs increase. Compared with three decades ago, most cropland is now fertilized and treated with other chemicals.

While irrigation spread fairly continuously over a larger area in the period 1935–70, this operation nearly peaked in the 1970s and there is no opportunity for equivalent productivity gains from it in the future.

These points suggest that the easy days in developing new technologies to obtain further yield increases are past. Only large "breakthrough" technologies will now allow discrete jumps to a much higher per acre production function. However, there is at present no quantitative proof to indicate that U.S. crop yields generally are now plateauing.

### Are We Approaching Yield Limits?

Earlier observations that indicated that yield limits were being approached were made before the favorable weather and yields of 1979 and 1981. Since there were extreme fluctuations of weather and yields in the 1970s, several more years of observations are needed to determine statistically whether yields will continue to increase at the absolute rate of the past few decades, or whether they will taper off. However, given current high yield levels, a continuation of historic absolute rates of increase would produce declining relative increases.

Except for cotton, available time series data provide no firm evidence of yield plateaus (figures 2-1 to 2-3). Rye yields have behaved somewhat similarly to those of cotton in recent years. And while sorghum, oats, and wheat yields seem to have tottered, statistical analysis does not yet provide a basis for concluding that yield plateaus have been reached. The favorable weather and high yields of 1979 and 1981 seem to have kept other commodities on their yield trends. Judgments on the extent to which rates of yield increase have begun to decline depend partly on the periods in which comparisons are made. For the crops in table 2-3, the annual absolute increase in yields of corn, soybeans, barley, oats, and hay was greater from 1973 to 1979 than from 1945 to 1972, and from 1970 to 1979 than from 1945 to 1970. Only for wheat and sorghum were annual yield increases less in the more recent periods than in the earlier ones.

Differences between average yields and highest yields ever recorded suggest that there is much room for additional yield growth. Pfeiffer shows that in the United States the ratio of highest recorded

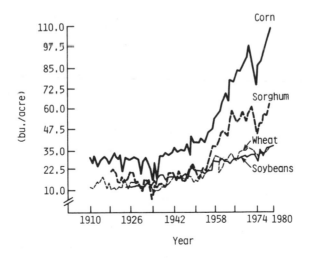

**Figure 2-1.** U.S. yields of corn, grain sorghum, soybeans, and wheat, 1910–79. (Data from U.S. Department of Agriculture.)

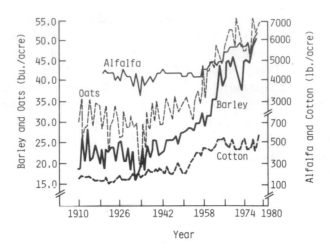

**Figure 2-2.** U.S. yields of alfalfa, barley, cotton, and oats, 1910–79. (Data from U.S. Department of Agriculture.)

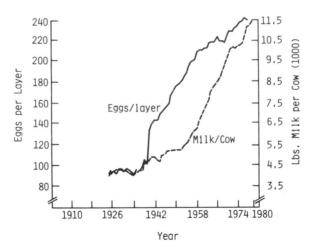

**Figure 2-3.** U.S. yields of milk per cow and eggs per hen, 1925–79. (Data from U.S. Department of Agriculture.)

**TABLE 2-3.** Average Annual Yield Increases for Crop and Livestock Products for Selected Periods

| Commodity | 1945–70 bushels | % | 1945–72 bushels | % | 1973–79 bushels | % | 1970–79 bushels | % |
|---|---|---|---|---|---|---|---|---|
| Corn/acre | 1.57 | 4.75 | 2.37 | 7.15 | 3.02 | 3.03 | 4.11 | 5.68 |
| Wheat/acre | 0.56 | 3.29 | 0.58 | 3.42 | 0.43 | 1.37 | 0.36 | 1.15 |
| Soybeans/acre | 0.35 | 1.93 | 0.36 | 2.02 | 0.73 | 2.64 | 0.61 | 2.29 |
| Sorghum/acre | 1.41 | 9.26 | 1.69 | 11.09 | 0.68 | 1.16 | 1.39 | 2.76 |
| Barley/acre | 0.69 | 2.71 | 0.67 | 2.64 | 1.68 | 4.16 | 0.87 | 2.03 |
| Oats/acre | 0.51 | 1.31 | 0.56 | 1.52 | 1.08 | 2.26 | 0.58 | 1.17 |
| Hay/acre[a] | 53.60 | 1.91 | 55.56 | 1.98 | 73.33 | 1.69 | 71.11 | 1.72 |
| Eggs/hen[b] | 2.64 | 1.74 | 2.78 | 1.83 | 2.17 | 0.96 | 2.44 | 1.12 |
| Milk/cow[a] | 198.56 | 4.15 | 202.67 | 4.23 | 225.33 | 2.23 | 191.11 | 1.96 |

*Note:* The percentages are *not* compounded rates of change.

*Source:* U.S. Department of Agriculture, *Agricultural Statistics* 1967, 1972 and 1979; USDA, Economics, Statistics and Cooperatives Service, *Crop Production, 1979 Annual Summary*, CrPr 2-1(80), January 1980; *Poultry and Egg Situation*, PES-307, August 1980; *Dairy Situation*, DS-380, May 1980.

[a] Measured in pounds.

[b] Measured in numbers.

yield of corn to 1975 average yield was 3.9.[31] For other crops the ratios were wheat, 7.0; soybeans, 4.0; sorghum, 6.5; rice, 5.8; oats, 6.2; barley, 4.8; and potatoes, 3.5.

The highest commercial yields in 1974–76 (with highest yield ever recorded in parentheses) were 225 (338) bushels for corn, 100 (216) bushels for wheat, 65 (110) bushels for soybeans, 250 (320) bushels for sorghum, 150 (296) bushels for oats, 150 (212) bushels for barley, and 1,000 (1,400) bushels for potatoes.

Some indexes of animal productivity show similar potential. Average milk production per cow per year only recently reached 11,500 pounds, but the record is 50,000 pounds. Pork has been produced with as little as 2 pounds of feed per pound of weight gain, a ratio well under the average for all pork production.

The resource costs and environmental conditions under which the high yields were obtained have not been documented. Evidently the technologies used are still too costly or they would have been adopted on a wider scale. However, the fact that these yield levels were obtained allows us to be somewhat optimistic about the future. It is possible that other technologies can allow these yields to be attained economically.

[31] R. P. Pfeiffer, "Record Yields and Your Operation," *Crops and Soil Science Magazine* vol. 28 (1976) pp. 5–7.

While yield limits are not yet quantitatively apparent in developed countries, they are even more distant in developing countries. Grain yields in developed countries increased from an average of 1.15 tons per hectare in 1934–38 to 3.0 tons in 1973–75. In developing countries, however, grain yields increased in this period from 1.14 tons to only 1.4 tons. Biologically, we might expect eventual yield limits to be higher in developing countries in general than in developed countries because the former are mostly located in the tropical regions of the world, while most of the developed countries are located in temperate climates where growing seasons are shorter.

Diminishing growth also is not yet apparent in total agricultural productivity. As table 2-4 shows, between 1935 and 1979, farm output grew by 148 percent, farm inputs by 19 percent, and agricultural productivity (output per unit of inputs) by 109 percent. With favorable weather at the end of the decade, there also was no hard statistical evidence of a decline in productivity growth in the period 1970–79.

### Prospects for Technology and Land Supply

Although the evidence does not indicate that either yields or total productivity has plateaued, the relative scarcity of the nation's land in the future will depend greatly on whether new technologies can be developed which are as effective in increasing yields as those of the past and whether these technologies are consistent with prevailing resource supplies and prices.

There are grounds for optimism that this can be done, but no room for complacency. Success will require vigorous research programs and a favorable pricing environment to reach yields that only approach the maximums so far recorded. If the growth rate for agricultural productivity that has been reached in recent decades is to be maintained, there must be breakthroughs in many areas, for example, improving the efficiency of photosynthate accumulation and partitioning to greatly increase the transformation of solar energy into plant production, and developing biological innovations that can become economic substitutes for fossil energy. Certainly research should be expanded to find out why soybeans produce only a third as much grain per acre as corn under the same environmental conditions. We are already too tardy in doing this. The possibility of inducing biological fixation of

**TABLE 2-4.**  Indexes of U.S. Farm Output, Input, and Productivity
(1967 = 100)

| Year | Output | Input | Productivity |
|------|--------|-------|--------------|
| 1920 | 51 | 98 | 52 |
| 1925 | 51 | 99 | 51 |
| 1930 | 52 | 101 | 51 |
| 1935 | 52 | 91 | 57 |
| 1940 | 60 | 100 | 60 |
| 1945 | 70 | 103 | 68 |
| 1950 | 74 | 104 | 71 |
| 1955 | 82 | 105 | 78 |
| 1960 | 91 | 101 | 90 |
| 1965 | 98 | 98 | 100 |
| 1966 | 95 | 98 | 97 |
| 1967 | 100 | 100 | 100 |
| 1968 | 102 | 100 | 102 |
| 1969 | 102 | 99 | 103 |
| 1970 | 101 | 100 | 102 |
| 1971 | 110 | 100 | 110 |
| 1972 | 110 | 100 | 110 |
| 1973 | 112 | 101 | 111 |
| 1974 | 106 | 100 | 105 |
| 1975 | 114 | 100 | 115 |
| 1976 | 117 | 103 | 115 |
| 1977 | 119 | 105 | 114 |
| 1978 | 122 | 105 | 116 |
| 1979 | 129 | 108 | 119 |
| | *Increase* | | |
| 1920-29 | 2 | 4 | 0 |
| 1930-39 | 6 | −3 | 8 |
| 1940-49 | 14 | 5 | 11 |
| 1950-59 | 14 | −2 | 16 |
| 1960-69 | 11 | 2 | 13 |
| 1970-79 | 28 | 8 | 17 |

*Source: Economic Indicators of the Farm Sector: Production and Efficiency Statistics, 1979, U.S. Department of Agriculture, Economics, Statistics and Cooperatives Service Statistical Bulletin no. 657, 1981 (Washington, D.C.).*

nitrogen in cereal grains falls in a somewhat similar category in terms of promise and required research investment.

Progress is needed on these fronts to offset rising real prices for energy and nitrogen fertilizer. There are many possibilities for the kind of genetic engineering of plant architecture that has been done in new rice varieties—changing the positioning and placing of the leaves to capture sunlight more effectively. It is estimated that the current efficiency of crops in fixing solar energy now is only 12 percent.[32]

[32]National Academy of Sciences, *World Food and Nutrition Study; the Potential Contributions of Research* (Washington, D.C., NAS, 1977) p. 12.

Genetic improvements have been most striking in hybrid corn and new rice varieties. Hybrid wheat also is now a reality and is in early stages of commercial production. In time, it can add as much to productivity as hybrid corn has. Work on other crops is much less advanced but similar progress should be possible. Included are the seed legumes, oilseed crops generally, and roots and tubers. Improvement in the latter would be particularly important for developing countries. Genetic improvements to increase the proportion of protein in cereal grains could help generate substitutes for meat, a food product that requires much land. For all crops, genetic, tillage, and other improvements are needed to increase the efficiency of plants in absorbing soil nutrients and fertilizer.

Other approaches to increasing crop yields and reducing the relative scarcity of land are both complex and promising. These include chemical growth regulators, alleviation of climatic and environmental stresses to allow crops to be grown over a larger land area, improved pest management and tillage practices, automated plant feeding through the nutrient film technique, controlled environment, hydroponic farming, greatly improved irrigation and water management, aquatic foods, nitrogen-fixing algae, and others.

Nonconventional foods also could substitute for conventional foods on a large-scale basis, or allow plant foods to be substituted for animal foods. Algae represent a possibility of using resources which otherwise cannot be utilized. Single-cell protein already is in commercial production on a small scale. Using plant proteins such as soybeans to simulate meats is an established technique that could have wider acceptance. These opportunities have been scarcely explored.

However inviting research on these technologies may appear, there is no way of knowing how difficult it will be or how much time it will take to obtain the new technologies. We do not know, at current levels of investment, whether marginal returns are constant, increasing, or decreasing for particular crops and technologies. Some persons maintain that the easy technologies have already been developed and that more complex and difficult tasks lie ahead. However, this is offset by an agricultural research profession that has become highly sophisticated and innovative.

Increases in productivity will be affected by levels of research funding. From 1939 to 1965, real public investment in agricultural research increased 3.8 percent per year. From 1965 to 1977, the annual rate of increase fell to 1.8 percent.[33] If expenditures on research and extension grow only enough to offset inflation, productivity growth in agriculture may slow to 1 percent by 2000.[34] With a real growth rate in research and extension (R&E) expenditures of 3 percent, which is equal to the average since World War II, the growth rate would be about 1.1 percent. With a real growth rate in R&E of 7 percent, agricultural productivity could grow at a rate of 1.3 percent (figure 2-4). Under these conditions, U.S. agricultural capacity would grow enough to meet domestic food and nonfood demands as well as those for exports without severe pressure on the supply of land.

### Orienting Research to Relative Resource Scarcities and Prices

United States' policy with respect to agricultural resources, research, and agricultural development generally has been consistent with relative supplies and prices of factors.[35] Its early developmental policy encouraged the use of more land and labor; its more recent policy encouraged the development of land substitutes.

During the early decades of the nation's history, the main resources used in agriculture were land and labor. Capital was largely produced on the farms where it was used. To develop agriculture and increase commodity supplies, the supply of land was kept large and its price was kept low through the land distribution system used. Similarly, the price of labor was kept low through a favorable immigration policy. As the supply of available land diminished, the foundations were laid for the research that would eventually provide technological substitutes for land. Land-grant colleges were established and research programs instituted in the U.S. Department of Agriculture, the Cooperative Extension Service, and the Bureau of Reclamation. At the same time, government agricultural credit programs lowered the cost of capital goods and encouraged farmers to use more of them. As we have seen, initially progress was slow, but from 1935 on the changes were rapid.

The technological changes that allowed these increases were a response to the relative supplies and prices of resources, just as in-

[33]Food and Agricultural Organization, United Nations, *Toward 2000* (Rome, FAO, 1979).

[34]Lu, Cline, and Quance, "Prospects for Productivity Growth."

[35]Earl O. Heady, *Agricultural Policy Under Economic Development* (Ames, Iowa State University Press, 1962) pp. 13–34.

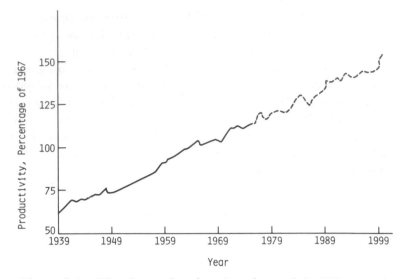

**Figure 2-4.** Historic trend and projected growth in U.S. agricultural productivity with a 7 percent real growth rate in agricultural research and extension expenditures. (From Yoo-chi Lu, Philip Cline, and Leroy Quance, "Prospects for Productivity Growth in U.S. Agriculture," U.S. Department of Agriculture, Economics, Statistics and Cooperatives Service, Report 435, 1979.)

creased use of land was a response to an earlier resource supply. Considering the accumulated knowledge that has resulted from agricultural research and our long experience in administering it, it should be possible to develop programs that respond to future resource supplies and prices. The task is to organize research in relation to these conditions. The speed and ability with which the capital technologies that can substitute for land are developed will depend on the level of investment in agricultural research, its organization, and our perspicacity in foreseeing scarcities of land and other resources.

*World Land Conversion to Agriculture*

While in the United States concern is centered on conversion of cropland to nonfarm uses, in the rest of the world the concern is over conversion of more land to crops. Since a major factor in the demand for land in the United States is grain exports, the scarcity of U.S. land will depend in part on how much land can be put into cultivation in the rest of the world and on the costs of this conversion. Some estimates of posssible conversions are extreme.

One estimate suggests that of the potentially arable land, only 22 percent of that in Africa, 11 percent of that in South America, and about 45 percent worldwide is now under cultivation.[36] The Wageningen group estimates that whereas 1.4 billion hectares currently are in cultivation, some 3.4 billion hectares potentially are arable.[37] They estimate that irrigated land could be increased from 200 million to 470 million hectares. Carter et al. estimated potentially arable land at 3.2 billion hectares if environmental problems were solved and sufficient investment were available.[38] Another estimate puts the world's potentially arable land at 9 billion hectares.[39] While these figures are too optimistic, and use of some fragile lands could cause unacceptable environmental deterioration, there still is land which can be converted. However, the capital requirements for leveling tropical jungles, controlling second growth, and maintaining soil fertility are heavy. There are also other problems of forest soils, processing facilities, and markets in some tropical locations. Boerma estimates that an additional 53 million hectares of new land could be cropped in ten years at a cost of $26 billion at monetary values of the early 1970s.[40] Another 46 million hectares could be renovated and improved for $21 billion, and irrigation schemes could be developed on 23 million hectares for $38 billion in ten years. These costs would be $8 billion annually over a ten-year period (in monetary values of the early 1970s).

Even the United States has a considerable amount of land that could be brought into grain cropping under sufficient capital investment and under sustained high commodity prices. Estimates suggest that there may be as many as 265 million acres which could be converted

[36]Ralph W. Cummings, Jr., *Food Production and the Energy Crisis*, Working Papers of the Rockefeller Foundation (New York, 1974).

[37]P. Buringh, H. P. J. van Heemst, and G. J. Staring, "The Absolute Maximum Food Production of the World," paper for the Third IIASA Symposium on Global Modeling; Food and Agriculture Organization, project on Food for a Doubling World Population, Free University, Amsterdam, 1975.

[38]Harold O. Carter, J. G. Youde, and M. L. Peterson, "Future Land Requirements to Produce Food for an Expanding Population," *Perspectives on Prime Lands* (Washington, D.C., U.S. Department of Agriculture, 1975) pp. 37–59.

[39]Colin Clark, *Population Growth and Land Use* (London, Macmillan, 1977).

[40]A. H. Boerma, "The World Could Be Fed," *Journal of Soil and Water Conservation* vol. 30, no. 1 (1975) pp. 4–11.

to the equivalent of capability class I-III land, with 135 million acres having good potential for conversion.[41] If soybean, wheat, and corn prices per bushel were to move to $15, $6, and $5 respectively and remain there (well above 1981 prices), the 115 million acres of U.S. land with greatest prospect for cropping would likely be cultivated. At higher real prices, other amounts from the initially estimated 265 million acres would be put under cultivation.

## Prospects for World Food Production

The outlook on the world food supply over the next thirty years is optimistic if appropriate investments are made in development of additional land and in agricultural research and education, and if organizations are provided to use effectively the additional resources and implement the new technologies. I believe that the yield potentials for 2000 suggested in our earlier work are still relevant.[42] Estimates by Rojko et al.[43] and Ray et al.[44] suggest a similar potential. The National Research Council indicates that food production in the developing countries could double by 2000, while in the high-income countries, grain production could be increased by an amount greater than U.S. current production.[45] These levels could be attained at reasonable costs even with the rising costs of energy, water, and other inputs. If agricultural development can be speeded up, food production in the developing countries has the potential of increasing 3.8 percent per year from the mid-1970s to 2000, according to the FAO,[46] with 28 percent of the increase obtained from added land, a fivefold increase in fertilizer use, a 150 percent increase in pesticides, and a doubling of labor. Other studies project more optimistic potentials. Buringh et al. estimate that the absolute maximum potential food production is

[41]Clark, *Population Growth and Land Use.*

[42]Leroy L. Blakeslee, Earl O. Heady, and Charles F. Framingham, *World Food Production, Demand and Trade* (Ames, Iowa State University Press, 1973). Also see Heady, "Social and Economic Conditions Surrounding Agriculture in Year 2000."

[43]Anthony Rojko et al., "Alternative Futures for World Food Production in 1985," in vol. 1, *World GOL Model Analytical Report,* Foreign Economic Report 146 (Washington, D.C., U.S. Department of Agriculture, 1978) pp. 24–31.

[44]S. K. Ray, R. W. Cummings, and R. W. Herdt, *Policy Planning for Development* (New York, McGraw-Hill, 1979).

[45]National Research Council, *World Food and Nutrition Survey; the Potential Contributions of Research* (Washington, D.C., National Academy of Sciences, 1977) pp. 39, 187.

[46]FAO, *Toward 2000.*

40 times greater than current production.[47] Clark's estimate of potential production is even larger.[48]

Optimistically, then, there is the potential for world food production to increase somewhat faster than population up to 2000. The existence of the potential does not guarantee implementation of policies to attain it, however. And in developing countries there is a shortage of trained manpower for agricultural research and education and its administration and management. Oram estimates that developing countries still need 30,000 new university graduates per year over the next twenty years for a sufficient agricultural research and education program and to promote agricultural development at a reasonable rate.[49] Over the past three decades, lack of management and trained intellect undoubtedly have been a greater restraint on development than lack of capital. However, while lack of trained manpower will still be a restraint over the next twenty years, the developing countries now have a vastly greater pool than they did thirty years ago and have the ability to train more people. I believe that there is enough managerial ability and unexploited production capacity so that food supplies, particularly with some slackening in birth rates, can grow faster than population over the next thirty years. This will restrain agricultural demand for U.S. land.

## Market and Policy Framework

Twenty years ago land scarcity was not a critical issue in the United States. The nation rapidly added to suburbs, highways, airports, and other nonfarm uses of land. Land now is more scarce relative to demand because exports have increased so greatly (table 2-5). Between 1970 and 1979, U.S. exports of wheat increased 85.6 percent; soybeans, 101.7 percent; cotton, 126.8 percent; corn, 370.6 percent; and feedgrains, 278.8 percent. Corn exports increased by 1.9 billion bushels, or the product of about 19 million acres at yield levels of recent years. The increase of 634 million bushels of wheat exports

[47]Buringh, van Heemst, and Staring, "Absolute Maximum Food Production of the World."

[48]Clark, *Population Growth and Land Use.*

[49]P. A. Oram, "Training Required for Research and Its Application," paper for consultative group on international agricultural research, World Bank (Washington, D.C., 1977).

**TABLE 2-5.** Exports of Grains and Cotton, 1940–79

| Year | Wheat[a] | Corn[a] | Soybeans[a] | Feed grains[b] | Cotton[b] | All grain and soybeans[b] | Exports as % of grain production |
|------|------|------|------|------|------|------|------|
| 1940 | 33.6 | 14.6 | NA | 0.5 | 0.29 | 1.5 | 1.2 |
| 1945 | 320.0 | 19.9 | 2.8 | 1.1 | 0.93 | 10.8 | 7.4 |
| 1950 | 334.3 | 107.2 | 27.8 | 6.1 | 1.07 | 17.0 | 11.1 |
| 1955 | 346.3 | 108.4 | 67.5 | 7.8 | 0.58 | 20.2 | 12.6 |
| 1960 | 661.9 | 276.0 | 134.7 | 12.3 | 1.71 | 36.1 | 17.0 |
| 1965 | 867.4 | 687.0 | 250.6 | 29.2 | 0.76 | 62.7 | 28.1 |
| 1970 | 741.0 | 517.0 | 433.8 | 20.8 | 0.97 | 56.1 | 23.2 |
| 1975 | 1,173.0 | 1,711.0 | 555.1 | 55.1 | 0.79 | 107.0 | 33.4 |
| 1979 | 1,375.0 | 2,433.0 | 875.0 | 78.8 | 2.20 | 144.5 | 37.7 |

Sources: U.S. Department of Agriculture, *Agricultural Statistics*, 1950, 1960, 1970, 1978; *Agricultural Outlook*, May 1981 (Washington, D.C., Government Printing Office).
[a] Million bushels.
[b] Million tons.

represented the product of about 20 million acres, while the increase of 441 million bushels of soybeans represents 14.5 million acres at recent yield levels.

The recent and prospective increases in the amount of land devoted to crop production are owed almost entirely to increased export demand. The rise in pressure on the land has stimulated mounting concern about conversions of farmland to nonagricultural uses and proposals that these conversions be slowed.

But should we intervene in the land market simply to accommodate increased demand for agricultural exports? The largest portion of U.S. grain exports in recent years has gone to developed countries such as Western Europe, Russia, Poland, and Japan—countries with relatively well-fed populations. As these countries import more grain, they are not eliminating malnutrition, but shifting their source of carbohydrates and protein. That is, the grain is going to feed livestock. It is legitimate to ask whether it is more important that an already well-fed consumer in Stuttgart or Moscow have a claim on U.S. land supply in order to shift more of his protein from plant to animal sources, than for a U.S. citizen to have an opportunity to convert the land to nonagricultural uses, such as a larger residential lot and garden or a park. The literature almost suggests that the use of land for the latter purposes is sacrilegious. This evaluation is simplistic, since the majority of U.S. marginal agricultural production is not directed to domestic families facing malnutrition or people of poor countries who suffer hunger.

If market forces are allowed to operate, land use will continue to conform with the desires of U.S. citizens and some agricultural land will continue to shift to domestic nonfarm uses. Theoretically, the reduction in agricultural land supply would tend to increase food prices in both domestic and export markets. However, with less than 3.5 percent of the nation's land supply used for nonagricultural purposes in the year 2000,[50] this price impact will be minor compared with the price impacts of rising world food demand. Whether the reduction in supply of agricultural land alone will have serious effects on food prices will depend on the extent to which land substitutes can be economically implemented in both developing and developed countries.

Some might argue that land uses which cut into U.S. grain exports (the country now exports over one-third of its grain production) will negatively affect the nation's foreign exchange position. But again, the exchange impact of using some land for nonagricultural purposes is small compared with that of our attachment to the automobile, which keeps petroleum imports high. The U.S. Energy Security Act of 1980 aims for production of 10 billion gallons of ethanol a year from grains by 1990. A program of this magnitude would have a much more serious impact on export supplies, grain prices, and exchange conditions than the continued modest use of more land for nonagricultural purposes.

Other questions can be raised about the effect of exports on domestic demand for land in the future. While the majority of U.S. grain exports go to developed countries, the continued rapid increase in the population of developing countries means that the United States may need to increase exports to the latter in the future. Population control is essentially a domestic matter for the developing countries. But, humanitarian considerations aside, it is legitimate to ask whether U.S. consumers should face restrictions on land use or its availability in order to accommodate the consequences of those policies if they lead to increased demand for imported grain.

If both populations and per capita incomes of developing countries continue to increase, markets can help reallocate land and its products so that land supply is more consistent with alternative demands or uses for it. This will be especially true if developing countries can resolve their poverty problems. More people in developing countries then

[50]Frey, "Major Uses of Land."

could bid higher prices for a share of grain from the United States and other exporters. With enough force in this direction, grain prices would be bid so high that more grain would serve directly as human food rather than as livestock feed.

Studies show that if diets in developed countries shift toward a greater reliance on plant proteins, large strides could be made in erasing malnutrition in developing countries.[51] More land also could be shifted from producing livestock feed to wheat and other human foods. Hence, the system would be "self-righting" to an extent, and this flexibility in extending human food production could make U.S. land available for nonfarm uses. There is no ethical, scientific, or political proof that a nutritionally adequate diet based primarily on plant sources with lower land requirements is inferior to one based more on animal products with higher land requirements. Neither is there any proof that allocating U.S. land to nonfarm uses is any less desirable than having consumers in developing countries maintain a diet based on plant sources rather than meat products.

In summary, the increase in demand for U.S. land to produce food over future decades will depend almost entirely on the increase in exports and on the political market and framework within which export needs are evaluated. From the standpoint of domestic food demands alone, U.S. land is in large supply and can continue to be diverted to nonfarm uses without forcing conditions of malnutrition, hunger, or suffering on the nation. The issue of preserving agricultural land to produce exports raises questions of whether priority in use of U.S. land should go to well-off consumers in other developed countries, or to U.S. citizens. In turn, the magnitude of exports will depend not only on world growth in population and income but also on the technologies used and the food produced in developing countries. As noted earlier, there is substantial potential for increased production in these countries if they adopt appropriate policies for research and development and for strengthening market incentives.

## Prices of Capital Goods Serving as Land Substitutes

An uncertain factor affecting the demand for land is energy. The supply and price of energy can affect the demand for U.S. land in two

[51]Earl O. Heady, Faber Doeke, and Steven C. Griffin, "Policies for Lessening World Food Deficits," in *Key Issues in Population and Food Policy*, Capon Springs, Conference 2 (Washington, D.C., University Press of America, 1978) pp. 375–379.

ways: (1) It could increase even more the price of some capital goods which serve as land substitutes, such as nitrogen fertilizer and chemicals with a petroleum base. With sufficiently high prices, use of land-substituting technologies based on fossil fuels would be depressed and demand for land would be relatively higher. (2) If the price of energy from alternative sources becomes competitive, the demand for land to produce these forms will increase. These include alcohol distilled from grains, beets, sugarcane, or biomass of current crops; current crops grown as a substitute for coal; and crops grown for energy purposes per se.

One could imagine an extreme scenario in which the Soviets overrun the Middle East oil fields, an entirely possible event, and retain the petroleum from them to ensure the extension of their sixty-five year dictatorship. With this petroleum held out of the world market, energy prices could skyrocket in the short run. The consequences could turn the United States to wide-scale use of agricultural land for energy production. High energy prices could also greatly retard the progress of agriculture in developing countries and to a lesser extent in developed countries.

The extreme marginal competition for U.S. agricultural land might be between domestic demand for energy, and demand by food consumers in developing countries. The intensity of this competition would depend on other decisions and policies which also are uncertain. Policies that would restrain the energy-derived demand for land include progressive taxes on horsepower or gasoline consumption of automobiles, greater public subsidy of and dependence on mass transit, systematic and large-scale R and D investments in solar energy, and so on.

The concern of the public and the values of particular consuming groups have fluctuated with respect to use of land and its products. During the "food crisis" of the mid-1970s, there was a fairly intensive outcry against feeding grain to cattle (or to any livestock according to some), rather than exporting it as food to persons suffering poverty and malnutrition in developing countries. However, there does not seem to be any suggestion to cease production of gasohol in order that more food might be sent to the world's hungry.

A high energy-derived demand for land is likely to be a short-run development. Over the long run, coal certainly can be a more economic source of energy than crops produced directly for this purpose. Similarly, in the long run, advances in the use of solar energy other than through agricultural crops seem a viable alternative.

The level of energy prices in the future will be extremely important in determining both the intensity of competition among demands for U.S. land and the extent to which land substitutes will be priced unfavorably. There currently is no econometric, statistical, or other quantitative basis for accurately predicting future petroleum and energy prices. These will depend on both domestic and international policy and political developments. Estimates by personnel from petroleum firms for increases in petroleum prices in 1990 range from two and a half to five times 1979 prices. If they continued their 1970–79 trend, 1990 energy prices would be three times higher than in 1979. There also is no quantitative base for predicting whether energy prices will continue to increase at this rate, or whether the past seven years represent a "one time thrust," with prices settling back under increased competition and stability among oil producing countries. In this scenario, real energy prices converge toward an equilibrium level by 1990. At least the rate of price increase over the next decade should be less than in the past decade, except in the case of extreme political scenarios. The wise thing for the nation is to expect prices of energy and of energy-intensive capital goods used in agriculture to continue to increase at a rate equal to or greater than that of recent history. Policies and programs for the future should be developed accordingly. It is better to follow this minimum regret strategy and be disappointed if high prices do not develop, than to become enmeshed in an impossible situation if they do.

It appears certain that the real price of energy and agricultural inputs derived from petroleum will increase considerably in the future. These inputs are now used at high levels, nearly at levels that maximize physical return per acre from their use. The elasticity of production this high on the yield curve is extremely low. These small elasticities near the economic optima of input have been illustrated with both earlier and recent data.[52] Hence, a small decline in the amount of input because of higher real prices will cause yield to decline by a smaller proportion than the decline in the use of the input. Thus relatively modest increases in real prices of capital goods which affect yields are not expected to depress production significantly.

[52]Earl O. Heady and Roger Hexem, *Water Production Functions in Irrigated Agriculture* (Ames, Iowa State University Press, 1978) chapter 6. Earl O. Heady and Luther W. Tweeten, *Resource Demand and Structure of the Agricultural Industry* (Ames, Iowa State University Press, 1963) pp. 106–116.

Unlike fertilizer, which can be used in varying amounts as its real price changes, other "discrete" technologies such as grain variety or hybrids are not likely to be affected by increasing real prices for capital goods. Similarly, new technologies which improve animal production and increase the rate at which feed is transformed into meat will be affected little by growing real prices for energy, chemicals, and similar inputs.

A fair portion of modern agricultural technologies relating to yield are insensitive to growing real prices related to fossil energy. The impact on the demand for U.S. land is likely to be less through the prices of capital goods that serve as land substitutes and more through the effect of these prices on the technology of developing countries. Farmers in these countries operate under a much more severe capital restraint than do the major commercial farmers of the United States. They use yield-increasing inputs in small quantities because they do not have the capital to buy more. While the elasticity of production and marginal profitability is still high at their level of use, increases in the price of inputs more rapidly exhaust their operating capital. This phenomenon is certainly much less restricting in American agriculture where capital is not an important restraint on the technologies used by the commercial farmers who produce the major portion of the nation's food supply. Looking out over the next fifty years, I believe that capital constraints in developing countries will contribute much more to the demand for U.S. land than higher real prices of land-substituting capital goods in our agriculture.

As mentioned previously, the level to which real prices of energy and capital goods derived from petroleum will rise is highly uncertain and depends on international and political variables. Under the most pessimistic scenario, the increase could be considerable. However, despite sharp price increases in the 1970s, the use of fertilizers and chemicals continued to grow. This suggests that if the increase in the price of fertilizer and other capital goods derived from petroleum is only as much in the next decade as in the past one (figures 2-5 and 2-6), U.S. agricultural technology in general is not likely to be restrained to any important extent. Fertilizers and other agricultural chemicals have not risen in real price as rapidly as fuels have (figures 2-5, 2-6, and 2-7), although chemical prices began to rise sharply in early 1980 and may take on a pattern paralleling that for energy.

While fuel for tractors increased sharply during the 1970s (figure 2-7), it is still not a large enough proportion of total production costs

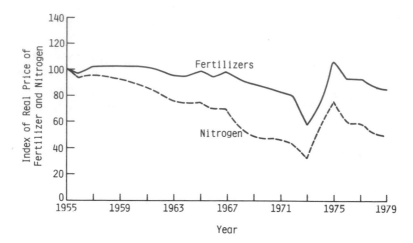

**Figure 2-5.** Index of real prices of all fertilizer and nitrogen (1955=100). (Index of prices paid for fertilizer and nitrogen divided by index of prices received for crops.)

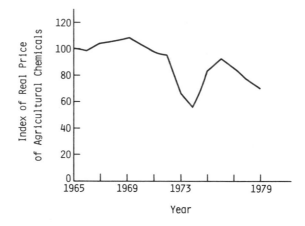

**Figure 2-6.** Index of real prices for agricultural chemicals (1965=100). (Index of prices for agricultural chemicals divided by index of prices received for all crops.)

52

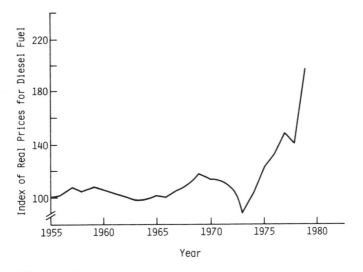

**Figure 2-7.** Index of real prices for diesel fuel (1955=100). (Index of price paid for diesel fuel divided by index of prices paid for all crops.)

and does not affect yield response directly enough to have a major impact on land demand. Studies indicate that the general demand for energy in agriculture is very inelastic, except for pump-irrigated crops.[53] The heaviest impact of high energy prices will be on agriculture irrigated by groundwater.

The increase of pump-irrigated agriculture has already started to slow. This process will continue across the Great Plains as energy prices increase further and mining of groundwater is brought to an end with withdrawal only at recharge rates. Even in the absence of higher fuel prices, the latter type of curtailment in irrigation would have come about as the water stock was exhausted. Our recent studies show that under high energy prices, the expected adjustment in U.S. agriculture is to use more land in total, with dry land substituted for irrigated land and a lower use of nitrogen.[54]

[53] Dan Dvoskin and Earl O. Heady, "U.S. Agricultural Production Under Limited Energy Supplies, High Energy Prices and Expanding Agricultural Production," CARD Report 76, Center for Agricultural and Rural Development (Ames, Iowa State University, 1976). Ronald Lacewell et al., "Impact of Natural Gas on Irrigated Agriculture," in W. Lockeretz, ed., *Agriculture and Energy* (New York, Academic Press, 1978).

[54] Ashok Chowdhury, "U.S. Agriculture Under Alternative Energy and Export Situations," unpublished Ph.D. thesis, Iowa State University, Ames, 1980. See also Dvoskin and Heady, "U.S. Agricultural Production."

With higher real prices for energy and inputs derived from it, this tendency alone will dampen expansion in use of land-substituting inputs. Fertilizer use did falter in the mid-1970s, then recovered to finish out the decade at record levels. In effect, fertilizer was still being substituted for land as the decade closed. While additional land went into grain production following 1972, this shift was due more to high commodity prices and the cessation of public land retirement programs during most of the period. With sufficiently high real prices for chemicals and fertilizers, as well as for farm commodities, farmers could increase the demand for land by substituting it for other inputs. This might be done by converting more pasture, range, and wooded land into cropland. This would come about anyway with sufficiently high real prices for agricultural commodities in the future. If it happens for the latter reason, added chemical and fertilizer inputs will be used to supplement the land.

I am optimistic that an experienced agricultural research organization in the United States can mesh its investigations and priorities with the changing prices of resources for food production. It will need to make an even more extended effort than in the past, but we should have the organization and experience to accomplish it. This same effort needs to be extended soon to the whole world if food export demands are not to dominate our choices of domestic land uses.

## Appendix: Modeling the Substitution of Nonfood Inputs for Land

Technologies that substitute for land may be represented by discrete functions (a new seed variety, for example) or by a continuous function. When this latter form of substitution is used, it gives rise to the conventional response curve or surface. The concept of substitution at various maginal rates can be illustrated by a simple production or yield function. Suppose the function is of the nature of equation (1)

$$Y = a + bN - cN^2 \tag{1}$$

where $Y$ is yield per acre and $N$ is the pounds of nitrogen applied per acre. Greater amounts of nitrogen applied per acre increase yield, but at a diminishing rate. Since yield and nitrogen application are measured in quantities per acre, the function can be restated as equation (2) where $A$, land acres, is equal

$$Y/A = a + bN/A - c(N/A)^2 \tag{2}$$

to 1.0 in equation (1). Now, to incorporate land in the production function, we multiply equation (2) by $A$, the amount of land, and simplify to obtain equation (3). This equation is a production function in which both nitrogen

$$Y = aA + bN - cN^2A^{-1} \tag{3}$$

and land area can be varied. From it we derive the isoquant equation (4) which indicates for a given yield, $\overline{Y}$, the combinations of land, $A$, and

$$A = (\overline{Y} - bN) \mp [4a\ cN^2 + (Y - bN^2)\ (2a)^{-1}]^{1/2} \tag{4}$$

nitrogen, $N$, which will produce this level of output. With $A$, land area, now expressed as a function of $N$, we determine the amount of land replaced, yield at a fixed level $\overline{Y}$, with increases in $N$.

More exactly, the substitution rates can be derived as in equation (5) which defines the marginal rates of substitution of nitrogen for land.

$$\frac{2A}{2N} = \frac{2\ cN^2A^{-1} - bN}{cN^2A^{-2}} \tag{5}$$

The marginal substitution rate of nitrogen for land declines as the ratio of $N$ to $A$ increases.

A corn production function from Colby, Kansas in 1972 can be used to illustrate these substitution quantities.[55] In equation (6), $Y$ is corn yield in pounds per acre, $W$ is acre-inches of water applied, and $N$ is pounds of nitrogen applied per acre. Setting the water level at 15 acre-inches

$$\begin{aligned} Y = 3040.3 + 684.00W + 36.25N - 19.951W^2 \\ - 0.0803N^2 + 0.6023NW \end{aligned} \tag{6}$$

[55]Heady, Doeke, and Griffin, "Policies for Lessening World Food Deficits."

and inserting land into the production function in the manner of (3)
we obtain the following land-nitrogen isoquant:

$$A = \frac{-(90574.6N - \overline{Y}) \pm [(90574.6N - \overline{Y})^2 + 35.09X\ 10^8N^2]^{1/2}}{5461.51} \tag{7}$$

Similarly, setting nitrogen at 180 pounds per acre, the land-water
isoquant is:[56]

$$A = \frac{-(792.41W - \overline{Y}) \pm [(792.41W - Y)^2 + 70503.03W^2]^{1/2}}{1766.90} \tag{8}$$

The respective marginal rates of substitution equations are given in
(9) and (10).

$$\frac{dA}{dN} = \frac{90574.6 - 642400.ONA^{-1}}{2730.76 + 321200.ON^2A^{-2}} \tag{9}$$

$$\frac{dA}{dW} = -\frac{792.41 - 39.902A^{-1}}{883.45 + 19.951W^2A^{-2}} \tag{10}$$

Hence it is quantitatively possible to illustrate the substitution of
these inputs for land. When nitrogen is fixed at 180 pounds per acre
and irrigation water is at 15 inches, an acre-inch of water substitutes
for 0.04 acres of land. However, when water is at 5 inches, the rate of
substitution of an acre-inch of water for land is 0.51. The marginal
rates of substitution of nitrogen fertilizer for land in Kansas and Iowa
(based on experimental data) are shown in table 2-6. A ton of fertilizer
is estimated (for the experimental location and year of the experi-
ments) to substitute for 24.3 and 16.1 acres of land respectively at the
irrigated Kansas and dryland Iowa locations at the low fertilizer/land
ratios. Even at the high ratios, the marginal substitution rate is rather
high.

**TABLE 2-6.** Isoquants and Marginal Rates of Substitution (MRS) of Nitrogen
Fertilizer for Land (Acres Land Replaced by a Ton of Fertilizer)

| Colby, Kansas 112 bushels of corn | | | Butler County, Iowa 116 bushels of corn | | |
|---|---|---|---|---|---|
| Nitrogen (tons) | Land (acres) | MRS dA/dN | Nitrogen (tons) | Land (acres) | MRS dA/dN |
| 0.047 | 1.674 | 24.3 | 0.028 | 0.792 | 16.1 |
| 0.094 | 1.000 | 5.4 | 0.055 | 0.610 | 3.3 |

[56]We also could hold the two inputs in some optimum or fixed proportion and derive
their combined substitution rate for land as illustrated in Heady and Tweeten, "Agricultural Policy Under Economic Development."

# Discussion

## Vernon W. Ruttan

The past decade has witnessed renewed uncertainty about the ability of American agriculture to sustain continued increases in productivity.[1] This concern draws on three sources. One is a perception that agricultural land resources are being rapidly lost to nonagricultural uses. A second is a perception that the land use practices of modern agriculture are leading to excessive loss of soil resources. The third is a perception that a pattern of technical change induced by declining energy prices, which so dramatically enhanced agricultural productive capacity over the past fifty years, is no longer sustainable.

Earl Heady has drawn on the accumulated experience of modeling the U.S. agricultural economy that has been undertaken under his direction at Iowa State University, plus a careful review of related literature, to examine the sources of demand for agricultural land during the coming decades. He concludes that one supply-side and one demand-side factor will dominate future demand for agricultural land in the United States. The supply-side factor will be the extent to which technical change will continue to be as strongly land-substituting as it was during the 1960s and 1970s. The demand-side factor will be the growth in export demand for U.S. agricultural commodities.

### Nonagricultural Land Use

Heady points out that if current trends continue, land devoted to urban and transportation use will rise from 2.6 percent of the U.S. land area in the late 1970s to 3.2 percent in the year 2000. In a paper presented at a Conservation Foundation conference in July 1980, Philip Raup pointed out that the 1950–80 trends in diversion of land

[1] National Association of Counties Research Foundation, *Disappearing Farmlands: A Citizen's Guide to Agricultural Land Preservation* (Washington, D.C. NACRF, 1979).

from agricultural to nonagricultural use will be sharply moderated during the next twenty years.[2] He gives several reasons.

1. The conversion of land to highway use, which occurred at an unprecedented pace from World War II until the mid-1970s, is now coming to a close. It is entirely possible that some land could be transferred from highway to other uses during the next twenty years.

2. Loss of agricultural land to dams and reservoirs, like loss of land for highways, has largely spent itself. There may be a few more Tellico reservoirs but no more Fort Pecks.

3. A major uncertainty is whether a period of consolidation in urban land use can be expected or whether the trend, accelerated by past expansion of the interstate highway network, toward the emergence of the "interstate city" can be expected to continue. Changes in demography, life-style, and transportation costs all point toward a slowing of the conversion of agricultural land to urban use.

4. If increasing travel costs produce changes in the demand for recreational land, there may be an intensification of competition between recreational and agricultural land use in or near metropolitan areas.

5. Changes in the demand for land for energy development also pose considerable uncertainty. Strip-mining can have dramatic impacts on local land and water use but its aggregate effect on agricultural production will be small. If, however, the current enthusiasm for the subsidized use of grains to produce motor fuel becomes firmly embedded in the political structure, the effects on land use could swamp any of the changes discussed here. On the other hand, if economic considerations dominate, the impact on land use will be hardly noticeable.

The conclusion that emerges out of an attempt to appraise the potential impact of diversion of land to nonagricultural use over the next several decades is that the aggregate effects are likely to be small. The impact of particular land diversions on the economies of individual communities and counties can, however, be large. The appropriate focus for policy should be on the management of local land use

---

[2] Philip M. Raup, "Competition for Land and the Future of American Agriculture," in Sandra S. Batie and Robert G. Healy, eds., *The Future of American Agriculture as a Strategic Resource* (Washington, D.C., The Conservation Foundation, 1980).

diversion and development rather than the more global concerns about agriculture's capacity to produce.

## Technical Change

My own inclination would be to place even greater emphasis than Heady does on the long-run implications that the closing of the fossil fuel frontier has for future expansion of agriculture's capacity to produce and for the elasticity of substitution between land and other inputs. In one sense, Heady's finding—that the general demand for energy in agriculture, except for pump irrigation, is very inelastic—is profoundly disturbing. An implication is that costs of agricultural production could rise rather substantially in response to continued growth in domestic and international demand, without substantial reductions in energy consumption. I find it hard to argue with this perspective in the short run. The major question for U.S. and world agriculture is whether it is also true over the longer run.

In the nineteenth century, when land was abundant relative to labor, research efforts were directed primarily to improving labor productivity. With the closing of the land frontier in the last years of that century, this single emphasis was no longer adequate. After a quarter century of stagnation in productivity, this thrust was complemented by efforts to improve land productivity (table D-1). The major factor focusing this effort was the declining real price of energy.

Let me review the situation that faced the nation during much of the quarter century after the closing of the frontier.[3] The domestic terms of trade turned in favor of agriculture—agricultural commodity prices rose relative to the general price level. Agricultural exports declined. By the end of the period, the United States was a net importer of agricultural commodities. Concern about soil and water conservation emerged as an important theme in policy discussion. The sources of future output and productivity growth were uncertain. It was not until the 1930s, when farmers began to plant hybrid corn, that the new biological and chemical technologies that have sustained production growth for the past half-century began to exert a measurable effect on production.

[3] Willard W. Cochrane, *The Development of American Agriculture: A Historical Analysis* (Minneapolis, University of Minnesota Press, 1979) pp. 99–121.

**TABLE D-1.** Annual Average Rates of Change (Percent per Year) in Total Outputs, Inputs, and Productivity in U.S. Agriculture, 1870–1979

| Item | 1870–1900 | 1900–25 | 1925–50 | 1950–65 | 1965–79 |
|------|-----------|---------|---------|---------|---------|
| Farm output | 2.9 | 0.9 | 1.6 | 1.7 | 2.1 |
| Total inputs | 1.9 | 1.1 | 0.2 | −0.4 | 0.3 |
| Total productivity | 1.0 | −0.2 | 1.3 | 2.2 | 1.8 |
| Labor inputs[a] | 1.6 | 0.5 | −1.7 | −4.8 | −3.8 |
| Labor productivity | 1.3 | 0.4 | 3.3 | 6.6 | 6.0 |
| Land inputs[b] | 3.1 | 0.8 | 0.1 | −0.9 | 0.9 |
| Land productivity | −0.2 | 0.0 | 1.4 | 2.6 | 1.2 |

*Sources:* From U.S. Department of Agriculture, *Changes in Farm Production and Efficiency* (Washington, D.C., Government Printing Office, 1979); and D. D. Durost and G. T. Barton, *Changing Sources of Farm Output,* USDA Production Research Report No. 36 (Washington, D.C.), February 1960. Data are three-year averages centered on year shown for 1925, 1950, and 1965.

[a] Number of workers, 1870–1910; man-hour basis, 1910–71.

[b] Cropland used for crops, including crop failure and cultivated summer fallow.

My own guess is that we are entering a period that is somewhat analogous to the 1895–25 period. The sources of future productivity growth are unclear. Heady quotes his colleague, Thompson, to the effect that yield increases in the 1980–2000 period may be more like those in the 1935–55 period than from 1960 to 1975. This is slightly more optimistic than the Lu–Cline–Quance projections showing that, if support for agricultural research continues to grow at the very low 1965–75 rate, total productivity growth can be expected to decline toward an annual rate of about 1 percent per year.[4]

## Some Concerns

I see no reason to quarrel with either the Thompson or the Lu–Cline–Quance perspective. I do, however, find several reasons for concern.

One is inadequate understanding of past sources of productivity growth in the United States. Public-sector research and agricultural extension work has accounted for about one-fourth to one-third of

[4] Yao-chi Lu, Philip Cline, and Leroy Quance, *Prospects for Productivity Growth in U.S. Agriculture,* U.S. Department of Agriculture, Agricultural Economics Report 435, September 1979.

productivity growth. Improvements in the education of farm people have accounted for a somewhat higher share. However, both formal education (schooling) and informal education (extension) tend to be effective in improving productivity only where there are rapid gains to be had from technical change itself. Our lack of knowledge about historical sources of growth does not make me very comfortable about our ability to design policies to assure future sources of growth.[5]

I continue to be troubled by the inability of this conference, and of the scientific community generally, to interpret the significance of the evidence on loss of soil resources. In my judgment, none of the participants in the current debate has succeeded in translating the physical measures into meaningful statements that can be interpreted either in terms of productivity or economic growth.

Nor am I greatly comforted by the list of potential sources of productivity growth, such as those suggested by Wittwer and employed as a basis for the Lu–Cline–Quance projections. Mansfield's studies in the industrial sector point to the weak ability to forecast either research costs or time to completion of research effort. He finds that even fairly sophisticated estimates of market penetration or diffusion have been extremely imprecise until at least five years after the introduction of products or changes.[6]

Finally, I am concerned about the difficulty that both the socialist economies and the developing countries have had in institutionalizing the research capacity and the policy regimes needed to sustain agricultural productivity growth in their countries. As a result, international commodity demand has been increasingly concentrated on North American agriculture. I am in complete agreement with Heady's final comment that this capacity needs to be extended to the whole world if we are not to let food export demand dominate our choices of domestic land uses.

[5] Vernon W. Ruttan, "Agricultural Research and the Future of American Agriculture," in Batie and Healy, eds., The Future of American Agriculture as a Strategic Resource.

[6] G. Beardsley and Edwin Mansfield, "A Note on the Accuracy of Industrial Forecasts of the Profitability of New Products and Processes," Journal of Business vol. 51 (January 1978) pp. 127–135.

# 3

# Growth in Demand for U.S. Crop and Animal Production by 2005

## *Martin E. Abel*

### Introduction

Growth in domestic and foreign demand for U.S. crops and livestock will determine to a large extent the pressures that will be placed on U.S. agricultural land resources in the next twenty-five years. In this chapter the principal crops examined are grains and oilseeds. The demand for different categories of meats is projected in order to estimate the growth in demand for feedgrains and protein meals as well as forage and pasture. The projections of growth in demand are based, not only on increased food requirements, but also on such nonfood uses as the production of ethanol from grains.

### Growth in World Grain Demand

Grains are the major source of food for most of the world. They are consumed directly or are used to produce meat, poultry, and dairy products. In the poor countries of the world, most grain is consumed directly as food. In the richer countries, grain fed to animals is the primary use. In these nations, growth in grain demand results mainly from increased meat, poultry, and milk production.

It is almost a universal phenomenon that as incomes reach a certain level, people want to eat more meat. Furthermore, meat demand is especially responsive to increases in income, as can be seen in figure 3-1.

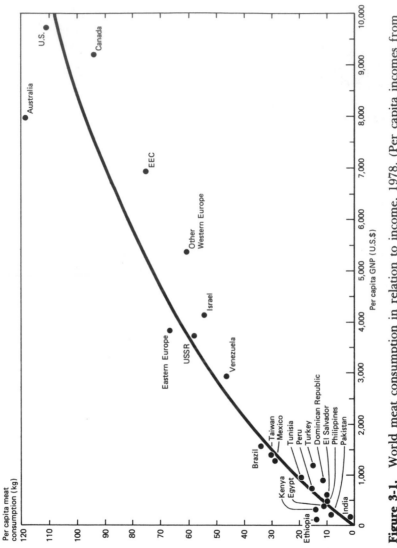

**Figure 3-1.** World meat consumption in relation to income, 1978. (Per capita incomes from World Bank Atlas. Per capita meat consumption from U.S. Department of Agriculture.)

The relationship between income levels, economic growth rates, and the demand for grain is also illustrated by the recent experience of a group of rapidly growing less developed countries. In these nations, growth in domestic grain production has not been able to keep pace with growth in demand. As a result, grain imports have increased rapidly, especially for coarse grains used to produce meat.

Wheat and coarse grain imports for fifteen of the most rapidly growing less developed countries, ranging from Algeria and Morocco to South Korea, Taiwan, Mexico, and Nigeria, have been examined, and the results summarized in table 3-1. Most of these countries had average annual rates of increase in per capita GNP of between 3 and 13 percent from 1970 to 1975. While many of them have relatively small populations, they accounted for about 325 million people in 1977, or about 8 percent of the world's population.

Taking the average rates for 1970–73 and 1976–79, the annual growth rate for coarse grain imports used as animal and poultry feed for these fifteen countries was 21 percent. For some countries, the annual growth rates of imports were extremely high: 50 percent for Tunisia; 47 percent for Mexico; 38 percent for Iran; and 38 percent for Algeria. In recent years, these fifteen nations have accounted for 13 percent of total world coarse grain trade, and almost all of this has been commercial trade.

Over the same period, wheat imports for these countries grew by 9 percent a year, ranging from a negligible annual growth rate in Taiwan to 25 percent for Iraq. Together, the fifteen countries accounted for 20 percent of total world wheat trade during the past few years.

Commercial grain imports by the rapidly growing less developed countries are expected to continue to increase at a fast pace, despite the increases already recorded. While some of the extremely high rates of growth in grain imports achieved during the 1970s cannot be maintained over a longer period, continued rapid economic growth in these nations will result in a generally strong import demand for grains. If some other less developed countries accelerate their rates of income growth, they too will become important cash markets for grain. Many nations that were formerly dependent upon food aid can no longer be looked upon as aid recipients; instead, they are now significant commercial markets and major contributors to growth in world grain consumption, including the consumption of coarse grains that usually must be imported for expanding meat production.

TABLE 3-1. Net Grain Imports, per Capita Income Growth, and Population for Selected Developing Countries

| | Wheat imports | | Coarse grain imports | | Annual growth of per capita (real) GNP: 1970–77 (percent) | Population 1977 (million) |
|---|---|---|---|---|---|---|
| | 1976/77–1978/79 average (1,000 mt) | Annual average growth rate[a] (percent) | 1976/77–1978/79 average (1,000 mt) | Annual average growth rate[a] (percent) | | |
| Algeria | 1,630 | 14.4 | 306 | 38.2 | 2.1 | 17.2 |
| Hong Kong | 153 | 0.8 | 153 | 0.2 | 5.8 | 4.5 |
| Iran | 1,283 | 11.4 | 927 | 37.9 | 13.3[b] | 34.8 |
| Iraq | 1,170 | 25.3 | 122 | — | 7.1 | 11.8 |
| South Korea | 1,833 | 0.4 | 1,841 | 17.6 | 7.6 | 36.0 |
| Libya | 500 | 12.3 | 122 | -2.0 | 4.5 | 2.6 |
| Malaysia | 434 | 4.5 | 329 | 8.0 | 4.9 | 13.0 |
| Mexico | 576 | 10.6 | 2,495 | 46.8 | 1.2 | 63.3 |
| Morocco | 1,349 | 14.9 | 48 | — | 4.2 | 18.3 |
| Nigeria | 995 | 17.6 | 60 | 9.9 | 4.4 | 79.0 |
| Saudi Arabia | 617 | 11.2 | 72 | 14.5 | 13.0 | 7.6 |
| Singapore | 167 | 6.4 | 365 | 28.0 | 6.6 | 2.3 |
| Taiwan | 636 | 0.3 | 2,826 | 13.7 | 5.5 | 16.8 |
| Tunisia | 686 | 14.7 | 208 | 50.4 | 6.5 | 5.9 |
| Venezuela | 767 | 2.4 | 992 | 14.8 | 3.2 | 13.5 |
| Total | 12,796 | 9.2 | 10,866 | 20.8 | | 326.6 |

Source: Grains, Foreign Agricultural Circular FG-20-78, U.S. Department of Agriculture, Foreign Agriculture Service, November 1978. Population and income data are from 1979 World Bank Atlas, World Bank, Washington, D.C.
[a] In preceding five years.
[b] Based on 1970–75 period.

The relationship between growth in per capita demand for grains or meat and per capita income is reflected in the income elasticity of demand, that is, the percentage increase in per capita consumption caused by a 1 percent increase in real income, all other things being held constant. The income elasticity of demand for different types of grain and for meat is shown in table 3-2 for developed, developing, and centrally planned economies.

In the developed countries, the income elasticity of demand for food grains is very low—about zero for wheat and about 0.2 for rice. The income elasticity of coarse grains, which are used primarily for feed, is essentially the same as the income elasticity for meat—approximately 0.4.

In the developing countries, the vast majority of grain is consumed directly as food and little is fed to livestock, except in the most rapidly growing countries. Income elasticities of demand for wheat and rice are about 0.4 and 0.3, respectively, and that for coarse grains consumed as food is about 0.2. We do not show an income elasticity of demand for meat and grain used as feed for these countries because these estimates are not readily available, and meat consumption in most developing countries, other than the most rapidly growing ones discussed above, is not yet significant.

In the centrally planned economies, the income elasticity for food grains is quite low, but for meat and feedgrains it is high, averaging about 0.6, or possibly more. In Eastern Europe and the USSR, wheat and rye, normally considered food grains, are also used for feed.

These basic grain consumption-income relationships are used in this chapter to project growth in grain consumption. They are modified somewhat for the centrally planned countries because those

**TABLE 3-2.** Income Elasticities of Demand

|  | Wheat | Rice | Coarse Grains | Meat |
|---|---|---|---|---|
| Developed countries | 0 | 0.2 | 0.4 | 0.4 |
| Developing countries | 0.4 | 0.3 | 0.2 | — |
| Centrally planned economies | 0.1 | 0.2 | 0.6 | 0.6 |

Sources: Donald W. Regier, *Livestock and Derived Feed Demand in the World GOL Model*, FAER No. 152, Economics, Statistics and Cooperatives Service, U.S. Department of Agriculture (Washington, D.C., 1978). Anthony Rojko, Donald Regier, Patrick O'Brien, Arthur Coffing, and Linda Bailey, *Alternative Futures for World Food in 1985: Volume I, World GOL Model: Analytical Report*, FAER No. 146, Economics, Statistics and Cooperatives Service, U.S. Department of Agriculture (Washington, D.C., 1978).

nations have not allowed meat production and consumption to keep
pace with growth in population and income. While most of the centrally planned economies in the 1970s followed policies to increase
meat supplies and are expected to continue such policies over the next
twenty-five years, political and economic considerations will continue
to prevent growth in meat production from being fully responsive to
growth in income and population.

## World Population and Income Growth

The demand for grains, oilseeds, and meats will continue to grow
rapidly as population and incomes grow. Increases in grain demand
for direct food consumption will continue in the poor countries of the
world where incomes are generally not high enough to permit rapid
increases in meats produced from grains, but where population
growth rates are fairly high. In the developed, centrally planned, and
high income developing countries, growth in meat production and
consumption will be the major source of increased demand for grains.

### Population Growth Rates

World population in 1980 was estimated to be 4.3 billion and is projected to increase to nearly 6.5 billion by 2005, or by nearly 1.7 percent
a year. Population growth rates in all regions of the world are expected to decline over the next twenty-five years, continuing a demographic trend that has already begun (table 3-3). The centrally
planned economies will show a significant decline in population
growth rates, with most of the decline occurring in China. While
declining, population growth in China still will contribute significantly
to the growth of food demand. Population growth rates in Eastern
Europe and the USSR are already quite low and are expected to
decline slightly, as are those in the developed countries. Thus, population increases will not be a major source of growth in food demand in
the developed countries or in the centrally planned countries other
than China.

On the other hand, population increases in OPEC members and

**TABLE 3-3.** Population Growth Rates

(annual average % change)

|  | 1960–73 | 1974–79 | 1980–90 | 1990–2005 |
|---|---|---|---|---|
| U.S. | 1.2 | 0.8 | 0.8 | 0.6 |
| Other OECD | 1.0 | 0.8 | 0.8 | 0.6 |
| Centrally planned | 1.5 | 1.4 | 1.2 | 1.0 |
| OPEC | 2.6 | 2.7 | 2.7 | 2.5 |
| Other developing | 2.6 | 2.7 | 2.4 | 2.1 |

*Source:* Population data and projections are based on the following: Food and Agriculture Organization of the United Nations, *World Population Estimates and Projections: 1950-2000* (Rome, FAO, 1975); Food and Agriculture Organization of the United Nations, *Agriculture: Toward 2000* (Rome, FAO, 1979).

other developing countries will continue to be a major source of growth in food demand, averaging 2.7 and 2.4 percent a year, respectively, in these two groups of countries in the 1980s and 2.5 and 2.1 percent annually by 2005.

*Income Growth*

In addition to population, growth in per capita real income is the other source of growth in the demand for food. Tables 3-4 and 3-5 show historical data and projections for real rates of growth in total and per capita gross national product (GNP), a common measure of income growth.

Growth in real GNP was significantly slower in the 1974–79 period than in the 1960–73 period in all regions of the world. These slower growth rates reflect:

Rapidly rising energy prices in the 1970s
A recession in 1974 and 1975 in almost all of the developed countries
A reversal in the 1970s of the long-term decline in real food prices
A general acceleration in inflation rates

We expect real economic growth in the next twenty-five years to be generally below that experienced in the 1970s. However, we still project substantial economic growth. Because of declines in population

**TABLE 3-4.**  Growth Rates in Real GNP

(average annual % change)

|  | 1960–73 | 1974–79 | 1980–90 | 1990–2005 | Growth 1990–2005 as % of growth 1974–79 |
|---|---|---|---|---|---|
| U.S. | 3.9 | 2.5 | 2.4 | 2.2 | 88.0 |
| Other OECD | 5.2 | 3.1 | 3.0 | 2.6 | 83.9 |
| Centrally planned | 5.3 | 3.7 | 3.5 | 3.2 | 86.5 |
| OPEC | 9.0 | 6.0[a] | 5.5 | 5.0 | 83.3 |
| Other LDC | 6.1 | 5.0 | 4.5 | 4.0 | 80.0 |

*Source:* Historical GNP growth rates are from *Economic Report of the President* (Washington, D.C., Government Printing Office, 1980) p. 325. Projected growth rates were developed by Schnittker Associates.

[a] The sharp decline in OPEC growth rates is explained by a −0.3 rate of growth in real GNP in 1974 and only a 2.6 rate of growth in 1978.

**TABLE 3-5.**  Growth Rates in Real GNP per Capita

(average annual % change)

|  | 1960–73 | 1974–79 | 1980–90 | 1990–2005 | Growth 1990–2005 as % of growth 1974–79 |
|---|---|---|---|---|---|
| U.S. | 2.7 | 1.7 | 1.6 | 1.6 | 94.1 |
| Other OECD | 4.2 | 2.3 | 2.2 | 2.0 | 87.0 |
| Centrally planned | 3.8 | 2.3 | 2.3 | 2.2 | 95.7 |
| OPEC | 6.4 | 3.3 | 2.8 | 2.5 | 75.8 |
| Other LDC | 3.5 | 2.3 | 2.1 | 1.9 | 82.6 |

*Source:* Derived from tables 3-3 and 3-4.

growth, growth in per capita income will not decline by as much as the expected decline in total economic growth.[1]

Most major economies in the world grew very slowly in 1980 and 1981. There are several reasons for this poor economic performance—tight fiscal and monetary policies in a number of industrialized countries designed to fight inflation; structural problems, large external debts and a shortage of foreign exchange in several Eastern European countries; and serious debt and foreign exchange problems in a number of developing countries. While many of these

[1] Twenty-five years is a sufficiently long period to permit progress in controlling inflation. Our assumption about inflation is not central to the analysis of this paper since we use real prices in it.

problems could exist for another few years, they do not appear to be insurmountable in the long run, and significant real economic growth in the world remains a good possibility over the twenty-five-year period for 1980–2005.

## Prospects for Increasing World Grain Supplies[2]

With continued growth in the demand for grains worldwide, it is imperative that production continue to expand at historical rates or even faster in some countries in order to avoid shortages and rising real prices of food. It is especially important for many developing countries to accelerate rates of growth in food production in order to arrest the trends toward an ever-rising need for imports.

### Expansion of Cultivated Land

Expansion of the area in crop production was once a major source of increased output in all countries and is still important in many developing countries. Several recent studies have indicated that there is a large amount of unused arable land in the world, including land in the developing countries. In spite of this, progress in bringing this land into production has been slow because of its low productivity and the high cost of making it usable for farming.

Where expansion has taken place, it has been principally on marginal, nonirrigated land with poor soils or low and variable rainfall. Crop production on such land may be quite unstable from year to year; therefore, this will not be a very dependable means of increasing total world food supplies.

It would require a significant increase in *real* crop prices to make marginal land profitable. Thus, the world is faced with the dilemma of not being able to rely on marginal land as a new source of crop production unless there is a substantial increase in real commodity and food prices. In addition, increased use of marginal land will

[2] For assessments of likely sources of growth in world agricultural production, see Pierre R. Crosson and Kenneth D. Frederick, *The World Food Situation: Resource and Environmental Issues in the Developing Countries and the United States*, Research Paper R-6 (Washington, D.C., Resources for the Future, 1977) especially pp. 35–74; and Peter Oram, Juan Zapata, George Alibaruho and Shyamal Roy, *Investment and Input Requirements for Accelerating Food Production in Low-Income Countries by 1990*, Research Report No. 10 (Washington, D.C., International Food Policy Research Institute, 1979).

intensify conservation and environmental problems associated with the cultivation of fragile land.

*Potential for Increased Irrigation*

Increased irrigation has been another major source of growth in agricultural output, but there are limits to how much additional land can be irrigated. Most of the easily developed sites for canal-type irrigation are in use. What remains are less desirable sites or those that depend on schemes that are too costly or are beyond available financial resources or engineering talents.

However, improving the efficiency of water use in existing irrigated areas is a promising and relatively low-cost way to increase agricultural production. This approach holds considerable promise for increasing food production, especially in Asia. Also, there are several areas in the world where use of groundwater for tube-well irrigation can expand food production without depleting available water supplies. Progress is being made along both of these lines.

*Technological Breakthroughs*

The technological advances that have led to dramatic increases in crop yield were discussed in the preceding chapter, and while no developments of a magnitude comparable to those of the past fifty years can be assumed, major breakthroughs in grain crop technology by 2005 cannot be ruled out. If they should occur, they would alter our projections in the following ways: (1) grain and oilseed production would be higher than projected, (2) the real price of grain would decline as a result of the new technologies, and (3) grain consumption would be higher than projected as a result of the lower prices.

*Rising Costs of Inputs*

Sustained increases in food supplies must come from consistently higher crop yields. This was achieved in Asia in the 1960s and early 1970s with the adoption of high-yielding varieties (HYVs) of wheat and rice. If these technologies were adapted to other areas, they would provide an important stimulus to output.

Much of the success of the so-called green revolution depended upon the extensive use of fertilizers, particularly nitrogen, but also phosphate and potash. Price increases in petroleum products resulted in sharply higher prices for nitrogen fertilizers in the mid-1970s. They subsequently declined, but then rose sharply again in 1980. Since further price increases seem inevitable, increased use of fertilizers is likely to be restricted by costs, especially in many of the poorer countries. Thus, grain prices will have to rise to keep pace with rising production costs and to maintain real grain prices, unless substantial technological breakthroughs in crop yields are achieved.

## World Grain Projections to 2005

Our projections for world grain production, consumption, and trade take account of likely expansion of land area, increased irrigation, and improved technology in different countries or regions. We assume constant real grain prices over the projection period at average 1978–79 levels.

The assumption of constant real prices is made for analytical convenience, and should not be interpreted as a forecast of prices for the next twenty-five years. Real prices could rise over time if either income and population growth are more rapid or production increases are slower than projected. It is also possible that real food prices could decline as a result of more rapid rates of technological change than assumed, or if slower growth rates in population and income occurred. Our projections for the United States and the world would have to be modified if alternative real price assumptions were used, and the modifications would depend on whether the price change was caused by factors affecting demand or supply.

Production of grains in most developed countries, centrally planned economies, and some developing countries that have experienced rapid increases historically is expected to grow at the same or slightly lower rates in the 1980–2005 period than during the 1960s and 1970s. For these countries, we assume that new crop land is unavailable, and where yields are already high, the rate of growth in future yield increases is slowed.

For some developing countries with low yields and relatively slow rates of growth in production historically, we assume some acceleration in production growth rates. The potential to increase yields through adapting existing crop technologies to local conditions and the pressure of growth in demand on domestic food supplies is likely to spur a number of these countries to invest more heavily in agricultural development and adopt price and other policies that are more conducive to increasing production.

Our projections of growth in demand are based on the population and economic growth framework discussed earlier. However, two exceptions in the demand projections are worth noting. In the centrally planned economies of Eastern Europe, the USSR, and the People's Republic of China, meat production and, therefore, grain feeding has not kept pace with the growth in demand. There is excess demand for meats in these economies; that is, consumers are willing to buy more at prevailing prices than is available. While we expect these nations to continue to increase per capita availability of meats, we do not expect growth in supplies to be sufficient to significantly reduce excess demand in these economies. This would require a rapid expansion in grain supplies, based heavily on growing imports, and this is unlikely on both political and economic grounds. Nonetheless, grain imports by the centrally planned economies are expected to grow.

In the case of the United States, projected production is the amount that would be required to maintain constant real grain prices, given our supply-demand projections for the rest of the world. Furthermore, these projections are for food and feed uses of grains. They do not assume major growth in industrial uses of grain, such as corn-based sweeteners and ethanol production. This possibility will be discussed later.

Tables 3-6 to 3-9 give our projections to 2005 for world production and consumption of coarse grains, wheat, and rice. Projected world and U.S. trade levels are also given for coarse grains and wheat. Rice trade is not projected because it has been only about 10 million metric tons (mmt) in recent years and is not expected to grow very rapidly. Rice will continue to be consumed principally in the countries in which it is produced.

World production and consumption of coarse grains and wheat will continue to grow, but not uniformly among countries or regions. As a result, world grain trade is expected to continue to increase rapidly over the next twenty-five years at annual rates of 2.7 and 2.6 percent, respectively, for coarse grains and wheat.

While wheat is normally considered a food grain, it is also used for feed in many countries, especially Western and Eastern Europe and the USSR. We expect this pattern of usage to continue.

We also expect the demand for coarse grains to grow more rapidly

**TABLE 3-6.** Summary of Projected World Grain Production, Consumption, and Trade[a]

(million metric tons)

|  | Average 1978–79 | Projections 2005 |
|---|---|---|
| **World production** | | |
| Coarse grains | 746 | 1,250 |
| Wheat | 434 | 660 |
| Rice | 380 | 600 |
| Total | 1,560 | 2,510 |
| **World consumption** | | |
| Coarse grains | 744 | 1,250 |
| Wheat | 437 | 660 |
| Rice | 380 | 600 |
| Total | 1,561 | 2,510 |
| **World trade[b]** | | |
| Coarse grains | 95 | 185 |
| Wheat | 79 | 145 |
| Total | 174 | 330 |
| **U.S. Exports** | | |
| Coarse grains | 64 | 145 |
| % of world trade | 67 | 78 |
| Wheat | 35 | 61 |
| % of world trade | 44 | 42 |

*Sources:* Historical data: Foreign Agricultural Service, U.S. Department of Agriculture; projections: Schnittker Associates.

[a] Crop year beginning July 1.

[b] World rice trade is relatively small, about 10 mmt a year, and is not expected to grow very rapidly in the next decade.

than production in a number of Western and Eastern European countries as growth in meat production and consumption exceeds domestic feed production capabilities. The USSR's coarse grain imports will increase from 14 mmt in the base period (1978–79/1979–80 average) to nearly 20 mmt. (These figures are derived from the difference between production and consumption adjusted for stock changes in the base period.) The long-term rate of growth in the USSR's imports is actually higher than indicated by these numbers because production in the base period was below normal and imports were correspondingly above normal levels. (Note that total grain imports by the USSR are projected to grow from 20 mmt in the base period to 30 mmt on average by 2005. In years of poor crops, imports could be substantially higher. Historically, imports in years of poor crops were about 10–15 mmt above average levels.)

**TABLE 3-7.**  World Coarse Grain Production, Consumption, and Trade[a]
(million metric tons)

|  | Average 1978–79 | Projections 2005 |
|---|---|---|
| World production |  |  |
| U.S. | 230.4 | 375 |
| USSR | 93.2 | 153 |
| W. Europe | 92.4 | 115 |
| E. Europe | 61.9 | 105 |
| Canada | 19.4 | 27 |
| Brazil | 17.9 | 30 |
| Argentina | 13.9 | 30 |
| South Africa | 10.2 | 14 |
| Australia | 6.7 | 9 |
| Thailand | 3.4 | 7 |
| Rest of world | 196.9 | 385 |
| World | 746.4 | 1,250 |
| World consumption |  |  |
| U.S. | 159.3 | 230 |
| W. Europe | 111.3 | 165 |
| USSR | 107.3 | 170 |
| E. Europe | 70.6 | 120 |
| PRC | 83.6 | 135 |
| Rest of world | 212.1 | 430 |
| World | 744.2 | 1,250 |
| Change in stocks | +2.2 | — |
| World trade | 95.2 | 185 |
| U.S. exports | 64.2 | 145 |
| % of world trade | 67 | 78 |

*Sources:* Historical data: Foreign Agricultural Service, U.S. Department of Agriculture; projections: Schnittker Associates.

[a] World crop year beginning July 1.

The most rapid growth in coarse grain imports is projected for the group of countries called the "rest of the world." Included in this group are the OPEC nations and other rapidly growing less developed countries such as South Korea, Taiwan, Mexico, and others. These nations and others that can increase economic growth rates and per capita income levels will continue to increase meat production and consumption. Imports of coarse grains for feeding will grow rapidly because domestic grain production is unlikely to keep pace with demand in these nations.

In our projections of world grain balances, we present estimates of

**TABLE 3-8.**  World Wheat Production, Consumption, and Trade [a]

(million metric tons)

|  | Average 1978–79 | Projections 2005 |
|---|---|---|
| World production |  |  |
| USSR | 105.5 | 130 |
| U.S. | 53.2 | 83 |
| W. Europe | 57.1 | 70 |
| PRC | 58.2 | 110 |
| E. Europe | 31.8 | 50 |
| India | 33.6 | 60 |
| Canada | 19.1 | 32 |
| Australia | 17.1 | 20 |
| Argentina | 8.1 | 17 |
| Rest of world | 50.7 | 87 |
| World | 434.4 | 660 |
| World consumption |  |  |
| USSR | 111.2 | 140 |
| W. Europe | 51.8 | 60 |
| PRC | 66.7 | 115 |
| E. Europe | 41.2 | 48 |
| U.S. | 22.0 | 22 |
| Rest of world | 143.9 | 275 |
| World | 436.8 | 660 |
| Change in stocks | −2.4 | — |
| World trade | 78.8 | 145 |
| U.S. exports | 34.8 | 61 |
| % of world trade | 44 | 42 |

*Sources:* Historical data: Foreign Agricultural Service, U.S. Department of Agriculture; projections: Schnittker Associates.

[a] World crop year beginning July 1.

U.S. grain consumption, production, exports, and its share of world trade for 2005. Consumption is discussed in detail in a later section.

The projected levels of U.S. wheat and coarse grain exports are based on U.S. export availability and are consistent with the projected import and export potentials for other countries or groups of countries. The U.S. share of total world trade is derived by expressing projected U.S. export levels as a percent of total world exports, the latter being derived from estimates of exportable quantities by 2005 for individual exporting countries.

It is worth noting that during the 1980–81 crop season U.S. exports

**TABLE 3-9.**  World Rice Production and Consumption (Rough Basis)[a]

(million metric tons)

|                    | Average 1978-79 | Projections 2005 |
|--------------------|-----------------|------------------|
| World production   |                 |                  |
| PRC                | 138.8           | 225              |
| India              | 72.0            | 120              |
| Indonesia          | 26.0            | 45               |
| Bangladesh         | 18.8            | 28               |
| Japan              | 15.3            | 11               |
| Thailand           | 16.6            | 26               |
| Brazil             | 8.3             | 15               |
| Burma              | 10.1            | 18               |
| S. Korea           | 7.6             | 12               |
| U.S.               | 6.0             | 8                |
| Pakistan           | 4.8             | 9                |
| Rest of world      | 55.7            | 83               |
| World              | 380.0           | 600              |
| World consumption  | 380.0           | 600              |

*Sources:* Historical data: Foreign Agricultural Service, U.S. Department of Agriculture; projection: Schnittker Associates.

[a] World crop year beginning July 1.

of wheat and coarse grains were 42.0 and 73.0 mmt, respectively. While these export levels were above the long-run trend because of relatively poor world crops, they nonetheless indicate the continued pressure of world demand on available supplies.

The U.S. share of world coarse grain trade is expected to rise from 67 percent in the base period to 78 percent in 2005. This increase in the U.S. share of world trade is based on the existing dominant position of the United States in world coarse grain trade and a more favorable climate or economic and technological environment for coarse grain production in the United States than in other major coarse grain-exporting countries such as Canada, Australia, and Argentina.

In the case of wheat, there is little change in the U.S. share of world trade over the projection period. Unlike coarse grains, the United States does not appear to have climatic or technological advantages over competing exporters, such as the three countries mentioned above and Western Europe. If other analyses indicate that the assumption of constant real grain prices is not valid, the consumption, production, and trade projections for the United States and other countries would have to be modified accordingly.

World demand for oilseeds is derived by separately estimating the growth in demand for meal and oil, with the former increasing in line with growth in meat production. Since oil and meal are joint products, the demand for oilseeds is determined primarily by the product whose demand is expected to increase most rapidly. Over the next twenty-five years we expect the demand for meal to grow slightly faster than the demand for oil.

World trade in oilseeds is difficult to characterize in simple terms because it consists of trade in both the oilseeds and their products. Our projections of U.S. exports of oilseeds (seeds plus the seed equivalent of products) are in soybean equivalents. We expect U.S. exports of oilseeds and oilseed products to grow from a soybean equivalent of 29 mmt in the 1978–79 crop year to 62 mmt by 2005, or by 2.8 percent a year. As with grains, the U.S. export projections are based on U.S. production and consumption and the projected export potential of other exporting countries.

## World Oilseed Production

World oilseed production consists of a wide variety of oil-bearing commodities. Oilseeds per se do not enter into consumption directly in any significant quantity, but they are processed to yield vegetable oils and protein meals. The relative importance of each product varies considerably among the different types of oilseeds.

The demand for oil is determined primarily by food demand, with industrial uses being rather unimportant. Oilseed meals are used as a protein supplement in livestock feed; demand, therefore, is dependent upon levels of livestock feeding. The value of some oilseeds, such as soybeans, is determined primarily by the value of the meal. The value of other oilseeds, such as palm kernels, is determined primarily by the value of the oil because the yield of meal is relatively small.

In terms of production, soybeans are the most important oilseed, accounting for 52 percent of world output in recent years. Cottonseed and groundnuts are next in importance, representing 15 and 11 percent, respectively, of world oilseed production. The other 22 percent is accounted for by sunflowers, rapeseed, copra, palm kernel, flaxseed, and a variety of other minor oilseed crops (table 3-10).

We project world oilseed production to grow from an average of 164 mmt in 1978–79 to 285 mmt by 2005, or by 2 percent a year, as

**TABLE 3-10.**   Relative Importance of Different Types of Oilseeds in World
Production

(percent)

|  | Average 1978–79 and 1979–80 |
|---|---|
| Soybeans | 52 |
| Cottonseed | 15 |
| Groundnuts | 11 |
| Sunflowers | 8 |
| Rapeseed | 6 |
| Copra | 3 |
| Palm kernel | 1 |
| Flaxseed | 2 |
| Other | 2 |
|  | 100 |

Source: Foreign Agricultural Service, U.S. Department of Agriculture.

indicated in table 3-11. The rate of increase varies among countries or regions, depending on the type of oilseed produced, availability of additional land for production, and expected rates of yield increases for different oilseed crops.

## U.S. Livestock Production

U.S. livestock production determines feed demand for grains and oilseed meals. Our projections (commercial slaughter) by type of livestock are presented in table 3-12. We assume that domestic production will keep pace with growth in demand. Trade in meats is relatively small, and we do not expect it to increase sharply in the next twenty-five years. The one exception may be continued growth in beef imports, but these will continue to be nongrain-fed beef and will not directly affect beef feeding in the United States; however, these imports may affect the demand for forage and pasture.

The income elasticities of demand for different types of meats in the United States are about as follows: beef, 0.7; pork, 0.2; and poultry, 0.9.[3]

Our production projections are normalized for livestock cycles in

[3] Donald W. Regier, *Livestock and Derived Feed Demand in the World GOL Model,* U.S. Department of Agriculture, Economics, Statistics and Cooperatives Service, Foreign Agricultural Economics Report 152 (1978).

**TABLE 3-11.**   World Oilseed Production [a]

(million metric tons)

| Country/Region | Average 1978–79 | Projections 2005 |
|---|---|---|
| U.S. | 65.2 | 109.5 |
| Canada | 4.2 | 8.3 |
| W. Europe | 2.5 | 4.5 |
| E. Europe | 3.7 | 7.1 |
| USSR | 10.6 | 18.0 |
| China | 17.0 | 30.8 |
| Argentina | 5.8 | 12.1 |
| Brazil | 14.2 | 26.0 |
| Others | 41.2 | 68.7 |
| Total | 164.4 | 285.0 |
| U.S. oilseed exports (Soybean equivalent) | 29.4 | 62.0 |

*Sources:* Historical data: Foreign Agricultural Service, U.S. Department of Agriculture; projections: Schnittker Associates.

[a] World crop year beginning October 1.

the case of beef and pork. In our base period, cattle numbers were at their cyclical low. The projection to 2005 assumes a level of production corresponding to the midpoint of the cycle. In the case of hogs, the base period production level was at about the midpoint in the cycle, and the same cyclical value is assumed for 2005.

We expect poultry production to continue to grow faster than either beef or pork, reflecting consumer preferences and the income elasticities for the different types of meat.

**TABLE 3-12.**   U.S. Livestock Production (Commercial Slaughter) [a]

(million head)

| | Average 1978–79 | Projections 2005 |
|---|---|---|
| (Cattle inventory) | (111) | (160) |
| Cattle | 33 | 48 |
| Hogs | 83 | 90 |
| Broilers | 3,788 | 6,950 |
| Turkeys | 148 | 285 |

*Sources:* Historical data: Economics, Statistics, and Cooperatives Service, U.S. Department of Agriculture; projections: Schnittker Associates.

[a] Calendar year

It is possible that our production projection for beef is too high and that for pork and poultry too low. Maintaining constant real grain prices over the next twenty-five years, as assumed in our projection framework, may limit the rate of growth in beef production because (1) economic returns on some land would be higher in grain and oilseed production than in forage production, and (2) better feed conversion ratios in hogs and poultry would favor their production over beef.

## Projected Demand for Grains and Soybeans

Table 3-13 presents projections of domestic and export demands for U.S. grains and soybeans based on U.S. export prospects, domestic feed and food uses based on our projection framework, and growing use of corn for both sweeteners and ethanol production. The latter two demands are discussed later in some detail, not only because they

**TABLE 3-13.**   Demand for U.S. Grains and Soybeans [a]

(million metric tons)

|  | Average 1978–79 | Projections 2005 |
|---|---|---|
| Wheat |  |  |
| Domestic demand | 22.0 | 22 |
| Export demand | 34.8 | 61 |
| Total | 56.8 | 83 |
| Rice |  |  |
| Domestic demand | 2.2 | 4 |
| Export demand | , 3.6 | 8 |
| Total | 5.8 | 12 |
| Feed grains |  |  |
| Domestic demand | 159.3 | 260–290 |
| Export demand | 64.2 | 145 |
| Total | 223.5 | 405–435 |
| Soybeans (beans only) |  |  |
| Domestic demand | 31.3 | 40–45 |
| Export demand | 21.4 | 24–31 |
| Total | 52.7 | 64–76 |

*Sources:* Historical data: Economics, Statistics, and Cooperatives Service, U.S. Department of Agriculture; projections: Schnittker Associates.
[a] Crop year beginning July 1.

affect the demand for grain, but also because the production of sweeteners and ethanol produces high-protein grain by-products that substitute for soybean meal and could reduce the demand for soybeans.

## Wheat

The domestic demand for wheat is expected to remain relatively stable over the next twenty-five years, as it has over the past decade or so. Per capita consumption of wheat and wheat products for food is expected to decline slightly, as reflected in the negative income elasticity for wheat, but this will be offset by continued population growth.

The quantity of wheat used for feed has shown no discernible trend over the years, but does vary from year to year depending on the relative prices of wheat and feedgrains. When wheat is cheap relative to feedgrains, more wheat will be used for feed. When the price of wheat rises relative to feedgrains, less of it is used for feed.

Exports of wheat projected to 2005 are based on our world supply-demand estimates discussed earlier.

## Rice

Domestic consumption of rice has been growing in both per capita usage and total quantities. Rice has substituted for other grains and nongrain starchy foods in U.S. diets and we expect this trend to continue. We also project an increase in rice exports, reflecting a continuation of the historical export trend.

## Feedgrains

We expect domestic feedgrain demand to grow because of increases in livestock and poultry production, continued growth in corn sweetener production (but at a slower rate than in the 1970s), and the use of corn (and possibly other feedgrains) to produce ethanol.

Because of uncertainties about the amounts of grain that will be used in sweetener and ethanol production over the next twenty-five years, we have estimated a range in projected domestic feedgrain demand by 2005.

The export demand for feedgrains is based on our analysis of world supply-demand balances for coarse grains discussed earlier.

*Soybeans*

The projected range in soybean demand, both domestic and export, reflects the possible range in grain used for ethanol projection, as well as the expected growth in demand for soybeans and other oilseeds for oil and meal production.

The use of corn in the production of corn-based sweeteners and ethanol produces high-protein grain by-products which can substitute for soybean meal in both the domestic and export markets. The higher the level of grain by-product feed production, the lower the level of soybean meal demand and, therefore, the demand for soybeans. In our analysis we assume that grain by-products will be priced competitively with other protein feed sources to ensure their use. A more detailed discussion of the interrelationships between corn and soybeans as a result of grain-based sweeteners and ethanol production follows.

*Corn Used for Sweetener and Ethanol Production*

We discuss here the interrelationships between corn used to produce sweeteners and ethanol, the resulting production of high-protein grain by-products, and their impact on the demand for soybean meal and, therefore, soybeans.

Ethanol and sweetener production from the corn wet-milling process results in gluten feed and meal, as well as corn oil. A dry-milling process for corn, appropriate only for ethanol production, yields distillers' dried grains (DDG). The yields for the various by-products are indicated in table 3-14.

Every metric ton of corn milled produces approximately 630 pounds of grain by-products which contain, on average, about half as much protein as an equal quantity of soybean meal. Thus, a metric ton of corn used to produce ethanol or sweeteners would reduce the demand for soybean meal by 315 pounds. Translated into the demand for soybeans, 1 metric ton of milled corn reduces the demand for soybeans by 0.179 metric tons.

Corn gluten feed and meal can be used as direct substitutes for soybean meal. However, DDG, which is a by-product of ethanol produced from dry milling, has to be used primarily as a protein supplement in cattle feed because of its high fiber content.

The quality of the protein in grain by-products is not quite as good as that of soybean meal since certain essential amino acids are lacking

**TABLE 3-14.**   By-Product Feed Yields from Corn Processed for Ethanol

|  | Wet milling (lbs/bushel) |  | Dry milling (lbs/bushel) |
|---|---|---|---|
| Gluten feed | 11.0 | Distillers' |  |
| Gluten meal | 4.5 | dried grains | 16.8 |
|  | 15.5 |  | 16.8 |

Sources:   *Cost of Producing High-Fructose Corn Syrup: An Economic Engineering Analysis,* Agricultural Experiment Station Bulletin No. 239, Purdue University, September 1979; and "Production of Fuel-Grade Ethanol From Grain," a paper presented by Secretary of Agriculture Bergland to the House Committee on Science and Technology, May 1979.

or are present only in small quantities in the by-product feeds. We would expect, therefore, that grain by-products would be fed in conjunction with soybean meal or other high-protein feed sources to ensure a proper nutritional balance. Taking protein quality differences into account, there is still ample scope for utilizing large amounts of grain by-product feeds in the United States and abroad.

As by-product feed production increases, we expect the prices of by-products to decline relative to soybean meal, reflecting not only the difference in protein quality but also the need to be price competitive.

In our projected production of ethanol and sweetener based on corn, we assume that one-half of the by-product feed production will be gluten feeds based on a wet-milling process and half will be DDG based on a dry-milling process. We also assume that 40 percent of by-product feed production will be consumed domestically and 60 percent will be exported. This is the same distribution that currently exists for soybeans and soybean meal.

*Sweetener Production.*   In the base period, about 400 million bushels of corn a year, or about 10 mmt, were used to produce approximately 2 million tons of corn sweeteners. We project sweetener production to reach 4–6 million tons by 2005, requiring 20–30 mmt of corn. The rapid growth in sweetener production is based on continued use of high fructose corn sweeteners (HFCS) in liquid form[4] and the recent technological breakthrough that permits HFCS to be produced in crystalline form and substituted directly for sugar.[5]

[4] Coca Cola, for example, has announced that it will shift from sugar to HFCS in its beverage production.
[5] HFCS is 1.7 times as sweet as sugar on an equal weight basis. Therefore, each ton of HFCS will replace 1.7 tons of sugar.

The United States currently consumes about 10 million tons of sugar annually and total sweetener consumption (sugar plus HFCS) is expected to continue to grow. HFCS in both liquid and crystalline form could replace a substantial part of U.S. current sugar consumption as well as accommodate growth in total sweetener demand.

*Ethanol Production.* Gasoline prices were already high enough in 1979 to make ethanol production based on corn profitable given the current tax subsidies being provided. Most projections indicate rising real prices of petroleum and gasoline to at least 1990 and probably beyond. Such real price increases would further increase the profitability of ethanol production, unless, of course, the real price of corn were to rise sharply.

In the base period about 1.5 million metric tons of corn a year were utilized to produce 150 million gallons of ethanol.[6] Several companies have announced plans to build new ethanol plants based on corn as a feedstock. Based on the energy price outlook in 1980, it appeared reasonable to assume that ethanol production could reach 1.0–1.5 billion gallons in 1985, 2 billion gallons in 1990, and perhaps 4 billion gallons by 2005. However, the outlook for ethanol production became decidedly less optimistic in 1981, as petroleum consumption declined in response to previous price increases and slow economic growth worldwide.

In our projections of feedgrain demand, we have assumed that ethanol production based on corn is in the 2–4 billion gallons per year range by 2005, requiring about 20–40 mmt of corn. There are, however, several reasons why this much corn may not be used for ethanol production by 2005.

First, the total demand for corn and other feedgrains could grow rapidly enough or production could slow enough to cause the real price of corn to rise significantly, thereby reducing its use in ethanol production. Other crops, such as sweet sorghum or sugarcane, may be more efficient feedstocks for ethanol production and eventually replace corn as a feedstock.

On another front, efforts are being made to develop efficient processes to convert cellulose to ethanol. There is a good chance that such processes would be available after 1985 or 1990. Cellulose would probably be a lower cost feedstock than corn and could account for a

---

[6] One bushel of corn yields 2.6 gallons of ethanol.

substantial part of the growth in ethanol production beyond 1990. Possible cellulose sources are by-products from timber and lumber production, crop residues such as straw and cornstalks, and garbage.

There is an increasing possibility that ethanol as an alcohol fuel may be replaced by methanol, an alcohol fuel produced from coal gasification. This is a promising technology and may become important by 2005. Finally, petroleum prices may not rise as rapidly as we have projected because the supply of petroleum and other fuels may be more responsive to price than we have assumed.

*Reduced Demand for Soybeans.*   The projected increases in grain by-product feed produced from ethanol and sweetener production will reduce the demand for soybeans by 12–24 mmt. These substitution effects are included in our projections of domestic and export demand for soybeans for 2005. In other words, if corn were not used for increased sweetener and ethanol production, the total demand for U.S. soybeans would be 88 mmt instead of the 64–76 mmt range shown above.


## Conclusions

We have projected the demand for U.S. grains and oilseeds (mainly soybeans) under the assumption that the real prices of these commodities will remain constant over the projection period in U.S. and world markets. The demands for domestic uses and exports for these commodities were estimated, including their uses for food, feed, sweetener, and ethanol production.

We have calculated the levels of U.S. grain and oilseed production that would be required to maintain real prices of these products over the next twenty-five years, but we have not tested the feasibility of these production levels under our price assumptions.

The real prices of grains and soybeans could rise over the next twenty-five years if demand in the United States and the world were to grow faster than projected, or if supplies were to increase at a slower than expected rate. This is a distinct possibility for at least the next decade because no major technological breakthroughs in crop production are in sight. On the other hand, an acceleration in rates of technological development, particularly by the latter part of the projection period, could result in lower real prices by 2005.

Based on our projection framework, we expect the demand for major agricultural products to continue to grow rapidly over the next twenty-five years. The total demand for wheat is expected to rise by 56 percent, or by 1.7 percent a year, with all of the growth occurring in exports. The total demand for rice will increase rapidly, by slightly over 100 percent for the projection period. Domestic demand is projected to grow by about 80 percent, or by 2.3 percent a year, and exports by about 120 percent, or 3.1 percent a year. Total feedgrain demand will grow by 80–90 percent in the next twenty-five years. Exports are projected to grow by nearly 110 percent and domestic use by 70–90 percent; the extent of increase will depend on the rate of expansion in grain-based sweetener and ethanol production.

The demand for soybeans will be influenced by the level of grain by-product feed produced from grain-based sweetener and ethanol production. In the absence of growth in production of corn sweeteners and ethanol, we would expect the total demand for soybeans to grow by nearly 70 percent, or by 2 percent a year. However, because of possible competition for soybean meal from grain by-products, soybean demand might grow by only 20–45 percent; the lower rate of growth in soybean demand would be associated with rapid growth in grain by-product feed supplies from grain-based sweetener and ethanol production, and the higher level of growth in soybean demand would be associated with more moderate rates of growth in grain by-product supplies.

The projected rates of growth in demand for these products are rapid enough to require substantial growth in output without an increase in real product prices. There should be a careful analysis of how much of the needed growth in production could come from improved technology that would increase per-acre yields and how much from expanded crop area and irrigation in order to test the validity of the constant real price assumption employed in our projections.

# Discussion

## Leroy Quance

Martin Abel has synthesized available projections of growth in the conventional "nonprice" factors (population and income) and some nonconventional factors (sweeteners and ethanol production) that will shift the demand schedule for U.S. farm output over the next quarter century. His treatment of the implications of potential ethanol production is especially interesting. With the addition of commodity and world regional detail, he has demonstrated a keen knowledge and perceptive analytical capability in world agriculture.

Based on a large amount of data from the USDA, FAO, the World Bank, and other sources and projections by Schnittker Associates, Abel rejects the sometimes popular "apocalypse now" viewpoint in favor of a supply-demand manageable future. This view results in part from his conclusion that population and real income growth around the world will slow.

With appropriate emphasis on world markets, Abel projects 52–69 percent increases in world grain production-consumption and even larger increases in world grain exports by the year 2005—91 to 95 percent. World coarse grain exports would increase from 95 million metric tons (mmt) in 1978–79 to 185 mmt in 2005, while world wheat exports would increase from 76 mmt in 1978–79 to 145 mmt in 2005. The United States would provide 78 percent (145 mmt) and 42 percent (61 mmt) of world exports of coarse grains and wheat respectively.

Projecting the midpoint in the U.S. livestock cycles for beef and pork, and assuming appropriate income elasticities of demand, Abel expects cattle, hog, broiler, and turkey production to increase 45, 8, 84, and 93 percent, respectively, from 1978–79 to 2005. These livestock projections appropriately reflect domestic population growth and a continuing trend by consumers to substitute poultry for some beef and pork.

The inclusion of fish consumption and production would provide a more complete picture of this dimension of the domestic food situation. I assume that Abel's main consideration was to project livestock production as a basis for deriving the projected demand for feedgrains, although he does not include or say much about projected domestic grain utilization for livestock feed.

Although he presents estimates of, and alludes to the impact of, income elasticities of demand for meats, Abel's projected livestock production does not appear to permit increases in per capita consumption of beef from the currently depressed consumption level. For example, using a carcass weight of 631.3 pounds per head, I translate Abel's 33 million head of cattle slaughtered in year 2005 into 20.8 billion pounds, or 112 pounds per capita. USDA projections made in 1979–80 indicate a production in year 2005 of 33.6 billion pounds or 126.4 pounds per capita, and those projections include a modest real price increase.

Abel's projections of feedgrain exports of 145 mmt in 2005 and wheat exports of 61 mmt are very reasonable in my opinion. His projection of only 24–31 mmt of soybean exports, however, is very low compared with the USDA's forecast for fiscal year 1981 of 28.7 mmt (beans and meal) and a projection of 42 mmt by 2005.

My biggest concern about Abel's analysis centers on the lack of a bottom line—the total increase in demand for U.S. farm output and thus the implications for resource use in U.S. agriculture. Central to this concern is the assumption of constant real prices. Relative price changes are the core of economic analysis, and economic processes play an important coordinating role in resource allocation.

Based on our own [USDA] projections and an evaluation of other projections such as those provided in Abel's paper, I expect that for the period to 2005, the nonprice or "constant price" shift in demand for U.S. farm output will be at least 2 percent per year—a solid 1 percent from domestic population and income growth and a solid 1 percent increase due to growth in exports. The domestic shift could be larger as a result of increased demand for such nonconventional uses of corn as in ethanol production and sweeteners.

Owing to sporadic weather-induced world grain production shortfalls and a competitive position in world markets, the export growth could cause more than a 1 percent increase in aggregate farm output demand.

The supply function for U.S. aggregate farm output will, on the average, shift to the right 1.5 to 2 percent per year as a result of productivity growth. This growth in supply could be partially or totally offset by inflation in input prices, environmental controls, and land and water constraints.

Thus, if we are extremely fortunate, both the demand and supply functions for aggregate farm output will shift to the right 2 percent per year. In this case, there would not be any real commodity price increases and Abel's projections could be interpreted as market projections. Then, with the exceptions noted above, Abel's projections would be on target as constant price projections but could also be taken as market projections. However, I suspect that if there were no real commodity price increases, almost all components of the demand for U.S. farm output would be larger, and Abel's projections for grains and soybeans would be too low.

If demand for grain for food, feed, and energy grows faster than Abel projects, inflation continues at high levels and raises the costs of inputs, the costs of environmental controls increase, or productivity growth slows, then the growth in demand will exceed that of supply and real prices received by farmers will increase. This would in turn dampen constant price quantities demanded in market equilibrating adjustments, especially in the export market. The odds greatly favor some combination of the above rather than the more optimistic scenario of supply increases keeping pace with growth in demand to maintain constant real prices. If constant prices prevail, I expect Abel's projections will turn out to be conservative, except possibly for feedgrains.

# 4

# The Potential Supply of Cropland

*Michael Brewer and Robert Boxley*

## Changes in Land Use

There are about 1.5 billion acres of rural land in nonfederal owner-
ships in the United States. Of this, 413 million acres were in crop use
in 1977 as measured by the National Resources Inventory (NRI).[1]
Land shifted between crop and other uses in response to economic,
technological, and institutional conditions. The dynamics of land use
differ throughout the United States, reflecting physical, demographic, and economic attributes of particular communities, locations,
and regions.

The Potential Cropland Study indicates that between 1967 and
1975 about 79.6 million acres of cropland were converted to other

Much of the material in this paper was developed by the National Agricultural Lands
Study (NALS) staff in its investigations of agricultural land availability. Initiation of this
study coincided with the release of data from the 1977 National Resources Inventory
(NRI), the latest of the series of inventories prepared by the Soil Conservation Service
(SCS). We have keyed our investigations to these data. At the outset, however, we should
note what students of U.S. land use statistics have long realized—that data sources are
fragmentary, incomplete, and often appear conflicting.

[1]The NRI was a random sample of 70,000 primary sample units, within which the
land uses on 210,000 locations were observed. The Iowa State University Statistical
Laboratory collated the results. See U.S. Department of Agriculture, *1977 National
Resources Inventories* (preliminary data, Soil Conservation Service, 1980). The other SCS
inventories, discussed later in the chapter, are the 1958 and 1967 *Conservation Needs
Inventories* and the 1975 *Potential Cropland Study.* The NRI defines cropland as nonfederal lands used to produce crops for harvest, either alone or in rotation. This may
include lands in crop rotation that are temporarily in pasture. An additional 1 million
acres of federal lands are also cropped under lease, permits, or other arrangements.

uses, two-thirds of which was pasture and range.[2] During that same period, 48.7 million acres of land were converted to cropland, 16.6 million acres to urban and built-up uses, and 6.7 million to water projects. Of the land converted to urban and built-up uses, about 30 percent came from cropland and 60 percent was in Soil Conservation Service classes I–III. Unfortunately, neither the NRI nor the Potential Cropland Study are fully satisfactory for quantifying urbanization. (This is discussed in the appendix.)

Data limitations notwithstanding, several trends in agricultural land use are apparent. The one that has attracted most public attention is the accelerated conversion of agricultural land to urban and other relatively irreversible uses. The two intervals during which average rates of such conversion can be estimated (1958–67 and 1967–75) indicate an 82 percent increase in the average annual conversion rate to urban, built-up, and transportation uses (table 4-1). Conversion to water uses also effectively removes land from agricultural production. Over these two periods, this rate increased as well, although the absolute acreage involved is substantially smaller. Though often discussed in the context of crises, the absolute acreage involved in these

**TABLE 4-1.** Conversion of Rural Land to Urban, Built-up, and Transportation Uses and to Water Bodies, 1958–75

(million acres)

|  | Year | | | Change (million acres/yr) | |
| --- | --- | --- | --- | --- | --- |
| Use category | 1958 | 1967 | 1975 | 1958–67 | 1967–75 |
| Urban, built-up, transportation | 50.77 | 60.99 | 77.64 | 1.14 | 2.08 |
| Water bodies | 49.20 | 55.79 | 62.51 | 0.73 | 0.84 |
| Total | 99.97 | 116.78 | 140.15 | 1.87 | 2.92 |

Sources: 1958 and 1967 U.S. Department of Agriculture, *Conservation Needs Inventories*, 1975; U.S. Department of Agriculture, Soil Conservation Service, *Potential Cropland Study*. "Water bodies" includes all water areas as measured by the Bureau of Census plus "small water areas" consisting of ponds and lakes of less than 40 acres and streams less than one-eighth mile in width.

[2]U.S. Department of Agriculture, *Potential Cropland Study*, Statistical Bulletin 578, October 1977. Over 3 million acres of the land converted to water was located in the southeastern states. Lee suggests that the large increase may be explained by Corps of Engineers reservoir and levee construction in swamp and marsh areas of southern Florida. (Linda K. Lee, *A Perspective on Cropland Availability*, U.S. Department of Agriculture, Agricultural Economic Report 406, July 1978, p. 16.)

shifts is modest—675,000 acres of cropland per year nationally, only 0.17 percent of the cropland reported by the 1977 NRI. Nevertheless, the conversions are not easily reversed, the rate appears to have increased, and the phenomenon warrants scrutiny.

As depicted in figure 4-1, cropland accounted for about 23 percent of the average annual conversion of rural land between 1967 and 1975. Soon after the National Agricultural Lands Study (NALS) was established, its research staff examined four hypotheses as possible explanations of these shifts or as possible harbingers of what may be expected in the future. They were:

1. Recent internal migration trends, coupled with the age structure of the U.S. population and changes in the housing market, have led to settlement patterns characterized by relatively more rapid growth in rural areas and larger lot sizes per new housing unit.

2. Substantial and increasing acreages were removed from agriculture by highways and rights of way for energy facilities.

3. Substantial and increasing acreages of unimproved land were removed from agriculture for speculative, recreational, or second home uses.

4. Substantial and increasing acreages of agricultural land became unavailable because of extractive activities.

Although incomplete, the available data permit at least an initial exploration of these hypotheses.

*Population Distribution*

Three population trends during the 1970s contributed to increases in agricultural land conversion: (1) continued metropolitan decentralization or suburbanization, (2) interregional shifts between the North and the South and West, and (3) renewed growth and vitality in rural areas. All three moved population and economic activity into less densely settled areas.[3]

Suburban growth continued at a rapid pace during the 1970s. Areas

---

[3]David L. Brown, "Agricultural Land Use: A Population Distribution Perspective," in Max Schnepf, ed., *Farmland, Food and the Future* (Ankeny, Iowa, Soil Conservation Society of America, 1979) p. 77.

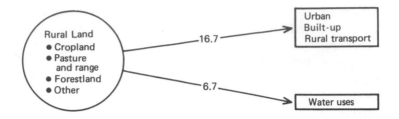

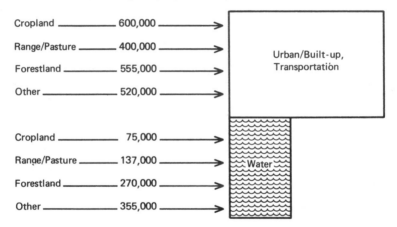

1967-1975

(acres per year shifted)

**Figure 4-1.** Net changes in use of rural lands, 1967–75 (million acres). Includes areas subsequently designated as "other nonfarm" in the *National Resources Inventory*. Approximately 50 million acres were so reported in 1977, between 2 and 3 million acres of which have cropland conversion potential. The extent to which "other nonfarm" land is reflected in recorded shifts in use over the 1967–75 period is not known. Change in water may have been overenumerated in 1975 because of a skewed population and/or classification errors in the Florida Everglades. New water control structures flooded large areas that were land in 1967. A comparison of the 1967 CNI and 1977 NRI data suggests that the 1975 PCS may have overnumerated change to water on the order of 1 to 3 million acres. (From Raymond Dideriksen et al., *Potential Cropland Study*, U.S. Department of Agriculture, Soil Conservation Service, 1977, p. 16).

peripheral to urban centers grew at an average annual rate of 1.6 percent between 1970 and 1977. This compares with an annual growth rate of less than 1 percent for the U.S. population overall. In contrast, central city portions of standard metropolitan statistical areas (SMSAs) declined by 0.7 percent a year during the period. This decline was mainly in central cities of SMSAs with a million or more population—the largest metropolitan areas. Central cities of smaller SMSAs declined much less rapidly.

Internal migration is the principal determinant of regional variations in population growth. Natural increase of the U.S. population, (births minus deaths), is low, and thus contributes little to regional variations in population change. The primary streams of interregional migration are from the North Central and Northeast regions to the South and West. Migration from the North to the South increased markedly after 1965–70, making the South a major locus of economic and population growth for the nation.

Increasing metropolitan concentration and declining small towns and rural areas no longer characterize population distribution in the United States. From 1970 to 1976, 2.3 million more people moved to nonmetropolitan counties than moved out of them. In contrast, these same counties had a net loss of 3 million persons through out-migration during the 1960s. Consequently, for the first time in the twentieth century, the rate of population growth in nonmetropolitan America (8 percent) exceeded that in metropolitan areas (4.7 percent). This turnaround affects most regions of the country—remote and completely rural areas as well as those that are partly urbanized or dominated by large cities.

Over 40 percent of the housing starts from 1970 to 1977 were in rural areas and two-thirds of those were located on lots serviced by septic systems, which typically require more land than houses in subdivisions served by central sewer systems.[4] Another factor contributing to the dispersal of rural housing has been the increasing share of the housing market captured by mobile and manufactured homes, many of which are located in rural areas outside mobile home parks.[5]

---

[4]U.S. Department of Commerce. *Annual Housing Survey, 1977* (Current Housing Reports Series H-150-77, September 1979) p. 66.

[5]James Mikesell, "Mobile Homes: More but Where, for Whom, Why," *Rural Development Perspectives,* U.S. Department of Agriculture, Agricultural Economic Report 373, June 1977.

Future settlement patterns are difficult to predict. Indications are that relatively rapid suburban growth and slow growth or a decline in central cities will continue into the twenty-first century.[6] If the magnitude, type, and location of new housing over the 1967–75 period claimed more agricultural land than was used for this purpose previously, there would be a tendency for that pattern to continue into the next decade since only 2 to 3 percent of the country's housing stock is produced each year.[7] Offsetting this is a probable slackening in the growth of new households after the mid-1980s, as the smaller birth cohorts of the 1960s come of age and the smallest of all cohorts from the 1930s reach retirement age.[8]

Underlying the housing market is a life-style of the American family that has been based on personal mobility. Speculation following the oil embargo and subsequent gasoline shortages of the early 1970s was that higher energy prices would force a consolidation of housing patterns. Current evidence suggests, however, that families continued to move out into the countryside in search of relatively lower priced housing. Greater fuel efficiency in the automobile has enabled such options to remain economically feasible. Persistence in this response would result in continuing pressure to convert rural land to built-up uses. The net effect of these demographic and economic trends on future conversion of cropland to built-up uses is problematical.

*Transportation and Energy Rights-of-Way*

Although the period 1967–75 was characterized by construction of the interstate highway system, the available data do not support the hypothesis that highway construction was a significant direct cause of the increased rate of conversion. On balance, acreages devoted to highway rights-of-way did not change dramatically between the two periods. It is possible, however, that the interstate highway system consumed more cropland than net change figures would indicate since, in contrast to earlier farm-to-market road systems, the federal

---

[6]Brown, "Agricultural Land Use," p. 79.

[7]Statistical Abstract of the U.S., September 1979, p. 782.

[8]David L. Brown and Calvin L. Beale, "The Social and Economic Context of Rural Land Use Change in the United States During the 1970's," Paper presented to the Association of American Geographers Conference on Land Use Issues of Non-Metropolitan America, College Park, Maryland, June 23–25, 1980.

interstate highway system has been superimposed over the rural land-scape, generally without regard to property lines or farm boundaries. Nevertheless, the interstate highway system is now largely in place and the taking of cropland for this purpose in the future will likely be less than in the past two decades.

Rights-of-way for other purposes, especially for transmission of electricity, frequently conflict directly with agricultural land uses. However, the land inventories from which conversion rates were computed did not separate transmission line corridors from surrounding land use classifications, and thus additional rights-of-way do not explain the change in rates of conversion as measured by the SCS inventory data.

### Conversion of Unimproved Land

Apart from area-specific analyses of rural land markets, such as the work by Healy and Short,[9] NALS found few national data with which to test the third hypothesis. One partial measure is the registration of subdivisions under the Interstate Land Sales Full Disclosure Act of 1968. Since the inception of the registration program, approximately 7.5 million subdivision lots have been registered. These are located on some 6.9 million acres of land. About 80 percent of this land reportedly was former ranch or other agricultural acreage.[10] Very few (3 percent) of the registered lots are actually built upon, and, of those, only 11 percent are used as primary residences. Despite this low rate of actual development, the remaining lots are effectively removed from other productive uses in most cases.

In the mid-1970s, subdivisions of 10,000 lots were not unusual. Currently, subdivision registration averages around 400 lots or less. This does not necessarily indicate that fewer lots are being offered for sale, though it probably does indicate that lots within developments of a size that requires their registration are not being offered to the public as frequently as several years ago. Various factors related to the general economy—high mortgage interest rates, the escalating cost of gasoline and automobile travel—might contribute to this slowdown.

[9]Robert G. Healy and James L. Short, "Rural Land: Market Trends and Planning Implications," *APA Journal* (July 1979) pp. 305–317.

[10]Estimate of the staff of the Office of Interstate Land Sales, Department of Housing and Urban Development.

*Extractive Land Use*

About 1.5 million acres of land are currently disturbed by surface mining of coal.[11] Increased dependence on coal for electricity generation and other fuel-related uses will undoubtedly increase strip-mining activity during the remainder of the century. Barse has estimated that about 1 million additional acres will be disturbed by the year 2000.[12] Further, another 800,000 acres will likely be needed for new coal and nuclear plants and associated facilities.

The amount of strip mining on cropland varies by regions. For example, in Illinois, 52 percent of the land on which coal strip-mining permits were granted was in crop use, 27 percent was in forest, and 21 percent in pasture.[13] In contrast, much less cropland is disturbed by strip mining in Appalachia or in Wyoming or Montana.

In the long run, the effects of strip mining on water quality may prove to be a more serious threat to agriculture than the acreage disturbed. In many instances land reclamation is technically possible, if not economically feasible. To date, however, few effective methods have been developed to deal with serious water quality problems associated with mining.

## Potential Cropland

As table 4-2 shows, there was considerable shifting of land between cropland and other agricultural uses over the period 1967–75. Specifically, 74.2 million acres of cropland were shifted to pasture and range, forestry, or other (nonurban) uses, while 48.7 million acres of land in these uses were shifted to crops.

More land is potentially usable for crop production than is now so used (table 4-3). The Plains states have the greatest number of potential cropland acres, but the relative potential is greatest in the Southeast. The Appalachian states also have a large cropland potential relative to their current base.

---

[11]J. Dixon Esseks, "Nonurban Competition for Land," in Max Schnepf, ed., *Farmland, Food and the Future* (Ankeny, Iowa, Soil Conservation Society of America, 1979) p. 57.

[12]J. R. Barse, "Agriculture and Energy Use in the Year 2000: Discussion from a Natural Resource Perspective," *American Journal of Agricultural Economics* vol. 59, no. 5 (December 1977).

[13]Esseks, "Nonurban Competition for Land," pp. 57–60.

**TABLE 4-2.** Land Use Shifts, 1967–75

(million acres)

| Farm production regions | Cropland to | | | | Pasture and range to | | | | Forest to | | | | Other to | | | |
|---|---|---|---|---|---|---|---|---|---|---|---|---|---|---|---|---|
| | Pasture and range | Forest | Other | Urban and water | Cropland | Forest | Other | Urban and water | Cropland | Pasture and range | Other | Urban and water | Cropland | Pasture and range | Forests | Urban and water |
| Northeast | 2.9 | 1.6 | 2.3 | 0.6 | 1.5 | 0.9 | 0.9 | 10.1 | 1.4 | 1.3 | 3.6 | 1.4 | 0.8 | 0.4 | 0.9 | 0.9 |
| Appalachia | 5.7 | 1.9 | 0.8 | 0.8 | 3.2 | 2.3 | 0.6 | 0.2 | 1.9 | 3.2 | 0.9 | 1.3 | 0.8 | 0.9 | 0.8 | 0.4 |
| Southeast | 3.2 | 1.8 | 1.6 | 0.7 | 1.9 | 1.4 | 0.7 | 0.6 | 2.2 | 6.2 | 1.4 | 1.9 | 0.4 | 0.4 | 0.6 | 2.7 |
| Lake states | 3.0 | 0.8 | 2.5 | 0.5 | 2.2 | 0.8 | 1.4 | <0.1 | 1.2 | 1.2 | 3.2 | 0.3 | 1.1 | 0.4 | 0.7 | 0.5 |
| Corn Belt | 8.4 | 1.0 | 2.7 | 0.9 | 4.9 | 1.7 | 1.5 | 0.5 | 1.3 | 4.5 | 1.1 | 0.4 | 1.2 | 1.4 | 0.6 | 0.9 |
| Delta states | 1.7 | 0.5 | 0.4 | 0.2 | 1.6 | 1.6 | 0.5 | 0.2 | 2.1 | 2.2 | 0.6 | 0.3 | 0.2 | 0.3 | 0.3 | 0.2 |
| Northern Plains | 8.8 | 0 | 1.2 | 0.2 | 6.0 | 0.2 | 0.8 | 0.3 | 0.2 | 1.2 | 0.1 | <0.1 | 0.6 | 0.6 | <0.1 | 0.7 |
| Southern Plains | 9.0 | 0.2 | 0.8 | 0.8 | 3.3 | 1.4 | 0.2 | 1.1 | 0.3 | 15.3 | 0.1 | 0.4 | 0.2 | 1.5 | 0.1 | 0.2 |
| Mountain | 5.8 | 0 | <0.1 | 0.1 | 5.6 | 2.0 | 6.3 | 1.1 | <0.1 | 22.6 | 0.7 | 0.1 | 0.4 | 6.7 | 0.1 | 0.1 |
| Pacific[a] | 4.4 | 0.5 | 0.7 | 0.6 | 1.7 | 1.8 | 1.2 | 0.2 | 0.4 | 4.8 | 4.1 | 0.4 | <0.1 | 0.6 | 0.2 | 0.4 |
| Total | 52.9 | 8.3 | 13.0 | 5.4 | 31.9 | 14.1 | 14.1 | 4.3 | 11.0 | 62.5 | 15.8 | 6.6 | 5.8 | 13.2 | 4.4 | 7.0 |

*Source: Potential Cropland Study*, U.S. Department of Agriculture, Soil Conservation Service, Statistical Bulletin No. 578, October 1977.

[a] Alaska and Hawaii not included.

Both the 1975 Potential Cropland Study and the 1977 National Resources Inventory assessed the ease with which land devoted to pasture, range, forest, or other uses could be converted to crops. These assessments were based on the collective judgment of USDA staff who served as enumerators. They were asked to classify noncropland into four qualitative categories having high, medium, low, or zero potential for conversion to crops.

The 1977 National Resources Inventory ratings for high and medium potential were based on commodity prices, production costs, and development costs prevailing in 1976. A "high potential" rating required favorable physical characteristics, and evidence of similar land in the vicinity being converted to cropland during the three preceding years. The latter criterion introduces ambiguity into the concept, for economic conditions may vary substantially over a three-year period. "Medium potential" land apparently has similar favorable physical characteristics but higher conversion costs.

Roughly similar procedures were used for the 1975 Potential Cropland Study except that 1974 prices were used. Thus, in both studies, cropland potential is pegged to prevailing economic conditions. Greater conversion incentives would be expected to exist in periods of high commodity prices. A particular parcel of land classified as having "medium potential" under less favorable economic circumstances might be labeled as having a "high" conversion potential under a more favorable agricultural economy. This may explain the reversal of proportions between acreage assigned high and medium classification in 1975 and 1977.[14] In 1975, 78 million acres had high potential and 33 million had medium potential. In 1977, the respective acreages were 36 and 91 million. The criterion used to distinguish between high and medium potential is insufficiently specified, as conversion costs are neither defined nor quantified. Indeed, the distinction between high and medium cropland conversion potential appears questionable.

Greater distinction was made by SCS between "medium" and "low" potential cropland. One of the yardsticks for the latter category given to the field examiners is that "conversion to cropland is unlikely in the foreseeable future"—defined as the next ten to fifteen years. In 1975, however, there were over 146 million acres of class I through III

---

[14]The ratio of the index of prices received to the index of prices paid was 1.17 in 1975 and 0.97 in 1977 [U.S. Department of Agriculture, *Agricultural Statistics* 1978, table 600, p. 416].

pasture, range, forest, and other land judged to have "low" cropland potential.[15] Some of this land presumably would be converted to cropland with sufficient increase in commodity prices (or decrease in conversion costs).

An estimation of the probability for future conversion depends both on anticipated commodity prices and conversion costs. Neither of these can be predicted beyond the short run, although the latter appears well suited to empirical investigation.

## Reversibility of Cropland Use

Overall, only about one-third of the lands that were in cropland in 1967 were identified as having high to medium potential for return to cropland use in 1975 (table 4-4). This was about 25 million acres, or only 20 percent of the 125 million acres of high and medium potential land. In part, this relatively low potential of former cropland reflected improvement in the quality of the cropland base (only 7.3 percent of

**TABLE 4-3.**  Current Cropland Acreage and Lands with High and Medium Potential for Conversion to Cropland

(thousands of acres)

| Farm production region | Current cropland base | With cropland potential[a] | Potential as percent of current acreage |
|---|---|---|---|
| Northeast | 16,916 | 4,637 | 12.5 |
| Appalachia | 20,753 | 14,349 | 69.1 |
| Southeast | 17,506 | 15,782 | 90.1 |
| Lake states | 44,141 | 8,121 | 18.4 |
| Corn Belt | 89,922 | 14,362 | 16.0 |
| Delta states | 21,191 | 9,967 | 47.0 |
| Northern Plains | 94,574 | 17,878 | 18.9 |
| Southern Plains | 42,222 | 20,020 | 47.4 |
| Mountain | 42,224 | 14,143 | 33.5 |
| Pacific[b] | 23,511 | 5,470 | 23.3 |
| Total | 412,960 | 124,729[c] | 30.2 |

[a]As enumerated by 1977 National Resource Inventory, based on 1976 price and cost relationships. Includes lands with "high" and "medium" potential.

[b]Includes Alaska and Hawaii.

[c]An additional 2 to 3 million acres of approximately 49 million acres of "other nonfarm" lands are also estimated to have cropland conversion potential.

[15]U.S. Department of Agriculture, Potential Cropland Study, p. 20.

**TABLE 4-4.**  Potential for Return to Crop Use of Lands that Were Cropland
in 1967

|  | Percent with high or medium cropland potential (by capability class) | | | |
| 1975 Land use | I–III | IV | V–VIII | Total |
| --- | --- | --- | --- | --- |
| Pasture and range | 51.1 | 26.7 | 22.2 | 42.7 |
| Forest land | 21.4 | 14.3 | 0 | 16.9 |
| Other land | 17.4 | 7.7 | 0 | 13.8 |
| Total—all uses | 40.1 | 20.3 | 7.3 | 32.3 |

Source: U.S. Department of Agriculture, Potential Cropland Study.
Definitions:
Class I land has few limitations restricting its use.
Class II and III lands have moderate to severe limitations restricting use and/or requiring conservation measures.
Class IV land has very severe limitations and generally is not suitable for cultivation without major treatment.
Class V–VII lands have moderate to very severe limitations not feasible to remove, which restricts their use to pasture, range, wood and/or wildlife refuge.
Class VIII land is precluded from plant production but may be used for recreation, wildlife, or water supply.

former cropland in capability classes V–VIII was viewed as having any potential for return to crop use), but even in the case of class I–III lands, only 40 percent of the former cropland was judged to have medium or better potential for return to crop use.

Possible explanations for the reduced rating of former cropland include:

1. Degradation of soil quality since 1967, from erosion or other causes.

2. Changes in the size or shape of the land parcel, or of the farm of which it was a part, so that it is no longer appropriate for crop use.

3. Changes in price/cost relationships, mix of farm enterprises, or technology which rendered the parcel uneconomic for cultivation.

4. The land was inappropriate for cultivation in the first place and after 1967 was moved into a more appropriate use.

This combination of physical and economic explanations indicates some of the hazards of defining "potential" cropland. Whatever the explanation, it appears that former cropland was only a small part of the potential cropland base in 1977.

## Significance of the Numbers

After all the inventorying activities have been completed, differences in acreage estimates reconciled, and the vagaries of potential convertibility noted, what inferences and conclusions can be drawn about the supply of cropland? Are policy guides implicit?

Much effort has been expended to address those questions. Congress, anxious to have some criteria for judging the appropriateness of soil protection programs, passed the Resources Conservation Act, which mandated an appraisal of the adequacy of the cropland base in light of future demands. State and local governments, perceiving a dwindling supply of farmlands and potential cropland, have stepped up their efforts to fashion statutes, ordinances, and other procedures for preserving cropland. Eleven federal departments joined in the National Agricultural Lands Study to explore an appropriate federal role, if any, in the management of agricultural land.

There are several critical factors that must be considered in interpreting these data for public policies. One of these is agricultural technology, which over time modifies the role of land relative to other factors or inputs in agricultural production. For example, recent developments in genetics, including techniques for recombining DNA and cloning, appear to promise accelerated rates of genetic improvement for both crops and livestock. If this promise is realized, land is unlikely to continue to play the same role in the production of agricultural commodities that it has in the past.[16] The optimal mix of land, labor, and capital in the future may be markedly different from that of today. This suggests that any national programs to preserve cropland or potential cropland should be flexibly designed to accommodate those changes once they become apparent.

A second factor is that substantial nonagricultural benefits may be derived from efforts to protect farmlands. For example, it costs more to provide public services to a dispersed population than one of similar size settled in a more compact pattern. It has been observed that a

---

[16]For further discussion of technological change and uncertainty, see the chapters by Abel, Crosson, and Heady in this volume.

strategem for agricultural land preservation that results in such a settlement pattern may yield considerable nonagricultural benefits, thus broadening its constituency.[17] It is appropriate to consider such possible benefits in judging the merits of public policies or investments in cropland protection. This is especially true for local governments in rapidly growing areas. Other nonagricultural benefits, such as the availability of near-by recreation and the amenity value of a farm landscape, serve to make preservation of agricultural lands a concern in many communities. Thus, though their objectives differ from those of farmers, urbanites often support similar programs.

Another consideration, although not necessarily third in importance, is that our understanding of the factors underlying shifting land use patterns is distressingly poor. Conceptual and methodological problems abound, giving rise to misinterpretation, but the paucity of data is also important. Disagreement and confusion have resulted. Agency budget constraints have resulted in very different levels of statistical reliability for given geographical units in the various resource inventories that have been made in recent years. Of greater importance is the fact that the entire process of data collection is poorly structured to assure relevant and reliable information. Many such data are generated by agencies for management purposes. A variety of specific program needs have guided past data collection efforts, with the consequence that comparable time series data, so critical for depicting and analyzing the dynamics of cropland use, often are not produced. These analytical needs have not yet been specified. Until they are, there is no basis for determining whether or not a single series can serve both managerial and analytical purposes.

A final consideration is that problems associated with cropland supply occur locally and regionally as well as nationally. National figures and central trends mask more extreme situations experienced at other levels. Too frequently the cropland supply situation is discussed in terms that consider the country as a single production entity. Given the importance attributed to regional and local problems, this is not very useful.

With these caveats posted, what can we say about the national supply

---

[17]The American Assembly, *The Farm and the City*. Report of the Fifty-Eighth American Assembly, Arden House, Harriman, New York, April 10–13, 1980.

of cropland? First, there is considerable flexibility in the major farm production regions of the country for adjusting land use to shifts in demand—nonagricultural as well as agricultural. The responses to such shifts are especially evident in the northern and southern Great Plains and the Southeast. Ebbs and flows in the demand for land to produce agricultural commodities have been accommodated in past years.

Of broader importance is the question of the extent to which measures should be undertaken to preserve the nation's undeveloped land for agricultural purposes. Agricultural land, including potential cropland, can be perceived as a stock resource capable of generating a flow of benefits over time. These derive from its use in various lines of production including, but not limited to, commercial agriculture. Some uses—for example, wildlife habitat, recreation, and scenic "open" lands—require little capital and labor input. Erosion, contamination, and other physical processes diminish the agricultural land base both quantitatively and qualitatively over time, although the severity and rate of degradation can be affected by management and conservation practices.

Two fundamental public policy questions arise in this regard: (1) Is the agricultural land base appropriately allocated among uses? (2) Is appropriate investment being made to maintain the flow of land services over time?

It is beyond the scope of this chapter to answer these questions. However, should the answers demonstrate a need for policy intervention, attention must be given to the instruments through which this intervention is effected. Policy tools may themselves introduce rigidities and irreversibilities that intensify the problems of future land use adjustments. Indeed, the central problem regarding the supply of potential cropland may be more closely related to the ease with which it can be shifted among uses rather than to the number of acres counted by enumerators.

## Appendix: Quantifying Changes in Land Use

Gauging changes in land use requires comparable measures of use at two points. A number of studies and data series bearing upon the conversion of land into and out of agricultural uses in the United

States are available but are not always comparable or comprehensive.[18] A frequently used series is that compiled by the Soil Conservation Service for the years 1977, 1975, 1967, and 1958. This series is tailored for specific SCS program applications, however, limiting their comparability and use as a time series for analytical purposes.

The 1958 Conservation Needs Inventory (CNI) was a 2 percent sample of nonfederal rural lands.[19] This size sample was designed to provide statistically reliable estimates at the county level. The principal objective for this data collection exercise (and the subsequent CNI effort in 1967) was to classify the sample plot by its land use and soil type, and to identify areas needing conservation treatment through physical measures or through improved management. A considerable amount of soil mapping was required to provide this information in the cells, or small areas of land, included in this survey.

CNI did not "inventory" the 1958 urban and built-up areas except in the sense of accounting for total land area of states and the nation. Enumerator instructions for the 1958 CNI permitted several procedures for developing estimates of urban and built-up areas. One of these involved use of county records describing incorporated areas. If followed, this procedure could overestimate the urban and built-up category of land use (relative to 1977 NRI procedures) since areas not in urban or built-up uses within the incorporated boundary would be treated as though they were developed. On the other hand, if applied to an entire county, this procedure would not record unincorporated built-up areas, tending toward underestimation. The extent to which enumerators elected to use this method is not known. In 1967, enumerators were instructed to update the 1958 estimates.[20] Again, a range of procedures was permitted. Both of these earlier series thus contain unspecified errors from this source.

[18]For an overview of major data series and analyses not discussed in this paper, see H. Thomas Frey, *Major Land Use in the United States: 1974,* U.S. Department of Agriculture, Agricultural Economic Report 440, November 1979); Kathryn A. Zeimetz, Elizabeth Dillion, Ernest E. Hardy, and Robert C. Otte, *The Dynamics of Land Use in Fast Growth Areas,* U.S. Department of Agriculture, Agricultural Economic Report 325, April 1976; and H. Thomas Frey and Robert C. Otte, *Cropland for Today and Tomorrow,* U.S. Department of Agriculture, Agricultural Economic Report 291, July 1975.

[19]U.S. Department of Agriculture, *Basic Statistics of the National Inventory of Soil and Water Conservation Needs,* Statistical Bulletin 317, 1958.

[20]U.S. Department of Agriculture, *Basic Statistics—National Inventory of Soil and Water Conservation Needs,* 1967, Statistical Bulletin 461, January 1971, p. 1.

The 1975 Potential Cropland Study was also based on a subsample of data points used for the 1967 CNI.[21] The principal objective of this study was to quantify the potential for new cropland, and to obtain information about the problems entailed in bringing such land into active cultivation. The study also collected data on land use changes (including conversions to urban and built-up uses) that had occurred since 1967. It was conducted under a stringent budget, and the sampling frame was designed to give statistical reliability only at the level of the farm production region.

The 1977 National Resources Inventory (NRI) was undertaken to address a far broader array of concerns, and measured more parameters than did the three earlier agricultural land surveys. It covered all nonfederal land (urban as well as rural), and was designed to address such subjects as: wetland availability, activity on floodplains, types of water use, erosion (by both wind and water), the potential for wildlife habitat, and other matters. It was a 1 percent sample and produced estimates accurate at the state level.

In the NRI, land in urban, built-up, or incorporated areas of more than 40 acres was derived from actual measurement while estimates of land in urban and built-up uses of less than 40 acres were based on sample points for which statistical confidence limits can be calculated. Enumerators were given explicit instructions for categorizing and recording their field observations within the sampled urban areas, and only those portions of an ownership tract that were actually in urban or built up uses were included in the urban and built-up category of land use.

Thus, the methods used to measure land in urban, built-up, or incorporated areas differed among the four inventories. As between the 1975 and 1977 data sets, we argue that the 1975 Potential Cropland Study is more appropriate for measuring the conversion of rural land to urban, built-up, transportation, and water uses since 1967. Land use data for 1975 and 1967 were assembled according to a common logic—namely to update earlier estimates. Both the 1967 and 1975 efforts thus focused on additional conversion to urban and built-up uses that occurred since the previous estimate, rather than revising earlier (1958) definitions or the techniques used for their measurement.

[21]U.S. Department of Agriculture, *Potential Cropland Study*, Statistical Bulletin 578, October 1977.

# Discussion

## Marion Clawson

Brewer and Boxley have plowed an old field but their furrow is straight, clean, and recent. Professional workers and scholars of many kinds have long been concerned over land area, use, productivity, and the capacity of land to provide needed food in this country. Over the decades there have been many attempts to develop and appraise data on these matters, and to estimate probable or possible future relationships or situations. I think we can be confident that such attempts will not end with the work represented in this volume. Demands upon the land and the capacity of the land to provide desired products change over time, as does our knowledge of such matters and our capacity to utilize land and other natural resources. No past and no present study, however accurate and incisive, can possibly be the final word.

While professionals have been studying the land use situation, farmers and others have been testing land use capabilities by trial and error. Farming has been attempted for centuries in a great many situations in North America, only to be abandoned for any of several reasons. Some of this land has been developed, farmed, and abandoned for cropping more than once in a long history. Knowledge of the land areas involved in this trial-and-error process—especially the lands discarded for agriculture—is limited indeed. There is little explicit consideration of these abandoned lands in this paper. In our concern with future land development it might have been instructive to have considered more fully past unsuccessful attempts at agricultural land use.

Brewer and Boxley do emphasize that the changes revealed by the available data are, for the most part, *net,* that is, they show the balance between additions to and subtractions from agricultural land use. The overall national picture is one of considerable stability when measured in total statistical terms. There have indeed been some net changes in land use, but they have been comparatively small in relative terms.

The extent of the changes seems to increase as one disaggregates national data to states and regions. The gross changes, into and out of agriculture or any other land use, have been substantially greater than the net changes. The authors rightly emphasize the dynamics of the situation. And, as they well point out, land use changes are often major for the tracts of land involved. The overall picture of statistical land use stability masks many changes of substantial importance to the land tract or to the community.

The paper makes a notable contribution by its description and analysis of the four relatively recent comprehensive agricultural land use inventories. The authors point to the limitations or deficiencies of these inventories, even for the purposes for which they were made, and even more when attempts are made to use the resultant data for other purposes. In particular, comparisons over time are clouded by lack of complete comparability in the data. The paper also makes a notable contribution by placing the issue of preservation of prime cropland in a reasoned and rational perspective. Preservation of prime farmland is important, but so are many other matters, including particularly the preservation and enhancement of the research capacity to deal with changing times.

To some extent, this paper is vulnerable to some of the criticisms the authors make of past attempts to measure agricultural land area, its productivity, and the opportunities for its extension. They examine the data and the land primarily from an agricultural point of view. They consider other land uses primarily as they impinge upon agriculture. Their paper is by no means a review and appraisal of the total land situation in the United States. It is, at best, an agricultural expert's view of total land use.

Over the years I have been much impressed, and sometimes more than a little amused, at the difference in the perception the city planners and the agricultural experts have of land use, especially of land use in the rather extensive suburban fringe areas of the country. The agricultural land use analyst is likely to group as "urban" or some other broad term all the land not now used or not under active consideration for farming use. Forty years ago, the first USDA surveys of total land use statistics grouped barren mountain tops, swamps, deserts, and city areas all together as "miscellaneous." In the intervening years, there has been more refinement, but not all that much, in the agriculturalist's view of urban land use. The city planner returns the compliment—he subdivides urban land use into many categories, but groups everything not of direct concern to him as "rural," and he considers hardly at all how that land is used. There are substantial gaps between these two approaches to land use.

There has never been, and I suspect never will be, in the United States a comprehensive national survey of *all* land for *all* uses, each considered equally legitimate. The difficulties of making any such survey and of compiling the information on a meaningful and useful basis would be very great. But I strongly suspect that every land use survey which focuses primarily upon one kind of use, whether it be cropping, forestry, recreation, residential, industrial, or any other, will have some flaws and inaccuracies simply because it is oriented to one major use. I mean here "flaws" not merely in the sense that a survey of agricultural land provides a poor base for judging recreational or urban land, but that every survey oriented to a particular land use will be adversely affected in some respects by its basic orientation.

Perhaps the most striking aspect of the paper by Brewer and Boxley is what it did not say. I am reminded of the Sherlock Holmes episode of the dog which did not bark—therein lay the solution to the mystery. In overall statistical terms, the land use situation in the United States, especially the agricultural situation, has been relatively stable for sixty years or more. As noted earlier, this overall statistical stability conceals a great deal of shifting back and forth of specific tracts of land. It is also true that most land in the United States is used today, and has been used in every intervening year, in the same general way it was used sixty or more years ago. During these sixty years population has more than doubled, GNP has increased more than six times in real terms, and the United States has emerged as a major international power. By any standards, these sixty years have been a period of important changes in the economy, social life, political structure, and international role of the United States. But agricultural land use, as measured by the usual statistics, has changed relatively little.

The use of agricultural land over the past two generations has been at the intensive, not at the extensive, margin of cultivation. I think it is likely that it will continue so. Concern over cropland area is merited, but concern over other aspects of agricultural land may be far more important.

# Discussion

## Robert G. Healy

Some environmental and natural resource problems become social and political "issues" because of the personal perceptions of individuals. People can see the air pollution in Los Angeles or Denver, the water pollution in the Ohio or the Potomac, or the rising price of energy at the gas pump or on a utility bill. Other problems become issues only when statistical data, usually the kind routinely collected by the national government, show that something is awry. The current controversy over the adequacy of the U.S. agricultural land base has origins in both factors, but seems to have been given a major push into public attention by release of the eminently quotable finding that the United States is losing 3 million acres of farmland yearly to nonagricultural use.

Urbanization has taken over farmland for decades, but public complaints focused on the type of development or the loss of open space, not the threat to food production. Only when USDA data began to show an expansion of the number of acres harvested, and at the same time an apparent jump in the rate of land conversion to other uses, was the agricultural land supply issue given its present vigor.

If, as I have suggested, the agricultural land retention issue depends heavily on the data base, those who collect and combine the data, and who frame the definitions by which it is collected, have effective control over whether or not an issue will develop. Thus I applaud the critical scrutiny that the Brewer–Boxley paper gives to the data concerning both the potential for expanding the cropland base and the rate at which land is being converted to other uses. It should not be surprising that figures on land supply and conversion are uncritically accepted by the press and in political debate, but I have noticed that they are used equally uncritically by land use researchers. This examination of the data is long overdue.

I share their conclusion that "our knowledge base is distressingly

poor," although I also agree that it is rapidly getting better. My remarks take two tracks. First, can we push the existing data a bit further
than Brewer and Boxley have done? Second, are there problems affecting the potential cropland supply that might not be fully appreciated, in part because current data do not touch on them?

On the first track, I would have liked to have seen Brewer and
Boxley make a much more explicit comparison of cropland conversion between the periods 1958–67 and 1967–75. They note in their
paper that the data for 1958, 1967, and 1975 are based on similar
collection techniques and hence are comparable. They also note that
these comparable data show a 55 percent increase in land conversion.
If the details in the 1958 data permit, I would have liked to have seen
changes during the two periods broken down both by type (how much
went into water impoundments in each period, for example) and by
region. The four possible explanations which Brewer and Boxley
advance for an acceleration in conversion are quite plausible, but I
think that it would not be impossible to quantify the individual forces
for each of the two periods and make an explicit comparison. Since
there has been a great deal of *regional* difference in such factors as
water projects and rates of rural housing growth, some regional disaggregation might make it possible to identify causes and effects.

One might also explicitly compare the amount of land conversion
revealed in these data and the estimates contained in the periodic
USDA survey, *Major Uses of Land in the United States,* which compares
changes at five-year intervals.[1] This survey uses very different
methods and definitions, but it provides a long time series of change,
and a certain amount of detail on uses. For example, I am intrigued
by the fact that the survey cites U.S. Census data showing that during
the period 1969–74 the amount of land in urbanized and incorporated areas grew at almost exactly the same yearly rate as it had
during the period 1959–69. If this is compared with the data examined by Brewer and Boxley, it provides an additional clue that the
alleged speedup in urban conversion is probably neither suburban
spread nor the growth of rural towns. Either land is being increasingly
converted outside town boundaries or the speedup did not occur.

[1]H. Thomas Frey, *Major Uses of Land in the United States: Summary for 1969,* Agricultural Economic Report No. 247, Economic Research Service (Washington, D.C., U.S.
Department of Agriculture, 1973); H. Thomas Frey, *Major Uses of Land in the United
States: 1974,* Agricultural Economic Report No. 440, Economics, Statistics and Cooperatives Service (Washington, D.C., U.S. Department of Agriculture, 1979).

Again, *regional* comparisons between the two periods for the two data sources would greatly increase the ability to test hypotheses of the kind advanced by Brewer and Boxley.

I also believe that existing data have something more to tell us with respect to potential cropland. I would take as a starting point the fact that this conference was ultimately interested, not in land supply for its own sake, but in its relation to the supply of agricultural products. This highlights the competition of various agricultural products for the same land. Looking at the 1975 Potential Cropland Study, for example (p. 5), it can be seen that most of the land with high and medium potential for conversion is now used for pasture and range.[2] If we know where this land is regionally and know something about soil types and rainfall, it should not be too hard to estimate its animal carrying capacity. That information, in turn, will help make it clear that when conversion of this land to crops moves the grain supply curve rightward, the need for grain to feed animals formerly grazed will move the *demand* curve for grain as well.

Another reason for focusing on product, not just acres, is that even after investment in conversion, potential cropland is not likely to be as productive as that presently used for crop production. Again using the 1975 Potential Cropland Study, we can calculate that 55 percent of current cropland is in soil capability class I or II. Of the land with "high" potential, 49 percent lies in those classes. Of land with "medium" potential, only 22 percent lies in the top two classes. An acre is not necessarily equal to an acre.

In addition to more thoroughly mining the data available, one might examine two other problems with respect to potential cropland supply. The first, and most susceptible to measurement, is erosion. Most of the land with high or medium potential for conversion is in soil classes IIe, IIIe, or IVe, and "e" stands for erodible. According to the 1980 RCA draft (p. 3-4), even the better of these soils are dangerously erodible when in crop production.[3] For example, IIe and IIIe soils, when in crops, exceeded tolerable erosion levels *on average* in approximately half of the United States. In eight states, cultivating

[2]Raymond I. Dideriksen, Allen R. Hidlebaugh, and Keith O. Schmude, *Potential Cropland Study*, Statistical Bulletin No. 578 (Washington, D.C., U.S. Department of Agriculture, Soil Conservation Service, 1977).

[3]U.S. Department of Agriculture, Soil Conservation Service, *Soil and Water Resources Conservation Act (RCA) Review Draft, Appraisal 1980, Part I* (Washington, D.C., U.S. Department of Agriculture, 1979).

IIIe soils created average erosion losses of more than 15 tons per acre per year. Class IVe soils are even worse. By contrast, when these soils are in pasture, they lose (RCA, p. 3-32) only 0.7 ton/acre, 1.6 ton/acre, and 2.7 ton/acre, respectively. RCA has also pointed out the eventual productivity loss caused by high erosion rates. Again, one acre is not comparable to another, or if it is in the beginning, because of erosion it may not remain that way for long.

Finally, existing data tell us very little about a serious constraint on long-term land availability, especially outside current commercial crop areas. This is the character of land ownership, its relationship to scattered rural settlement patterns, and the sizes of parcels in which land is held. Within 30 miles of Washington, one finds thousands of acres of corn each summer. This land has surely been counted as agricultural in the Agricultural Census and perhaps land use surveys. Yet it bears price tags of $10,000 per acre and above, and is owned by urban speculators and developers. Similarly, much crop and timberland in truly rural areas is held in 20-, 30-, and 50-acre hobby farms and recreational parcels. This land may well look agricultural, but in terms of parcel size and owner intentions, it is as surely converted out of modern commercial agriculture as it would be if it were at the bottom of a reservoir or covered with residences. Or consider the areas in which buckshot urbanization has surrounded agricultural parcels so that farmers can neither expand acreage nor use the full range of farming practices. Trying to measure a future land supply when it is subject to these kinds of constraints requires not only new data sources, but whole new definitions and concepts of measurement.

I think that it is the responsibility of the federal statistical community to make their definitions and working procedures more explicit than they have. And it is the responsibility of the research community to provide some new concepts that describe land conversion not just as a physical process but as an economic and institutional process as well.

# 5

# Irrigation and the Adequacy of Agricultural Land

*Kenneth D. Frederick*

## Introduction

Irrigation is a land-conserving technology. It gives higher yields by reducing losses attributable to the vagaries of the weather, encourages the use of complementary inputs such as fertilizers and improved seed varieties, and improves the prospects for multiple cropping. Irrigation also is a land-creating technology in that it opens up arid and semiarid areas to high-yielding agriculture. Consequently, it might be expected to become increasingly important as agricultural expansion presses upon the limits of a nation's land resources.

This chapter examines whether irrigation will indeed be an important technology for relieving the overall pressures on the agricultural land base or, alternatively, whether pressures on irrigators in the form of rising energy and water costs will curtail the role of irrigation and add to the overall pressures on agricultural lands.

Past expansion of U.S. irrigation has been aided by easy access to low-cost water, which has commonly been treated as a free good available to anyone able to transport it to the place of use. Indeed, in addition to having access to water without charge, in the western states the original users were granted rights to use similar quantities as long as the water was put to beneficial use. Moreover, sizable subsidies were provided for the water development costs on federal irrigation proj-

This paper draws on research partially financed by a grant from the Environmental Protection Agency's Environmental Research Laboratory in Athens, Georgia.

ects, which comprise about one-fifth of the West's irrigated acreage, and until recently, low energy prices made it relatively inexpensive to move water.

Past expansion of irrigation has not been the result of pressures on the agricultural land base. On the contrary, irrigated acreage has doubled since 1950, a period commonly characterized by surpluses and policies designed to reduce the acreage under crops. It cannot be assumed, however, that an increase in the pressure on the agricultural land base will result in a faster or even a comparable growth of irrigation in the future. Water, just as prime agricultural land, is becoming increasingly scarce and costly. Energy costs, water supplies, and salinity must be taken into account in projecting the future role of irrigation.

Despite the importance of irrigation in U.S. agriculture, surprisingly little is known about its impact on agricultural land needs, the factors accounting for its growth, or those likely to affect future growth. This chapter addresses these issues.

## The Current Role of Irrigation

Before attempting to analyze what is likely to happen to the overall level of irrigation and its impacts on agricultural production and land needs, it would help to know the current situation—that is, the acreage under irrigation, the crops grown, the yields, and the importance of irrigation to the national production of major crops. Unfortunately, acquiring this information is not easy. There are wide variations among the estimates of irrigated acreage and there are no recent and comprehensive data differentiating between irrigated and dryland production and yields. For reasons discussed in the appendix, this chapter uses the Soil Conservation Service's 1967 and 1977 inventories for data on total irrigated acreage and the censuses of agriculture for data on the relative acreage planted to specific crops.

Of the estimated 60.7 million acres irrigated in the United States in 1977, 55.7 million were cropland and 5 million were pasture. Nearly 14 percent of the nation's cropland and 11 percent of the combined cropland and pasture was irrigated (see table 5-1). More than 25 percent of the value of U.S. crops is grown on irrigated lands. Nearly 83 percent of the irrigation is in the West, where it is essential to high-productivity farming in much of the area. Irrigated lands ac-

**TABLE 5-1.** 1977 Irrigated and Dryland Agricultural Land Use by Farm Production Region (millions of acres)

| Farm production region | Irrigation | | | Dryland | | | Total | | |
|---|---|---|---|---|---|---|---|---|---|
| | Cropland | Pasture | Total | Cropland | Pasture | Total | Cropland | Pasture | Total |
| Northern Plains | 10.6 | 0.1 | 10.7 | 83.9 | 9.4 | 93.3 | 94.6 | 9.5 | 104.1 |
| Southern Plains | 8.6 | 0.4 | 9.0 | 33.6 | 27.1 | 60.7 | 42.2 | 27.5 | 69.7 |
| Mountain | 15.2 | 2.0 | 17.2 | 27.1 | 5.5 | 32.6 | 42.2 | 7.4 | 49.6 |
| Pacific | 11.9 | 1.4 | 13.3 | 11.2 | 2.8 | 14.0 | 23.2 | 4.1 | 27.3 |
| 17 Western states | 46.4 | 3.9 | 50.2 | 155.8 | 44.7 | 200.5 | 202.2 | 48.5 | 250.7 |
| Northeast | 0.4 | 0 | 0.4 | 16.5 | 5.8 | 22.3 | 16.9 | 5.8 | 22.7 |
| Appalachia | 0.4 | 0 | 0.4 | 20.4 | 18.5 | 38.9 | 20.8 | 18.5 | 39.3 |
| Cornbelt | 1.1 | 0 | 1.1 | 88.8 | 25.2 | 114.0 | 89.9 | 25.2 | 115.1 |
| Lake states | 1.0 | 0 | 1.0 | 43.2 | 6.9 | 50.1 | 44.1 | 6.9 | 51.0 |
| Southeast | 2.4 | 1.0 | 3.4 | 15.1 | 13.1 | 28.2 | 17.5 | 14.1 | 31.6 |
| Delta states | 4.0 | 0.1 | 4.1 | 17.2 | 12.6 | 29.8 | 21.2 | 12.7 | 33.9 |
| 31 Eastern states | 9.3 | 1.1 | 10.4 | 201.2 | 82.1 | 283.3 | 210.4 | 83.2 | 293.6 |
| National total | 55.7 | 5.0 | 60.7 | 357.2 | 127.8 | 486.1 | 412.9 | 132.7 | 546.9 |

Note: Minor differences in totals are due to rounding.
Source: U.S. Department of Agriculture, Soil Conservation Service, *Basic Statistics: 1977 National Resources Inventory* (NRI), Revised February 1980, tables 3a, 4a.

counted for about 23 percent of western cropland, 8 percent of their pasture, and half the value of their crop production.[1]

From 1950 to 1977 there was virtually no change in the total cropland harvested in the United States, yet average crop yields rose 68 percent and irrigated acreage more than doubled.[2] To learn more about the impacts of irrigation on the overall agricultural performance over this period, the irrigated and dryland production and yields of four crops—corn, sorghum, wheat, and cotton—are examined for seventeen western states. For these four crops, total harvested cropland was virtually unchanged, average yields rose about 122 percent, and irrigated acreage rose 383 percent.[3] These crops accounted for about 44 percent of the nation's irrigated cropland and 52 percent of all harvested cropland in 1974.

The focus on western irrigation is prompted by several factors—the West accounts for about 96 percent of the irrigated acreage of these crops, the differences between irrigated and dryland yields are much greater in the West than in the East, and the steps required to estimate 1977 irrigated and dryland crop acreage and yields make it desirable to limit the regional focus of this analysis.

Data from the 1974 census, the 1977 NRI, and various state crop and livestock reporting boards are combined to estimate the 1977 dryland and irrigated harvested acreage of corn, sorghum, wheat, and cotton.[4] The yield estimates are based on trends which eliminate or at

[1] Dallas Lea, "Irrigated Agriculture: Past Trends, Present State, and Problems of Future Expansion," second review draft, August 1977. Table 11 estimates the value of production coming from irrigated lands. Lea is with the Economics and Statistics Service of the U.S. Department of Agriculture.

[2] Data on total cropland harvested and an index of crop production per acre are in U.S. Department of Agriculture, Economics, Statistics, and Cooperatives Service, *Changes in Farm Production and Efficiency, 1977*, Statistical Bulletin No. 612, prepared by Donald D. Durost and Evelyn T. Black, Washington, D.C., November 1978. The 1977 irrigation data are from table 2 of this paper. The 1950 acreage data for the United States, the East, and the total West are from U.S. Department of Agriculture, *Agricultural Statistics 1952* (Washington, D.C., Government Printing Office, 1952). The relative breakdown between western irrigated and dryland acreage is based on the data in the 1950 Census of Agriculture.

[3] The average yield increase is the weighted average of the change in trend yields where the weights are the mean of the 1950 and 1977 acreage harvested.

[4] The 1977 acreage estimates start with the 1974 census data on irrigated and dryland crop acreage for each of the seventeen western states. The 1974 census data are not used directly since they understate irrigated acreage. The Soil Conservation Service's 1977 NRI has irrigated and dryland acreage data for the broad categories of row and close-grown crops. For each state the ratio of 1977 NRI irrigated (dryland) row crops

least reduce the impact of short-term fluctuations caused by the weather or other factors.[5] The resulting acreage and yield estimates, along with the implied production levels, are presented in table 5-2.

Irrigation provides much higher yields than western dryland farming for all four crops, but especially corn and cotton. While the yield advantage over eastern production is smaller, with the exception of wheat it is still sizable. For example, in 1977, western irrigated trend yields exceeded comparable dryland West and all eastern yields for corn, sorghum, wheat, and cotton by the following percentages:

|              | Corn | Sorghum | Wheat | Cotton |
|--------------|------|---------|-------|--------|
| Dryland West | 139  | 70      | 45    | 135    |
| East         | 30   | 26      | 3     | 37     |

One way of illustrating the importance of irrigation to the agricultural land base is to speculate on the amount of additional land that

---

to 1974 census irrigated (dryland) row crops is multiplied by the 1974 census irrigated (dryland) acreages for corn, sorghum, and cotton. The 1974 census wheat acreages of each state are adjusted by a similarly calculated ratio for close-grown crops. These adjustments are intended to compensate for three factors—the growth from 1974 to 1977, the underenumeration of the census irrigation data, and the fact that the census crop data include only farms with sales of $2,500 or more.

The above adjustment assumes that the acreage of each crop grew at the same rate as the acreage of the entire crop group. This assumption seems reasonable for wheat, which comprises the great majority of the close-grown crops. A further adjustment is required, however, to allow for differences in growth of the individual row crops from 1974 to 1977. Unfortunately, there are only partial data available for determining these differences. For corn the ratio of irrigated (dryland) corn acreage to irrigated (dryland) row crop acreage in 1977 was divided by the comparable ratio for 1974. This ratio was then multiplied by the initial estimate of 1977 irrigated (dryland) corn acreage. Similar adjustments were made for sorghum and cotton. The state crop and livestock reporting boards are the only sources of data required to calculate these ratios but only some of the states have such data. Consequently, the available data were combined to estimate a regional adjustment factor for each of the row crops.

Since the NRI crop acreage estimates include temporarily idled land and all acreage planted, further adjustment of the 1977 crop acreages was made to convert the estimates to a harvested acreage basis. This was done by assuming that the previously calculated figures correctly reflect the ratio of irrigated to dryland acres and that the U.S. Department of Agriculture's Statistical Reporting Service data are the most accurate estimates of total harvested crop acreage.

[5] Estimated yields for both irrigated and dryland production are based on fitting a linear regression to actual yields in 1950, 1954, 1959, 1969, 1974, and 1977. Census data are used for the 1950 through 1969 observations. The more recent yield data are based on crop and livestock reporting board data for all those western states providing data which differentiate between irrigated and dryland acreage and yields.

**TABLE 5.2.** Irrigated and Dryland Acreage, Yields, and Production of Corn, Sorghum, Wheat, and Cotton for 1977

| | Acreage harvested (1,000 acres) | Trend yields (bushels/acre) | Production (millions of bushels) |
|---|---|---|---|
| Corn [a] | | | |
| Irrigated West | 8,838 | 115.2 | 1,018 |
| Dryland West | 4,572 | 48.3 | 221 |
| East | 56,596 | 88.6 | 5,014 |
| U.S. total | 70,006 | 89.3 | 6,253 |
| Sorghum [a] | | | |
| Irrigated West | 1,847 | 77.4 | 143 |
| Dryland West | 10,774 | 45.5 | 490 |
| East | 1,444 | 61.4 | 89 |
| U.S. total | 14,065 | 51.3 | 722 |
| Wheat | | | |
| Irrigated West | 3,899 | 39.4 | 154 |
| Dryland West | 49,387 | 27.1 | 1,338 |
| East | 12,930 | 38.4 | 497 |
| U.S. total | 66,216 | 30.0 | 1,989 |
| | | (bales/acre) | (1,000 bales) |
| Cotton | | | |
| Irrigated West | 3,868 | 1.41 | 5,454 |
| Dryland West | 5,212 | 0.60 | 3,127 |
| East | 4,199 | 1.03 | 4,325 |
| U.S. Total | 13,279 | 0.97 | 12,906 |

*Sources:* The total acreage estimates for the West and United States are from U.S. Department of Agriculture, *Agricultural Statistics 1978,* Washington, D.C., Government Printing Office). Derivation of the irrigated and dryland acreages and the trend yields are explained in notes 2 and 3.

[a] For grain only.

would be required to produce the same level of output without irrigation. The answer, of course, depends on what happens to dryland yields both on the intensive (i.e., the lands already in production) and extensive (i.e., the additional lands devoted to dryland production) margins. Assuming no change on the intensive margin and yields equivalent to the 1977 combined average of the East and dryland West, an additional 7.1 million harvested acres would be required to compensate for the irrigated production of these four crops. This estimate contains two somewhat offsetting biases. On the one hand, it is unlikely that a 25.6-million acre increase in dryland acreage could produce such yields since the quality of the lands would be inferior to those already under dryland production. On the other hand, this estimate makes no allowance for increasing yields on those lands previously under dryland farming. On balance, 7 million acres may be a reasonable estimate of the land-conserving implications of the 18.5 million acres irrigated to these four crops. If the land-conserving impacts of the rest of the West's irrigated acreage were proportional to those of these four crops, irrigation would reduce the harvested acreage required to produce the 1977 agricultural output by about 17.8 million acres. Of course, this simple illustration ignores the difficulties of dryland farming some of the high-value specialty crops which are grown almost exclusively under irrigation.

### Impacts of Irrigation on the Production and Yields of Corn, Sorghum, Wheat, and Cotton

While many factors affect crop production, the focus here is on the role of irrigated and dryland acreage and yields. Western irrigation generally requires more intensive use of complementary inputs such as fertilizers and pesticides, and the higher yields on irrigated lands are the result of a combination of inputs. However, no attempt is made to explain the effect of these other inputs. Indeed, the data do not differentiate between the use of these inputs in irrigated and dryland farming. At least in the arid and semiarid West, water control is essential for high-yielding agriculture and thus is a necessary element in the region's agricultural expansion.

The percentage changes in dryland and irrigated production of corn, sorghum, wheat, and cotton from 1950 to 1977 are indicated in table 5-3. Nationally, corn, sorghum, and wheat output at least doubled while cotton output rose by only 18 percent. Irrigated production generally grew much faster than the total; for example, the percentage increases in irrigated production were 4,748 for corn, 251 for sorghum, 470 for wheat, and 175 for cotton. The rapid growth of irrigated output is partly due to relatively low base year levels. Thus, despite the rapid growth, irrigation accounted for only 28 percent of the national increase in corn production, 20 percent for sorghum, and 12 percent for wheat. Eastern cotton production declined sharply over this period, and irrigation accounted for 175 percent of the national increase in cotton production.

Table 5-4 differentiates between the impacts of changing acreage and yields within the irrigated West, the dryland West, and the East

**TABLE 5-3.** Changes in Irrigated and Dryland Acreage, Yields, and Production of Corn, Sorghum, Wheat, and Cotton, 1950–77

(percentages)

|  | Change in estimated acres harvested | Change in trend yields | Change in production |
|---|---|---|---|
| Corn |  |  |  |
| Irrigated West | 1,842 | 144 | 4,748 |
| Dryland West | −73 | 78 | −51 |
| East | 2 | 126 | 130 |
| U.S. total | −4 | 145 | 136 |
| Sorghum |  |  |  |
| Irrigated West | 107 | 70 | 251 |
| Dryland West | 16 | 151 | 191 |
| East | 1,028 | 190 | 3,185 |
| U.S. total | 36 | 150 | 241 |
| Wheat |  |  |  |
| Irrigated West | 328 | 31 | 470 |
| Dryland West | 2 | 96 | 99 |
| East | 7 | 77 | 90 |
| U.S. total | 7 | 92 | 107 |
| Cotton |  |  |  |
| Irrigated West | 148 | 11 | 175 |
| Dryland West | −25 | 50 | 12 |
| East | −55 | 56 | −30 |
| U.S. total | −26 | 59 | 18 |

*Sources:* The text and accompanying notes indicate the sources of the data used for this table.

on the overall change in the production of these four crops.[6] Yield rather than acreage increases were the major factors underlying the changes in national production. Indeed, total acreage declined for two of the four crops and, therefore, acreage changes had a negative impact on production in these cases. On the other hand, increased acreage accounted for more than one-half of the increase in the irrigated output of these crops.

[6] The changes in irrigated West, dryland West, and eastern production initially were divided into three components each: that due to the change in acreage with yield held constant, that due to the change in yield with acreage held constant, and that due to the impact of the change in acreage on the change in yield, which is referred to as the interaction effect. The sum of these three components is equivalent to the total change in production for each category. This can be demonstrated by starting with the following definition:

$P_t^i \equiv A_t^i Y_t^i$ where $P_t^i$ is irrigated production in year $t$; $A_t^i$ is irrigated acreage in year

**TABLE 5-4.**  Sources of Corn, Sorghum, Wheat, and Cotton Production Growth, 1950–77

| | Change in acres harvested | Change in yields | Total[a] |
|---|---|---|---|
| **Corn for grain** | | | |
| Irrigated West | 19 | 9 | 28 |
| Dryland West | −13 | 6 | −6 |
| East | 2 | 77 | 79 |
| U.S. total | −5 | 104 | 100 |
| **Sorghum for grain** | | | |
| Irrigated West | 12 | 9 | 20 |
| Dryland West | 9 | 54 | 63 |
| East | 11 | 6 | 17 |
| U.S. total | 26 | 74 | 100 |
| **Wheat** | | | |
| Irrigated West | 10 | 2 | 12 |
| Dryland West | 2 | 63 | 65 |
| East | 2 | 20 | 23 |
| U.S. total | 10 | 89 | 100 |
| **Cotton** | | | |
| Irrigated West | 156 | 19 | 175 |
| Dryland West | −44 | 61 | 17 |
| East | −218 | 126 | −92 |
| U.S. total | −182 | 281 | 100 |

*Note:*  Figures are percentages of the change in the U.S. production of each crop.

*Sources:*  The underlying data are explained in notes 2, 4 and 5. Note 6 explains the derivation of the acreage and yield contributions.

[a] The components of the totals may not add due to rounding.

---

$t$; and $Y_t^i$ is the average yield on irrigated land in year $t$. If $\Delta$ indicates the change between years 0 and $t$, then

$$\Delta P^i \equiv P_t^i - P_0^i = \Delta A^i Y_0^i + \Delta Y^i A_0^i + \Delta A^i \Delta Y^i \tag{1}$$

Thus, the change in irrigated production equals the sum of the three components on the right-hand side of the equation: the change in dryland West and eastern production also can be divided into three comparable components.

Since irrigated acreage was relatively small in the initial year (1950) and grew much faster than dryland acreage in the following decades, use of the equation in this form gives much greater weight to nonirrigated as opposed to irrigated yield changes. Furthermore, much of the production change is not attributed specifically to either yield or acreage changes because of the sizable interaction term. Consequently, the interaction term has been eliminated by rewriting equation (1) in the following but equivalent form:

$$\Delta P^i = \Delta A^i \bar{Y}^i + \Delta Y^i \bar{A}^i \tag{2}$$

where $\bar{Y} \equiv (Y_0 + Y_t)/2$ and $\bar{A} \equiv (A_0 + A_t)/2$. This equation weights the change in acreage

Average yields rose for all four crops in all regions considered. Nationally, corn and sorghum yields more than doubled, wheat yields rose 92 percent, and cotton yields rose 59 percent. Both dryland and irrigated yield trends were up, and with the exception of irrigated cotton, which rose 11 percent, and irrigated wheat, which rose 31 percent, yields rose by 50 percent or more (see table 5-3).

The change in aggregate crop yields can be divided into four contributing factors. Three of these factors—the yield changes in the irrigated West, the dryland West, and the East—are included in table 5-4, which shows their contribution to the change in production. The fourth factor results from changes in the relative regional and irrigated/dryland distribution of the total acreage. That is, since irrigated yields are generally higher, average crop yields rise as the percentage of the land irrigated rises. This occurs even with no change in average irrigated and dryland yields.

Table 5-5 presents the percentage changes in aggregate crop yields between 1950 and 1977 and indicates the percentage contributions of the four factors to these yield increases. It is evident from this table that the increases in dryland yields, both in the East and West, were the dominant factors underlying the rise in national average yields. Dryland yield increases accounted for 80 percent or more of the total increase in corn, sorghum, and wheat yield increases and 67 percent of the cotton yield increases. While the growth rate of yields was higher for dryland wheat, sorghum, and cotton than for irrigated production of these crops, the principal reason for the dominance of dryland yields is that nationally the great majority of the acres harvested are dryland. Thus, an increase in average dryland yields has a much greater impact on national production and yields than does a comparable increase in irrigated yields. The importance of the percentages of land irrigated and nonirrigated is most strikingly

---

(yield) terms by the average yields (acreages) rather than by the initial year levels. By eliminating the interaction term, the entire change in irrigated (dryland) production is divided among two terms, the change in yield and the change in acreage. The change in the total production of a given crop is equal to the sum of the changes for the irrigated West, dryland West, and East. Thus, total production change for each crop within a given region is divided into six components in table 5-4.

There are no "correct" weights for separating out the contribution of dryland and irrigated acreage and yield changes to the change in crop production. In contrast to the results presented in table 5-4, initial year weights decrease and final year weights increase the role attributed to irrigation yields.

illustrated in the case of corn. In spite of a 144 percent rise in irrigated corn yields, a 1,842 percent rise in irrigated acreage, and a 4 percent decline in total acreage, the increase in irrigated corn yields accounted for only 8 percent of the national increase in corn yields.

Table 5-5 indicates that for corn, wheat, and cotton the change in the acreage mix had a greater impact on aggregate yields than did the change in yields on irrigated lands. The most notable case is cotton; the change in the acreage mix accounted for 27 percent of the national yield increase. With the exception of sorghum, the largest acreage increases were for the irrigated West; irrigated acreage for all four crops rose as a percentage of the total. Consequently, much of the contribution to yields stemming from the changing acreage mix is attributable to the increased role of irrigation. Table 5-6 separates the

**TABLE 5-5.**  Changes in Total Crop Yields and the Sources of Changes, 1950–77

|  | | Sources of crop yield changes (percentages of total change in yields) | | | |
|  | % Change in aggregate yield | Growth of yields in irrigated West | Growth of yields in dryland West | Growth of yields in East | Change in acreage mix |
|---|---|---|---|---|---|
| Corn | 145 | 8 | 6 | 74 | 12 |
| Sorghum | 150 | 12 | 74 | 8 | 6 |
| Wheat | 92 | 3 | 71 | 23 | 4 |
| Cotton | 59 | 7 | 22 | 45 | 27 |

**TABLE 5-6.**  Impact of the Change in Acreage Mix on National Crop Yields, 1950–77 (as a percent of the change in national yields)

|  | Shift from dryland to western irrigation | Shift between dryland West and East |
|---|---|---|
| Corn | 5 | 7 |
| Sorghum | 4 | 2 |
| Wheat | 4 | 0 |
| Cotton | 37 | −10 |

contribution of the change in the acreage mix to the growth of total yields into that attributable to (a) the shift from dryland (i.e., dryland West plus East) to irrigated acreage and (b) the shift from dryland West to eastern acreage.[7] Adding the impact of increased western irrigation (from table 5-6) to the impact of the change in western irrigated yields (table 5-5) suggests that the total effect of irrigation on the growth of national yields was 13 percent for corn, 16 for sorghum, 7 for wheat, and 44 for cotton.

## Principal Factors Affecting the Future Growth of Irrigated Agriculture

The days of cheap water are ending in the West. In many areas, irrigation now depends on nonrenewable water supplies. The combination of declining groundwater tables and sharply rising energy prices is making groundwater pumping much more expensive, and the demands on the western rivers and streams already commonly exceed available supplies. Moreover, nonagricultural water demands are rising rapidly and undoubtedly will divert some water out of irrigation, which accounts for about 84 percent of the withdrawals and 90 percent of the consumption of western water.

The future of irrigated agriculture is threatened by changes in the terms on which farmers are able to secure water and the quality of the water received. The next three sections examine (1) the relation between the demand for and supply of western water, (2) the impact of rising energy costs and increasing pumping depths on the economics of irrigation in the West, and (3) the extent of salinity problems and their importance for irrigation.

---

[7] The impact of the increasing role of irrigation on national crop yields is determined by aggregating the dryland West and East and redoing the component analysis of yield changes described in note 6. With only two types of farming considered, irrigated West and all other, the yield impact of change in the acreage mix is equivalent to the impact of the change in the role of western irrigation. The difference between the yield changes attributable to the change in the acreage mix (from table 5-5) and that attributable to the shift from dryland to irrigated acreage (from table 5-6) is caused by the relative shift from dryland West to eastern production (presented in table 5-6). With the exception of cotton, all the relative shifts in acreage had positive impacts on national yields. While the changes in the role of irrigation explained 37 percent of the growth of national cotton yields, the change in relative dryland West and all East acreage reduced national yields by 10 percent over this period.

*The Availability of Water in the West*

The early development of western irrigation was based primarily on diverting surface waters to neighboring fields. Level valley lands that could be irrigated with gravity flows were the first to be developed because the costs were low. Subsequent expansion often required the construction of canals, dams, and pumps to transport water longer distances and to increase the assured supply.

The Bureau of Reclamation was established in 1902 to reclaim arid western land through irrigation. The Bureau helped ensure that the financial and engineering requirements of major water projects did not prevent the spread of irrigation. By 1975, Bureau projects were supplying 26 million acre-feet of water annually for the irrigation of over 9 million acres. In addition to providing financing and technical expertise, and enabling farmers to benefit from the economies associated with large-scale water projects, the Bureau further ensured the availability of inexpensive water for irrigation through direct subsidies. One estimate suggests that at current collection rates and costs, of the $3.62 billion the Bureau has spent for irrigation construction, roughly 56.7 percent will be paid from electricity sales, 40 percent from general tax revenues, and only 3.3 percent by the farmers.[8]

Western surface water withdrawals for irrigation peaked at about 88 million acre-feet in 1955.[9] In subsequent years, irrigation withdrawals fluctuated between 78 and 88 million acre-feet, reaching this higher level again only in 1975. This leveling off of stream flow diversions for irrigation reflected a number of factors, including the rising costs associated with developing new supplies, the competition from non-farm users for undeveloped supplies as well as water previously used for irrigation. Finally, as will be shown, relatively little surface water remained to be developed within the areas with the most favorable growing conditions.

Groundwater started to become an important water source for irrigators in the 1930s. The spread of groundwater irrigation was stimu-

[8] E. Phillip LeVeen, "Reclamation Policy at a Crossroads," in *Public Affairs,* Bulletin of the Institute of Governmental Studies, University of California, Berkeley, vol. 19, no. 5 (October 1978) pp. 2–3.

[9] The historical data on ground and surface water withdrawals in this section are from U.S. Department of Interior, Geological Survey Circulars 765 (1977), 676 (1972), 556 (1968), 456 (1961), 398 (1956) and 115 (1951).

lated in the late 1930s by the combination of advances in engine and
pumping technology and widespread drought, and in the 1950s and
1960s by the availability of cheap energy and further technological
advances, such as development of the center pivot. Groundwater withdrawals for western irrigation rose from negligible levels in the early
1930s, to about 10.7 million acre-feet in 1945, and over 56 million
acre-feet by 1975, when groundwater accounted for 39 percent of
total irrigation withdrawals. This rapid growth was largely due to
expansion of irrigation in the Northern and Southern Plains states.
These two regions, which obtain nearly 80 percent of their irrigation
water from the ground, accounted for about 60 percent of the growth
in western irrigation since 1950.[10]

This expansion of groundwater use has led to the mining of
aquifers underlying some important irrigation regions. In some cases
depleted water tables already have forced a reduction in groundwater
use. For example, in the Southern Plains, annual groundwater withdrawals for irrigation rose from less than 1 million acre-feet in 1945
to a peak of 13.3 million acre-feet in 1965; declining groundwater
tables were in part responsible for a subsequent decline in withdrawals
to 9.6 million acre-feet in 1970 and 11.1 million in 1975.

Market price is the normal measure of scarcity, but since water is
seldom allocated within a competitive market, there are no simple
ways to measure the seriousness of a region's water problems. Two
indications of the pressures on water resources—the relation between
total water use and total stream flow and the relation between offstream water use and total stream flow—are presented in table 5-7. A
third indicator—groundwater mining (that portion of groundwater
withdrawals that exceeds recharge) as a percentage of annual water
consumption—is presented in table 5-8.

All three indicators are based on average year precipitation (defined
as the quantity that will be equaled or exceeded 50 percent of the time)
and 1975 consumption levels under average conditions. Total water
use is the sum of offstream and instream uses. Offstream uses are
estimated as the total water that would have been consumed or lost
assuming 1975 demand and average precipitation. Instream uses are

[10] The regions refer to the U.S. Department of Agriculture's farm production regions. The Northern Plains includes North and South Dakota, Nebraska, and Kansas;
the Southern Plains includes Texas and Oklahoma. The growth of irrigated acreage is
based on 1950 census and 1977 NRI data.

defined as the higher of navigational water requirements or the stream flow required to maintain habitat for aquatic and riparian plants and animals. Data on these indicators are available in the Second National Water Assessment by the U.S. Water Resources Council for 21 water resource regions and 106 subregions. These water resource regions and subregions are defined according to drainage basins and no combination of these basins conforms exactly to the boundaries of the seventeen western states. However, ten of these regions, which are divided into fifty-three subregions, provide a useful approximation of the western states.[11]

In twenty-four subregions, including about 66 percent of the West's irrigated land, total water use exceeds stream flows. Furthermore, in most of the other twenty-nine western subregions, there is little slack between stream flows and total use. Total use is less than 75 percent of stream flows in only three subregions and these are areas with relatively poor agricultural potential.

A comparison of the percentages in the two columns of table 5-7 suggests the importance of instream flows to the degree of water scarcity. In thirty-three of the subregions, instream flow requirements are more than half of total water use. Although there is no consensus as to how much water should be allocated to instream uses such as fish and wildlife, this does not mean that including these uses in the total overstates water scarcity. There is also no general agreement on the amount of water that should be allocated to irrigation or any other use. Society has placed increasing importance on instream flows in recent years and their value may increase further in the future. Even though these uses do not compete for water in the marketplace, this must be taken into account if scarce water supplies are to be efficiently allocated among alternative uses.

In many areas of the West groundwater has become the principal source of supply. Pumping commonly exceeds recharge and in an average year groundwater mining exceeds 20 billion gallons per day.[12]

---

[11] These ten regions include three subregions which are either totally or largely within the eastern states and another five which include some parts of the East. The lands that are not common to both the seventeen western states and water resource regions 9 to 18 are relatively insignificant in terms of irrigation, water use, and water supply problems. Consequently, little distortion is introduced by using all ten western water resource regions as a proxy for the seventeen western states.

[12] U.S. Water Resources Council, *The Nation's Water Resources 1975–2000, Second National Water Assessment*, vol. 1, p. 18.

**TABLE 5-7.** Indicators of the Demand Pressures on Western Water Resources in an Average Year

| Region number | Subregion number | Name | Total water use as a % of total stream flow | Offstream water use as a % of total stream flow |
|---|---|---|---|---|
| 09 | | SOURIS-RED-RAINY | 62 | 2 |
| | 01 | Souris-Red-Rainy | 62 | 2 |
| 10 | | MISSOURI | 87 | 27 |
| | 01 | Missouri-Milk-Saskatchewan | 82 | 23 |
| | 02 | Missouri-Marias | 82 | 22 |
| | 03 | Missouri-Musselshell | 81 | 21 |
| | 04 | Yellowstone | 96 | 21 |
| | 05 | Western Dakotas | 84 | 24 |
| | 06 | Eastern Dakotas | 82 | 22 |
| | 07 | North and South Platte | 140 | 85 |
| | 08 | Niobrara-Platte-Loup | 103 | 69 |
| | 09 | Middle Missouri | 91 | 32 |
| | 10 | Kansas | 123 | 63 |
| | 11 | Lower Missouri | 87 | 27 |
| 11 | | ARKANSAS-WHITE-RED | 83 | 12 |
| | 01 | Upper White | 84 | 1 |
| | 02 | Upper Arkansas | 134 | 85 |
| | 03 | Arkansas-Cimarron | 114 | 56 |
| | 04 | Lower Arkansas | 83 | 19 |
| | 05 | Canadian | 122 | 62 |
| | 06 | Red-Washita | 129 | 68 |
| | 07 | Red-Sulphur | 83 | 12 |
| 12 | | TEXAS-GULF | 100 | 33 |
| | 01 | Sabine-Neches | 85 | 5 |
| | 02 | Trinity-Galveston Bay | 89 | 18 |
| | 03 | Brazos | 142 | 84 |
| | 04 | Colorado (Texas) | 119 | 82 |
| | 05 | Nueces-Texas Coastal | 96 | 26 |
| 13 | | RIO GRANDE | 136 | 88 |
| | 01 | Rio Grande Headwaters | 110 | 69 |
| | 02 | Middle Rio Grande | 140 | 96 |
| | 03 | Rio Grande-Pecos | 148 | 102 |
| | 04 | Upper Pecos | 144 | 94 |
| | 05 | Lower Rio Grande | 136 | 88 |
| 14 | | UPPER COLORADO | 84 | 20 |
| | 01 | Green-White-Yampa | 87 | 22 |
| | 02 | Colorado-Gunnison | 80 | 17 |
| | 03 | Colorado-San Juan | 84 | 20 |
| 15 | | LOWER COLORADO | 225 | 114 |
| | 01 | Little Colorado | 80 | 21 |
| | 02 | Lower Colorado Main Stem | 225 | 114 |
| | 03 | Gila | 304 | 254 |
| 16 | | GREAT BASIN | 125 | 66 |
| | 01 | Bear-Great Salt Lake | 102 | 44 |

| | 02 | Sevier Lake | 186 | 127 |
| | 03 | Humboldt-Tonopah Desert | 177 | 117 |
| | 04 | Central Lahontan | 116 | 56 |
| 17 | | PACIFIC NORTHWEST | 84 | 4 |
| | 01 | Clark Fork-Kootenai | 62 | 2 |
| | 02 | Upper/Middle Columbia | 79 | 8 |
| | 03 | Upper/Central Snake | 91 | 33 |
| | 04 | Lower Snake | 78 | 16 |
| | 05 | Coast-Lower Columbia | 85 | 5 |
| | 06 | Puget Sound | 81 | <1 |
| | 07 | Oregon Closed Basin | 101 | 41 |
| 18 | | CALIFORNIA | 83 | 37 |
| | 01 | Klamath-North Coastal | 65 | 3 |
| | 02 | Sacramento-Lahontan | 76 | 28 |
| | 03 | San Joaquin-Tulare | 109 | 89 |
| | 04 | San Francisco Bay | 91 | 24 |
| | 05 | Central California Coast | 83 | 37 |
| | 06 | Southern California | 107 | 101 |
| | 07 | Lahontan-South | 243 | 100 |

Source:   U.S. Water Resources Council, *The Nation's Water Resources: The Second National Assessment*, vol. 3, appendix II, table II-5. (Washington, D.C., Government Printing Office, 1978).

In twenty-one water resource subregions, groundwater mining is equivalent to 10 percent or more of total water consumption (see table 5-8). Not surprisingly, there is a close parallel between these subregions and the twenty-four others where average year water requirements exceed stream flow; seventeen subregions belong to both groups and these seventeen account for about 86 percent of the total western groundwater depletions. Groundwater mining supplies 30 percent or more of consumption in eleven subregions and 50 percent or more in five subregions. The five subregions with the highest rates of groundwater mining include most of the High Plains of Texas, Oklahoma, New Mexico, Colorado, and Kansas, and Arizona's principal agricultural areas. These five subregions alone account for 20 percent of the West's irrigated lands.

Despite the enormous quantities of water involved, groundwater mining does not threaten the available water stored in any of the water resource regions or subregions during the foreseeable future. Groundwater stocks are large, and only in the California region does annual mining for an entire region approach 1 percent of available

**TABLE 5-8.** Groundwater Mining as a Percentage of Annual Water Consumption in an Average Year

| Region number | Subregion number[a] | Name | Groundwater mining as a % of annual consumption |
|---|---|---|---|
| 10 | | MISSOURI | 17 |
| | 03 | Missouri-Musselshell | 1 |
| | 05 | Western Dakotas | 2 |
| | 06 | Eastern Dakotas | 7 |
| | 07 | North and South Platte | 13 |
| | 08 | Niobrara-Platte-Loup | 13 |
| | 09 | Middle Missouri | 16 |
| | 10 | Kansas | 41 |
| | 11 | Lower Missouri | 5 |
| 11 | | ARKANSAS-WHITE-RED | 68 |
| | 01 | Upper White | 2 |
| | 02 | Upper Arkansas | 3 |
| | 03 | Arkansas-Cimarron | 103 |
| | 04 | Lower Arkansas | 2 |
| | 05 | Canadian | 85 |
| | 06 | Red-Washita | 55 |
| | 07 | Red-Sulphur | 1 |
| 12 | | TEXAS-GULF | 50 |
| | 01 | Sabine-Neches | 8 |
| | 02 | Trinity-Galveston Bay | 19 |
| | 03 | Brazos | 78 |
| | 04 | Colorado (Texas) | 38 |
| | 05 | Nueces-Texas Coastal | 26 |
| 13 | | RIO GRANDE | 16 |
| | 02 | Middle Rio Grande | 21 |
| | 03 | Rio Grande-Pecos | 46 |
| | 04 | Upper Pecos | 16 |
| | 05 | Lower Rio Grande | 1 |
| 15 | | LOWER COLORADO | 53 |
| | 01 | Little Colorado | 7 |
| | 02 | Lower Colorado Main Stem | 27 |
| | 03 | Gila | 61 |
| 16 | | GREAT BASIN | 16 |
| | 01 | Bear-Great Salt Lake | 3 |
| | 02 | Sevier Lake | 40 |
| | 03 | Humboldt-Tonopah Desert | 27 |
| | 04 | Central Lahontan | 3 |
| 17 | | PACIFIC NORTHWEST | 5 |
| | 01 | Clark Fork-Kootenai | 2 |
| | 02 | Upper/Middle Columbia | 8 |
| | 03 | Upper/Central Snake | 4 |
| | 04 | Lower Snake | 7 |
| | 05 | Coast-Lower Columbia | 2 |
| | 07 | Oregon Closed Basin | 2 |

| 18 | | CALIFORNIA | 8 |
|----|----|----|----|
| | 02 | Sacramento-Lahontan | 4 |
| | 03 | San Joaquin-Tulare | 10 |
| | 05 | Central California Coast | 10 |
| | 06 | Southern California | 8 |
| | 07 | Lahontan-South | 43 |

Source: U.S. Water Resources Council, *The Nation's Water Resources: The Second National Assessment*, vol. 3, appendix II, table II-6. (Washington, D.C., Government Printing Office).
ᵃ Includes only subregions with percentages of 0.5 or above.

storage.[13] Of course, the percentages for individual subregions may exceed the regional averages. Nevertheless, mining is 1 percent or more of available storage in only four subregions—the North and South Platte River Basin (subregion 1007) with 2 percent, the San Joaquin Valley (subregion 1802) with 1.8 percent, the central California coastal area (subregion 1805) with 1 percent, and the Arikaree-Republican River area of northern Kansas and southern Nebraska (subregion 1010) with 1 percent. The comparable percentages for the subregions which include the High Plains are generally between 0.6 and 1.

This does not mean, however, that irrigators will have plenty of water for the foreseeable future. Aggregate data for areas as large and diverse as the water resource subregions are inadequate for analyzing the implications for irrigated agriculture. Much of the water included as available storage underlies areas with low agricultural potential or is located at depths and in quantities that make it too costly for use in irrigation. Higher energy costs reduce the quantities of water that can be extracted profitably for irrigation. Furthermore, seemingly modest reductions in the groundwater stocks of a large water resource subregion obscure the damage experienced in a particular area when the reductions are localized.

Future changes in irrigated acreage will vary widely, depending in large part on the relation between the supply and demand for water in a particular area. Although water can be transported, the costs of doing so are high in relation to its value in agriculture. Consequently, irrigators in a given area must rely largely on the water currently

[13] Available storage is that portion of total groundwater storage which can be tapped with conventional wells, methods, and machinery. The data on storage and annual mining are from the Second National Water Assessment.

available either naturally or through transport structures already in place. This suggests that some disaggregation of the West according to areas of water scarcity would be useful for forecasting likely changes in irrigation.

Twenty subregions where water already is particularly scarce are indicated in figure 5-1.[14] They account for nearly 60 percent of the West's water consumption, and within this area irrigation accounts for nearly 92 percent of consumption. However, in view of the tight water situation, there is likely to be little expansion of irrigated acreage over the next several decades. Indeed, the Second National Water Assessment projects irrigation consumption in this area to decline by 3 percent from 1975 to 1985 and by an additional 3 percent from 1985 to 2000. Total water consumption in this area is projected to decline by nearly 1 percent over the last quarter of this century, yet consumption for all other purposes is projected to rise by 55 percent.[15] This illustrates an important aspect of the dominance of irrigation in western water use—large percentage increases in water allocations to other uses can be accommodated with relatively small percentage reductions in irrigation consumption.

In contrast to the outlook in the twenty water-scarce subregions, there are opportunities for expanding both total and irrigation water consumption in the rest of the West. Indeed, the Second National Water Assessment projects irrigation consumption to increase a total of ·22 percent between 1975 and 1985 in the other thirty-three subregions. However, no significant further expansion of irrigation consumption is projected for this region from 1985 to 2000. Over the next twenty-five years, the assessment projections of water consumption suggest that the total for the thirty-three subregions will rise 34 percent and consumption for purposes other than irrigation will more than double.

Total western water consumption is projected to rise nearly 14 percent from 1975 to 2000, with irrigation accounting for 62 percent of the increase. However, the implied annual water consumption growth rates are only 0.2 percent for irrigation and 2.4 percent for all other uses.

[14] All twenty of these subregions have either high ratios of water requirements to stream flows or high ratios of groundwater mining to consumption, and in most of these subregions both conditions prevail.

[15] Calculated from data in the Second National Water Assessment, vol. 3, appendix II, table II-4.

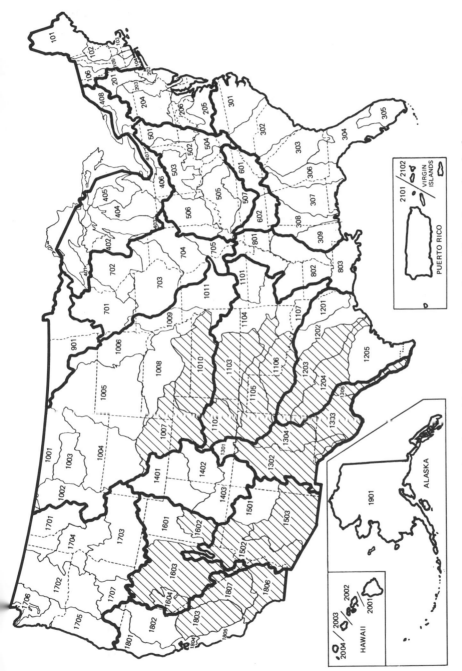

**Figure 5-1.** Twenty water resource subregions with serious water supply problems (cross-hatched area).

Development of the West's vast energy resources, especially coal and oil shale, is expected to place particularly heavy demands on western water. The water consumption projections of the Second National Water Assessment include an allowance for steam electric production, petroleum refining, and mining fuels. Concern that the assessment had not taken adequate account of all likely energy developments and associated water requirements led to a supplementary study by the Aerospace Corporation.[16] The Aerospace Report (AR) accepts all the assessment's water supply data and all the demand projections except those relating to energy. The AR report uses four federally generated energy development scenarios to determine the maximum feasible limits for energy development and the associated water requirements, assuming standard-sized plants and no special provisions to adopt water-conserving technologies. Consequently, the AR estimates are higher than any likely levels. In contrast to the assessment projections discussed above, the resulting nonirrigation water consumption levels are 7 percent higher by 1985 and 39 percent higher by 2000.

In terms of total western water demand, the AR estimates represent a 1 percent increase by 1985 and a 6 percent increase by 2000. Although these are only modest percentage changes in total western water demand, they would be local, and within certain regions major new demands on water supplies are implied. Where demand already exceeds renewable supplies, any increase requires either compensating reductions among other users or additional groundwater mining. The actual impacts on irrigation will depend in large part on the institutions, including the legal system, affecting water use, and these vary widely among states.

The earliest irrigators start from a preferred position in this struggle in that they commonly own the most senior water rights.[17] Potential

---

[16] Aerospace Corporation, *Water Related Constraints on Energy Production*, Aerospace Report No. ATR-78 (9409)-1, June 1978.

[17] In some areas of the West, even the rights of some of the earliest irrigators are threatened by Indian water claims. Rulings of the nation's highest courts have consistently held that Indian lands have sufficient accompanying water rights to accomplish the purpose for which the lands were reserved and that these rights predate those of other users. Indian water rights have not been quantified but they are potentially large and will require diversions from other uses to satisfy. However, the effect of satisfying Indian claims is not likely to be large since irrigation is likely to be the primary use of Indian water.

new irrigators have no such legal advantage and face a major economic disadvantage in that irrigation in general is a relatively low-value use of water. For example, water costs of $100 or more per acre-foot are insignificant in the costs of mining or processing western coal while water costs of half these levels are prohibitive for many irrigators, especially those growing relatively low-value crops. Thus, if market forces are allowed to operate, water will tend to move out of irrigation as demand starts to exceed an area's supply. Some farmers already have found it profitable to sell their water rights, and unless they are legally constrained from doing so, many others are likely to follow suit.

*Additional Sources*

Both the water supply and demand situations described above assume that there will be no major new sources of water. However, weather modifications and interbasin transfers are possible means of increasing water supplies in specific areas. Of the two options, weather modification is more promising economically for agriculture but it is less certain technically. Preliminary research suggests that winter cloud seeding under some conditions can augment water supplies. More specifically, studies suggest that a coordinated program to seed the clouds of six mountain ranges in the Upper Colorado River Basin can increase snowfall sufficiently to provide an additional 1.4 to 2.3 million acre-feet of water a year at a cost of about $5 to $10 per acre-foot. While the cost is attractive compared with most alternatives,[18] the technology is still speculative and likely to be limited in its transferability to other regions and seasons.

Increasing rainfall through summer cloud seeding has turned out to be a much tougher scientific problem. Although there has been some encouraging evidence from seeding of summer clouds, the results have not been definitive and it is difficult to know when a breakthrough might occur.[19] Even if a weather modification technology is established and the economics are favorable, there will be major

---

[18] In California the dams and reservoirs under consideration will cost $200 to $300 per acre-foot of water added to the effective supply.

[19] The discussion of weather modification is based largely on information provided by Bernie Silverman, Chief, Atmospheric Water Resources Management, Bureau of Reclamation, Denver, Colorado during a February 1980 conversation.

institutional obstacles to adoption of a program. Paying for the program, compensating the losers, allocating the additional water, and eliminating the fears that are sure to emerge among the people downwind from the cloud seeding are difficult problems that are likely to stall efforts to modify the weather until long after scientists and economists are comfortable with the technology.

The task for winter seeding is complicated since the losers (e.g., those with higher snow removal costs) are closer in both location and time to the seeding than are the beneficiaries (i.e., farmers perhaps hundreds of miles downstream who presumably receive more water many months later). Nevertheless, cloud seeding is done in a few western areas today, and its use is likely to spread as the value of water increases and the technology improves. Conservative estimates suggest that winter cloud seeding might add nearly 10 percent to the flow of the upper Colorado River, which may be a reasonable target for the turn of the century. Such an increase, however, would have little impact on the overall course of western irrigation. While this would represent a significant increase for that area, it would be equivalent to only 0.3 percent of total western stream flows.

The scarcity of indigenous water resources in relation to demand has prompted a call for water imports from regions more amply endowed. Water importation has broad support within the Lower Colorado River Basin and the High Plains areas where current activities are dependent on nonrenewable water sources. However, if the net water supplies within the West's water-scarce southern belt are to be increased, the water will have to be transported long distances.[20] The Mississippi, Columbia, and upper Missouri rivers are the closest water bodies from which large quantities might be obtained, although the availability of water for export would be contested vigorously in these areas. But even if there were plenty of water for export, the costs of transporting it to the High Plains or Southwest would far exceed its value in agriculture. Although economic feasibility has not been a necessary requirement for western water projects, the economics of such a water transfer project appear poor even by the standards of

[20] The Central Arizona Project currently under construction will make it possible to transport Colorado River water into the Phoenix–Tucson area. However, this project will not increase effective water supplies within the water-scarce areas of the West. The water is already being fully utilized; the project largely will divert water currently going to southern California to central Arizona.

other water projects. For example, the value of the energy required to move water from the Mississippi to the Texas and New Mexico High Plains would be over $400 per acre-foot at 1980 electricity prices in the area.[21] This cost is well over ten times the prices farmers say they can afford to pay for water and still irrigate profitably.

## Changing Groundwater Costs and the Economics of Irrigation

The preceding section indicates that the recent expansion of western irrigation has been based largely on groundwater and that current levels of water use are depleting many groundwater tables. Although groundwater supplies are still large in relation to use, the combination of increasing pumping depths and rising energy costs is changing the economics of groundwater irrigation. This section examines these changes and their significance for the future role of irrigation.

The overall impact of changing water supply conditions and energy prices on irrigation depends on the decisions of thousands of farmers who are responding to a wide variety of conditions, prices, and opportunities. They are affected differently and can be expected to respond differently to changing energy costs and groundwater conditions. Nevertheless, the qualitative nature of the impacts are similar. Consequently, insights as to the likely direction and pace of future irrigation changes can be gained by seeing how alternative energy prices and pumping depths affect water costs under specific assumptions.

The impacts on water costs are considered in two stages—the costs of lifting water to the surface and the costs of distributing the water to the plants. The alternative energy prices are selected to represent actual levels in 1970 and 1980 and projections for 2000, all in 1977 constant dollars. Alternative pumping depths of 100, 200, and 300 feet are considered; this range includes the conditions facing many but by no means all farmers.

Table 5-9 indicates the cost of the energy required to pump 1 acre-foot of water from various depths with alternative fuels and fuel

---

[21] A water import study done by the Bureau of Reclamation in the early 1970s estimated that nearly 47 billion kWh of power would be required to deliver 5,794,000 acre-feet of water to the High Plains annually. At 5 cents per kilowatt hour, approximately the average 1980 cost of electricity in Texas, the cost per acre-foot is over $400 (U.S. Department of Interior, *West Texas and Eastern New Mexico Import Project,* June 1973).

**TABLE 5-9.**    Energy Costs to Pump 1 Acre-Foot of Water from Different Depths with Alternative Fuels and Fuel Prices

(1977 $)

| | Pump lift (ft) | Energy costs under alternative fuel prices | | |
|---|---|---|---|---|
| | | 1970 | 1980 | 2000 |
| Natural gas | 100 | 1.13 | 4.56 | 9.12 |
| | 200 | 2.30 | 9.29 | 18.58 |
| | 300 | 3.43 | 13.86 | 27.72 |
| Electricity | 100 | 7.52 | 8.88 | 17.76 |
| | 200 | 15.03 | 17.76 | 35.52 |
| | 300 | 22.55 | 26.64 | 53.28 |
| LPG | 100 | 7.32 | 12.60 | 25.20 |
| | 200 | 14.65 | 25.20 | 50.40 |
| | 300 | 21.98 | 37.80 | 75.59 |
| Diesel | 100 | 5.24 | 14.96 | 29.92 |
| | 200 | 10.59 | 30.00 | 60.00 |
| | 300 | 15.74 | 44.96 | 89.92 |

*Note:* The technical assumptions, such as the amount of fuel and the pressure required to lift an acre-foot of water, are based on information in U.S. Department of Agriculture, Economics, Statistics and Cooperatives Service, *Energy and U.S. Agriculture: Irrigation Pumping, 1974-77,* prepared by Gordon Sloggett, Agricultural Economic Report No. 436, September 1979. Other assumptions include a 60 percent pumping efficiency. The fuel costs in 1977 constant dollars are: natural gas ($/mcf) 0.39 in 1970, 1.58 in 1980, and 3.15 in 2000; electricity ($k/Wh), 0.033 in 1970, 0.039 in 1980, and 0.078 in 2000; LPG ($/gal) 0.25 in 1970, 0.43 in 1980, and 0.86 in 2000; diesel ($/gal) 0.28 in 1970, 0.80 in 1980, and 1.60 in 2000. The 1970 prices for LPG and diesel are national averages obtained from U.S. Department of Agriculture, Economics, Statistics and Cooperatives Service, *Agricultural Prices,* June 1977. The 1980 price for electricity is from the October 1977 issue of this USDA publication. There was a wide range in the natural gas prices paid by High Plains irrigators in 1970; the table assumes a price of $.25/mcf in 1970 dollars. The 1980 prices reflect average prices paid by farmers in Nebraska, Kansas, Oklahoma, and Texas in January 1980. The prices were obtained through phone conversations with several officials in those states. Based on a conclusion of a recent major energy study (Hans Landsberg and coauthors, *Energy: The Next Twenty Years* Cambridge, Mass., Ballinger, 1979, p. 71), it is assumed that real fuel prices will double between 1980 and 2000.

prices and a 60 percent pump efficiency. The table suggests that at least historically the type of fuel used has been as important as the pumping depth and the price in determining a farmer's energy costs. Natural gas continues to be the cheapest means of pumping. At 1980 energy prices, pumping natural gas from a given depth costs only slightly more than one-half the cost of the next cheapest alternative, electricity. Even when total annual pumping costs are considered, natural gas is generally preferred although the margin of its advantage over electricity is narrowed considerably.[22] With the exception of farmers benefiting from very inexpensive electricity, such as those in the Pacific Northwest, natural gas would be the choice of virtually all groundwater users. However, it has not been available to all farmers, and as of 1977 only about 34 percent of the acreage irrigated with on-farm pumped water used natural gas.[23] This percentage is likely to decline as farmers find it increasingly difficult to arrange gas hookups for new irrigation. The resulting shift to more expensive fuels will be an additional factor increasing average water costs to new irrigators.

Rising energy prices are changing the economics of irrigation regardless of the fuel used. From 1970 to 1980, the real cost of pumping an acre-foot of water 200 feet rose an estimated $6.99 for natural gas, $2.73 for electricity, $10.55 for LPG, and $19.41 for diesel. The assumptions of table 5-9 suggest that additional cost increases over the next two decades for a 200-foot lift may exceed $9 for natural gas, $17 for electricity, and $25 for both LPG and diesel. The greater the pumping lift, the higher the cost increases.

Once the water reaches the surface, additional energy is required to distribute it to the plants. The energy requirements vary widely, depending on the system used and the pressure at which it is operated. Table 5-10 illustrates the impacts of higher energy prices on the costs of distributing 1 acre-foot of water with five different systems. Surface irrigation requires only enough energy to lift the water to the highest point on the field, where gravity takes over. Center pivot and big gun systems, on the other hand, distribute the water under high pressure, which requires considerable energy. Of course, the operating costs of such systems are more susceptible to changes in energy prices. For example, the difference between the electricity costs for distributing 1 acre-foot with a center pivot and a surface system rise from $11.28 at

[22] Different fuels, of course, require different power units. The annualized per acre fixed costs of alternative power units to irrigate 130 acres with a center pivot system have been estimated at $6.10 for electric, $9.41 for natural gas, $9.39 for LPG, and $14.37 for diesel. The combined capital and energy costs of a natural gas unit were less than those for electric. Total water costs would include the cost of a pump and well but these costs would be comparable among the various fuels. See Leslie Sheffield, "Energy—Is it the Achilles Heel for Irrigated Agriculture?" a paper written for *Irrigation Age* (September 1979) table 1.

[23] In 1977 about 49 percent of the acreage in the West used electricity, 5 percent LPG, 10 percent diesel, and 1 percent gasoline (U.S. Department of Agriculture, Economics, Statistics and Cooperatives Service, *Energy and U.S. Agriculture: Irrigation Pumping 1974–77*, prepared by Gordon Sloggett, Agricultural Economic Report No. 436, September 1979, pp. 21–22).

**TABLE 5-10.**   Energy Costs to Distribute 1 Acre-Foot of Water per Acre with Different Distribution Systems and Alternative Fuels and Fuel Prices

(1977 current $)

| Distribution system | Energy costs under alternative fuel prices | | |
|---|---|---|---|
| | 1970 | 1980 | 2000 |
| Natural gas | | | |
| Big gun | 4.36 | 17.60 | 35.20 |
| Center pivot | 1.85 | 7.46 | 14.92 |
| Other sprinkler | 1.06 | 4.26 | 8.52 |
| Drip | 0.39 | 1.60 | 3.20 |
| Surface | 0.13 | 0.54 | 1.08 |
| Electricity | | | |
| Big gun | 28.64 | 33.84 | 67.69 |
| Center pivot | 12.15 | 14.36 | 28.72 |
| Other | 6.94 | 8.20 | 16.41 |
| Drip | 2.61 | 3.08 | 6.15 |
| Surface | 0.87 | 1.03 | 2.05 |
| LPG | | | |
| Big gun | 27.93 | 48.04 | 96.08 |
| Center pivot | 11.85 | 20.38 | 40.76 |
| Other sprinkler | 6.77 | 11.65 | 23.29 |
| Drip | 2.54 | 4.37 | 8.73 |
| Surface | 0.84 | 1.46 | 2.91 |
| Diesel | | | |
| Big gun | 20.01 | 57.16 | 114.31 |
| Center pivot | 8.48 | 24.25 | 48.50 |
| Other sprinkler | 4.85 | 13.86 | 27.71 |
| Drip | 1.82 | 5.20 | 10.39 |
| Surface | 0.61 | 1.73 | 3.46 |

*Note:*   The energy cost estimates assume the following PSI levels: 165 for big gun, 45 for other sprinkler, 5 for surface, 70 for center pivot (U.S. Department of Agriculture, *Energy and U.S. Agriculture*) and 15 for trickle (K. L. Chen, et al., "A Model to Predict Total Energy Requirements and Economic Costs of Irrigation Systems," Presentation to the American Society of Agricultural Engineers, Chicago, December 1976). Other assumptions are listed in the notes to table 5-9.

1970 prices, to $13.33 at 1980 prices, and to $26.67 at prices projected for the year 2000.

Cost comparisons among irrigation systems should be based on delivering a given amount of water to the root zone of the plants. Therefore, the efficiency of the system needs to be considered; surface irrigation is generally considerably less efficient than any of the sprinkler systems and much less efficient than drip. To deliver 14 acre-inches of water to the root zone, a surface system with a 50 percent application efficiency has to pump 28 acre-inches of water while a center pivot system with an 80 percent efficiency has to pump only 17.5 acre-inches of water. In this case the difference between the total energy required to pump and distribute water with a center pivot and surface system depends on the pumping depth. Under current prices and the assumptions of tables 5-9 and 5-10, the energy costs associated with a center pivot system drop below those of a surface system when the pumping lift rises to about 250 feet.

Farmers have a number of opportunities for offsetting some of the impacts of higher energy prices short of abandoning irrigation or switching to a completely different distribution system. A tailwater recovery system can increase the application efficiency of surface distribution to levels comparable to those of sprinkler systems, thereby reducing the amount of water that must be pumped. Rising energy costs have made such recovery systems economically attractive, and their use has spread rapidly over the past decade. The capital costs of the system can be recovered through energy savings in about 2.5 years with current electricity prices and a 200-foot pumping lift. Energy needs also are being reduced by lowering the pressure used with center pivot systems, although there may be some offsetting problems such as poorer distribution of the water associated with lower water pressure. Improving pump efficiency is another means of reducing energy needs. Table 5-9 assumes a 60 percent pump efficiency, which is probably close to the average. Commonly, a $2,500 investment in new bowls and an engine tuneup are sufficient to improve pumping efficiency to about 75 percent. At current electricity prices and a 200-foot lift, the capital costs could be recovered from the energy savings in about two years. Scheduling irrigation to apply water only when the crops need it may reduce the water used without reducing yields. Services which use computers to analyze weather, soil moisture, and plant water requirements now are available in many irrigation areas.

The impacts of rising costs of energy and pumping lifts on profitability are illustrated with 1977 crop budget data for a farm in western Kansas where irrigated corn or dryland wheat are the primary crops. The returns to risk were $14.50 per acre for irrigated corn (assuming a yield of 104.2 bushels per acre, a price of $2.47 per bushel, pumping 2 acre-feet a height of 215 feet, a surface water distribution system, and natural gas for fuel costing $1.20/mcf) compared to $6.88 per

acre for dryland wheat (assuming a yield of 25.3 bushels per acre and
a price of $3.09 per bushel). If pumping depth increases by 2 feet per
year, energy prices increase according to the assumptions of table 5-9,
and all other factors affecting profitability are unchanged, then the
per acre returns to risk are reduced by 1980 to $1.35 for irrigated corn
and $3.82 for dryland wheat; by the year 2000 there would be losses
of $46.59 for irrigated corn and $3.32 for dryland wheat.[24]

The above example overstates the likely impacts on irrigated profitability by assuming no adjustments to the rising water costs. Farmers
already have made some adjustments to higher energy and water
costs. Overirrigating and other wasteful practices which were prev-
alent when water was cheap have been largely phased out among
many groundwater users. Also, cropping patterns are changing
slowly, with low-value, high water-using crops declining in importance. In the future, new technology should provide farmers with a
wider range of options for adjusting to high water costs. It has been
only within the past decade that significant numbers of agricultural
scientists have focused their efforts on developing more efficient irrigation systems, crop varieties with more efficient evapotranspiration
rates, and other technologies appropriate for high energy and water
prices. The fruits of these research efforts should provide irrigators
with new ways to adjust in the coming decades. Nevertheless, the
available adjustments are not likely to alter the basic facts that rising
water costs are reducing the profitability of irrigated farming relative
to dryland techniques and that the combination of higher energy
costs and increasing water scarcity is limiting the opportunities for
profitably expanding irrigated acreage in the West.

*Salinity*

Failure to adequately dispose of the salts which inevitably emerge with
irrigation can lead to declining productivity and in extreme cases can
destroy the land's productivity. All water used for irrigation carries
salts and the salt content of the water rises as it evaporates, is con-

---

[24] The returns to risk are net of the costs of management, general farm overhead, and
rent. Higher energy prices also increase the cost of crop drying, which accounts for the
decline in dryland profits. The assumptions are based on the budgets for the Kansas
100 region. The crop budget data are from U.S. Department of Agriculture, Economics, Statistics and Cooperatives Service, Firm Enterprise Data System, prepared in
Cooperation with Oklahoma State University, unpublished.

sumed by the plants, or passes over saline soils. If the salt concentrations become too high, they inhibit plant growth. Where drainage is adequate, salts can be flushed from the root zones if there is sufficient rainfall or by applying additional irrigation water, but this seldom eliminates the salinity problem. When the salts are washed off the land, the return flows have higher salt concentrations. This adversely affects downstream users as well as plants and wildlife dependent on the stream. In areas lacking good drainage, repeated irrigation raises the level of the underground water table. If the water table reaches the root zone of the plants, capillary action carries water close to the soil surface, where it evaporates and leaves a salt residue. Over time, this process reduces and eventually destroys the productivity of the land.

All western river basins except the Columbia are confronted with high and generally rising salt levels. In much of the Colorado, parts of the Rio Grande, and the western portion of San Joaquin river basins, the salt concentrations in either the water or the soils are approaching levels that threaten the viability of irrigated agriculture. Groundwater salinity is not yet a widespread problem in the West. However, the problem is growing and already is serious in parts of California, New Mexico, and Montana. Although groundwater tables are less susceptible to pollution than surface waters, the problems are much more difficult to correct underground.[25]

A rough but informed guess suggests that 25 to 35 percent of the irrigated lands in the West have some type of salinity problem, and they are getting worse.[26] Two large irrigated areas where salinity already is a serious concern for agriculture are the Lower Colorado River Basin and the west side of the San Joaquin Valley in California. The underyling cause differs in these cases.

The salt content of the Colorado River increases progressively downstream as a result of the salt-concentrating effects of irrigation and the salts picked up as the water passes other saline formations. About two-thirds of the salts delivered to the Colorado are from natural sources, and these can be eliminated only through expensive investments to either divert the river and its tributaries around some of the areas contributing the salts or to construct and operate desalini-

[25] Groundwater salinity from irrigation may result from the infiltration of irrigation waters or from the intrusion of sea water as the fresh water is pumped out of coastal aquifers.

[26] This guess is based on a February 1980 conversation with Jan van Schilfgaarde, Director, U.S. Salinity Laboratory, Riverside, California.

zation plants. Irrigation accounts for most of the salts attributable to human activities. These could be curtailed by reducing irrigation return flows. Ideally, water applications would be limited to the quantities required by the plants and to flush the salts just beyond the root zone. However, there is no incentive for farmers to adopt such practices since they derive no benefit from using less water and the resulting damages are passed downstream. Annual damages from salinity in the Colorado River have been estimated at between $75 and $104 million in 1980 and $122 and $165 million in 2000 if no control measures are taken. While most of the damage would be incurred by municipal and industrial users, farmers would face decreased crop yields, increasing leaching requirements, and higher management costs. Four initial control projects costing a total of $125 million have been proposed.[27]

In the San Joaquin Valley, the principal contribution to salinity is poor drainage that prevents salt-laden waters from being carried away from the fields. High water tables already reduce the productivity of about 400,000 acres and threaten more than 1 million acres in the valley. A $1.26 billion drainage system to carry irrigation runoff from the western side of the valley to the delta has been proposed as a solution. Since farmers would have to install their own underground drainage to get the waters to the central drain, the total costs of an effective system would be considerably higher than this figure.[28]

There are nonstructural measures that might be undertaken to reduce salinity levels as well as the damage from any given level. Agricultural scientists have developed crops and irrigation techniques which enable farmers to irrigate successfully with high salt levels, and more efficient on-farm water use can reduce the salt-loading impacts of irrigation. Van Schilfgaarde suggests that the amount of San Joaquin Valley saline drainage water that must be disposed of could be reduced to one-third or less of current levels and a long-term equilibrium reached through an integrated irrigation system whereby the best water is used first on salt-sensitive crops, with the increasingly salt-laden runoff applied to increasingly salt-tolerant crops. The remaining highly saline waters would be reduced to quantities that

[27] U.S. Department of Interior and U.S. Department of Agriculture, *Final Environmental Statement: Colorado River Water Quality Improvement Program*, vol. I, section 1, May 1977.

[28] U.S. Department of Interior, California Department of Water Resources, and California State Water Resources Control Board, *San Joaquin Valley Interagency Drainage Program*, Final Report, June 1979.

could be disposed of through a greatly scaled-down drainage system or perhaps in evaporation ponds.[29]

As long as farmers pay only a small fraction of the social value of water, do not bear the costs of their own additions to salt loads, and expect the federal government to pay most of the costs of structural solutions, their responses to rising salinity levels will be largely to press for the government investments required to provide good quality water. Only when these efforts fail or when the government response lags will farmers be forced to modify irrigation and cropping practices to cope with the salts. Undoubtedly, there will be some decline in productivity and profitability. From a national perspective, basinwide irrigation management schemes probably offer the most efficient means of controlling salinity, but the institutional obstacles to adopting such schemes are enormous. Consequently, the acreage adversely affected by salinity is likely to rise and much greater emphasis is likely to be placed on costly government projects than should be required or is desirable.

Salt levels are likely to rise in many irrigated areas and agricultural productivity will be adversely affected. The impacts within some areas may be devastating to farmers and local economies. More generally, salinity can be expected to continue to have a negative impact on the productivity and growth potential of irrigated agriculture. Two factors, however, suggest that the impacts of salinity on the overall role of irrigation will be modest and gradual. First, science will provide more ways of irrigating successfully with saline water. Second, the more seriously affected areas may be rescued through government projects before the problems force large tracts out of production.

## Conclusions and Policy Implications

The irrigation of an additional 30 to 35 million acres was an important factor in the ability of American farmers to increase crop production by 70 percent from 1950 to 1977 without any increase in total harvested acreage.[30] A conservative but rough estimate suggests that the

---

[29] Personal communication with Jan van Schilfgaarde, February 1980.

[30] The Census of Agriculture indicates there were 25.9 million irrigated acres in the United States in 1950 and the 1977 NRI indicates the total had grown to 60.7 million irrigated acres, suggesting an increase of 34.8 million acres. These figures include irrigated pasture as well as cropland. The growth of crop production is based on data from U.S. Department of Agriculture, Economics, Statistics and Cooperatives Service, *Changes in Farm Production and Efficiency, 1977*, Statistical Bulletin No. 612 (November 1978) table 1.

land-conserving impact of irrigation was equivalent to about 18 million acres as of 1977. If cropland irrigation in Arizona, California, Nevada, New Mexico, and Utah, which are predominantly arid states, is used to estimate the land-creating implications of irrigation, it appears that the acreage suitable for agriculture has been expanded by about 13 million acres. Furthermore, analysis of four principal crops suggests that irrigation had a significant impact on the increase in yields achieved from 1950 to 1977.

While recognizing irrigation's importance to past growth and current production, two other points should be borne in mind in drawing conclusions and examining policy implications. First, it is apparent that dryland farming continues to and undoubtedly will always dominate U.S. agriculture. Irrigated lands still account for only 13 to 14 percent of the nation's cropland; the combined land-conserving and land-creating impacts are equivalent to less than 8 percent of national cropland; and of the four crops considered here, cotton is the only one for which irrigation accounted for more than 16 percent of the national crop yield increase. Second, irrigation's role would not be as large as it is if farmers had paid the full costs of delivering water to the fields. The most notable subsidies have been in Bureau of Reclamation projects, for which irrigators pay only a tiny fraction of the total costs. Some groundwater users have benefited from artificially low energy costs. Furthermore, private pumping costs are less than social costs in areas with declining water tables. When groundwater is being depleted, a farmer's costs do not include the loss to either neighboring farmers or future users. Consequently, groundwater is used at rates well in excess of socially efficient levels.

The future growth of irrigation should be very different from the past when irrigated farming was stimulated by the availability of cheap water and energy. Water requirements exceed stream flows in the area of the West with the most favorable growing conditions, and nonagricultural demands for western water are growing rapidly. Although total groundwater stocks are large in relation to use, the economics of groundwater irrigation deteriorated sharply with the rise in energy costs and pumping depths. Furthermore, much of the groundwater is at depths and locations that make it unusable for profitable irrigation.

Although the available water supply is a physical constraint to expansion in most of the traditional irrigated areas, there are other western lands with access to water supplies, especially groundwater, that can be irrigated. Most notably, the Nebraska sandhills have vast water resources, relatively low pumping depths, and low land prices. Those features have just recently started attracting sizable investments in center pivots. State irrigation experts estimate that the state has a long-term sustainable physical limit of at least 15 million irrigated acres, an area twice that currently irrigated in Nebraska, and that 10–12 million acres can be profitably irrigated at current prices.[31]

The overall growth of irrigation will depend largely on the real price levels of agricultural products. Significant increases in product prices would erase the negative effects of rising energy prices and pumping depths and accelerate the development of new lands. For example, on the hypothetical western Kansas farm considered earlier, a 25 percent increase in the real price of corn would offset the production cost increases associated with a doubling of energy prices and a 40-foot increase in pumping depth. On the other hand, no foreseeable crop price levels will make irrigation competitive with most municipal and industrial water uses. With no significant changes in relative agricultural output and input prices from 1980 levels, the overall level of western irrigation should increase slowly for about another decade; expansion in Nebraska and a few other areas should more than compensate for modest declines in surface water allocations to irrigation and declines in areas such as the southern High Plains where farmers are dependent on rapidly diminishing groundwater supplies. Institutional factors favoring agricultural water uses and the fact that small percentage changes in irrigation water use can accommodate large percentage increases in other uses suggest that increasing water scarcity will affect surface irrigation gradually.

Irrigation in the East has grown considerably faster than in the West in recent decades. A 3 percent annual growth rate from 1980 to 2000 is not an unreasonable expectation. Such a growth would add about 8.5 million acres to eastern irrigation. Much of this expansion is likely to be for rice and soybeans in the Delta states, multiple cropping (such as corn or soybeans with a vegetable) in northern Florida and southern Georgia, and high-value crops such as fruits and vegetables throughout the East.

Almost regardless of what happens to crop prices, irrigation cannot be expected to make the contribution to agricultural expansion that it

[31] This assessment is based on a February 1980 conversation with Raymond J. Supalla and other irrigation experts from the University of Nebraska.

has in the past three to four decades. Rising crop prices do tend to improve the profitability of irrigated farming relative to dryland agriculture since yields tend to be higher with irrigation. Indeed, higher crop prices could offset the negative effects high energy and water costs have on the relative profitability of irrigation. Nevertheless, the long-term role of irrigation is threatened by resource and environmental factors. Water use already exceeds stream flows in much of the West; perhaps one-fourth of the land currently under irrigation is heavily dependent on nonrenewable water supplies; and the productivity of several million additional acres is threatened by rising salt levels. These problems are spreading and increasing in intensity.

New water projects are not likely to make a major contribution to the future growth of western irrigation. Structural measures to develop new water sources, reduce salinity, or improve water distribution efficiency often are not cost effective when the water is to be used for agriculture. Most of the best water projects have been completed and recent changes in the criteria for evaluating new projects should make it more difficult to get new ones approved. New projects are likely to do more to preserve the productivity of existing irrigation than to expand the acreage under irrigation.

Irrigation's future contributions to U.S. agriculture will depend increasingly on improving the returns per unit of water. More efficient water distribution systems, improved farm management practices, different cropping patterns, and new seed varieties may offer such improvements. The possibilities for increasing the returns to water are significant in part because they received little attention from either farmers or researchers when water was cheap and accessible. In recent years, scientists have started devoting considerable effort to developing technologies that improve the yields to water and farmers have demonstrated that they do adopt water conservation measures when water is expensive.

Although irrigation is an important part of U.S. agriculture, its current role and contributions to past growth are not valid reasons for adopting policies and programs designed to insulate farmers from the changing resource conditions. When the Reclamation Act was passed in 1902, national objectives may have been served best by subsidizing irrigation to stimulate settlement of the arid West. Currently, however, these subsidies, together with the legal and institutional factors insulating many surface water users from higher prices, encourage an inefficient use of western water by reducing the incentives and opportunities for transferring water to higher valued uses. These institutional constraints threaten to curtail the development of agricultural as well as nonagricultural resources in the West. Although greater opportunities for transferring water among sectors undoubtedly would reduce irrigation water use, these negative impacts on irrigation might be more than offset by the added incentive to get higher returns from the water used. In addition, improved water management practices adopted in response to higher costs would have beneficial environmental impacts. For example, reducing water run-off reduces sediment loads in streams as well as ground and surface water pollution from agricultural chemicals.

Western irrigation will not make the contributions to agricultural growth that it did when water was abundant and cheap. However, if the transition from water abundance to scarcity allows for an efficient use of the resources over time, irrigation will contribute to agricultural production and growth for many more decades. The serious problems will emerge if we attempt to keep water cheap when it is not. Such a policy will ensure its inefficient use and push the social costs of irrigated production to levels well above those of the dryland alternatives, thereby further limiting the long-term role of irrigation. Indeed, studies done at Iowa State University indicate that the nation's agricultural output could be produced at a lower total cost with less irrigation.[32]

Water policy is dominated by entrenched beneficiaries of a system developed when water was plentiful in relation to demand. Although the underlying resource conditions as well as the national interests in the use of western water have changed dramatically within the past several decades, there has not been a corresponding adjustment in the laws and institutions that control and manage the re-

[32] Results of the national agricultural model developed at Iowa State University suggest that if "allowed to be distributed in terms of competitive conditions and interregional comparative advantage (no supply control), the nation's domestic and export food demands could be met more economically by using less water in agriculture and by a wide redistribution of crop acreage." See Earl Heady, "U.S. Supply Situation for Food and Fiber and the Role of Irrigated Agriculture," an unpublished paper prepared for Texas A&M Conference, March 25–26, 1976. A July 21, 1979 run of the Iowa State model suggests that the least-cost way of meeting a moderate growth of demand for U.S. agricultural output would have only 33.4 million acres irrigated in the year 2000. This result was a part of a model run done for the U.S. Department of Agriculture's response to the Soil and Water Resources Conservation Act of 1977 (RCA). The irrigated acreage projected for this model run is only 56 percent of the 1977 NRI level.

source. The scientific community is proceeding with research which may provide farmers and others with more effective ways of responding to higher energy and water costs and rising levels of salinity. However, innovations will be adopted in a timely way only if institutional factors provide the correct incentives. There is a need to identify and develop strategies that will overcome the opposition to reform of water development, allocation, and pricing policies and practices. In particular, the equity implications of alternative reforms and the possible measures for compensating those whose livelihood is adversely affected by such reforms need to be analyzed and taken into account in policy formulations if reform is to succeed.

## Appendix: Data Problems [33]

The primary sources of irrigated acreage data for all states are the agricultural census (taken about every five years), the decennial irrigation surveys (in recent years done after every other agricultural census), and the 1966 and 1977 Soil Conservation Service inventory data, known as the 1967 Conservation Needs Inventory (CNI) and the 1977 National Resources Inventory (NRI). In addition, there are several secondary sources of data for irrigated acreage. Some of these are accorded considerable attention if not credibility because they are part of major government water studies. The first and second national water assessments contain estimates for 1965 and 1975, respectively, and the U.S. Geological Survey provides estimates for five-year intervals, with 1975 being the most recent. In addition, the *Irrigation Journal* publishes its own annual survey of irrigated acreage.

As table 5-11 indicates, there is a wide range in the estimates of the acreage irrigated in the nation and the seventeen western states. The uncertainty as to the extent of irrigation is evident in the Second National Water Assessment, which provides alternative estimates of 45.3 and 51.9 million acres irrigated in 1975 in the United States.

---

[33] Since the conference, the discussion of data problems has been moved to an appendix and revised to incorporate preliminary data of the 1978 Census of Agriculture and to qualify the assessment of the Soil Conservation Service inventory data. The qualifications stem in part from comments by Bruce Beattie, who served as conference discussant of this paper.

Even this range is not sufficiently wide to encompass the alternative estimates for 1975 or the neighboring years. If the 41.2-million-acre estimate of the 1974 Agricultural Census were adjusted for likely expansion between 1974 and 1975, it would still fall below this range. The 1975 national estimates of the U.S. Geological Survey (USGS) and the *Irrigation Journal* (IJ) of about 54 million irrigated acres exceed the range of the Second Assessment. Yet both of these estimates are lower than the 60.7-million-acre estimate of the 1977 NRI, even allowing for likely expansion from 1975 to 1977. Furthermore, even when two sources give virtually identical regional and national estimates such as the 1975 USGS and IJ data, a comparison of the state estimates shows that the aggregates mask wide differences among the sources.

The most detailed and widely cited data on irrigated agriculture are those of the agricultural census, which include county-level irrigation figures by crop for every state. One might expect the census data to be the most accurate since they are supposed to be based on a survey of all farms. Unfortunately, this expectation is not fulfilled for at least the 1969 and 1974 agricultural censuses, which were the most recent available in June 1980. The 1974 agricultural census understates the level of irrigated acreage in the United States, a situation recently noted by the Bureau of the Census itself.[34] The failure to achieve full farm coverage is the explanation the Bureau of the Census offers for the underenumeration. Another reason for underenumeration of irrigation in the censuses, including the 1978 census, may be that some farmers believe it is in their interest to understate the level of irrigation. The accuracy of a mail response system which has been used for the agricultural censuses since 1969 depends on individual responses, which are bound to be inaccurate if farmers believe it is in their interest to distort the responses. Possible reasons for this are that they believe their responses will be used for tax purposes or, in the case of farmers receiving federally subsidized water, they want to conceal how

---

[34] Preliminary data of the 1978 Census of Agriculture recently have been released which show the United States with 50.7 million irrigated acres in 1978. This figure implies an increase of 9.5 million acres over just four years, a very significant and unprecedented rise. The Bureau of the Census, however, suggests that a comparison of the 1978 with the 1974 and 1969 agricultural censuses overstates actual growth of irrigation. In an open letter dated December 12, 1980, Arnold L. Bollenbacher, Chief, Agriculture Division, Bureau of the Census, states "Because of improvements in coverage for the 1978 census, comparisons with the previous two censuses taken by mail (1969 and 1974) must be approached with caution so that improved counts are not misinterpreted as dramatic changes occurring between censuses. . . ."

**TABLE 5-11.** Alternative Estimates of Irrigated Acreage, Various Years (millions of acres)

| | Year | 17 Western states | U.S. total |
|---|---|---|---|
| Census of Agriculture | 1964 | 33.2 | 37.1 |
| First National Water Assessment | 1965 | 38.8[a] | 42.1 |
| USGS | 1965 | 39.5 | 44.0 |
| Conservation Needs Inventory | 1967 | 41.5 | 47.6 |
| Census of Agriculture | 1969 | 34.8 | 39.1 |
| USGS | 1970 | 43.7 | 50.0 |
| Census of Agriculture | 1974 | 36.6 | 41.2 |
| *Irrigation Journal* | 1974 | 47.0 | 53.3 |
| Second National Water        NF[b] | 1975 | 40.6[a] | 45.3 |
| Assessment                   SRF[c] | 1975 | 46.2[a] | 51.9 |
| USGS | 1975 | 47.3 | 54.0 |
| *Irrigation Journal* | 1975 | 47.6 | 54.0 |
| National Resources Inventory | 1977 | 50.2 | 60.7 |
| *Irrigation Journal* | 1977 | 49.9 | 58.5 |
| *Irrigation Journal* | 1978 | 51.3 | 60.7 |
| Census of Agriculture (preliminary) | 1978 | 43.4 | 50.7 |

*Sources:*
Census data:
    1964 and 1969: U.S. Department of Commerce, *1969 Census of Agriculture, vol. IV, Irrigation,* July 1973, table 1, p. 2.

    1974: U.S. Department of Commerce, *1974 Census of Agriculture, vol. 1, part 51, United States: Summary and State Data,* December 1977, p. II-5.

    1978: preliminary data released by the Bureau of the Census, U.S. Department of Commerce, undated.

*(footnote continued on p. 157)*

much water they actually receive.[35] The 1978 census used a direct enumeration area sample to make statistical estimates for farms missed in the initial mailing response but had no means of adjusting for underreporting among the respondents.

The 1978 agricultural census is being supplemented by the 1979 Farm and Ranch Irrigation Survey undertaken by the Bureau of the Census. This is a survey of about 10 percent of the irrigated farmers

---

[35] Several people interviewed in connection with this study suggested that underreporting is common because many farmers believe the data are used for tax purposes, and showing higher levels of irrigation may make their operations more susceptible to scrutiny by local or federal tax authorities. Fred Ruggles, Bureau of Census, Agriculture Division, also indicated that underreporting of irrigated acreage is a problem among California farmers receiving more federally subsidized water than they are entitled to receive.

National Assessment data:
   1965: U.S. Water Resources Council, *The Nation's Water Resources, The First National Assessment of the Water Resources Council* (Washington, D.C., Government Printing Office, 1968) p. 4-4-1.

   1975: U.S. Water Resources Council, *The Nation's Water Resources 1975–2000: Second National Water Assessment,* vol. 3: appendix 1 (December 1978) p. 59.

USGS data:
   1965: U.S. Department of Interior, Geological Survey Circular 556, prepared by C. Richard Murray, *Estimated Use of Water in the United States, 1965,* 1968, table 11.

   1970: U.S. Department of Interior, Geological Survey Circular 676, prepared by C. Richard Murray and E. Bodette Reeves, *Estimated Use of Water in the United States in 1970,* 1972, table 7.

   1975: U.S. Department of Interior, Geological Survey Circular 765, prepared by C. Richard Murray and E. Bodette Reeves, *Estimated Use of Water in the United States in 1975,* 1977, table 7.

Conservation Needs Inventory:
   U.S. Department of Agriculture, Soil Conservation Service, *Basic Statistics—National Inventory of Soil and Water Conservation Needs, 1967,* Statistical Bulletin No. 461, January 1971, table 3c and the a and c state tables.

*Irrigation Journal* data:
   The 1974, 1975, 1977, and 1978 IJ data from *Irrigation Journal,* vol. 28, no. 6, Survey/December 1978, pp. 46A to 46H.

National Resources Inventory:
   U.S. Department of Agriculture, Soil Conservation Service, "Basic Statistics—1977 National Resources Inventory (NRI)," Revised February 1980, in mimeograph.

   [a] Regional estimates in the National Water Assessments are for water resources regions which do not correspond to state boundaries. These figures include regions 9–18.
   [b] NF: National future—Estimates of present and future conditions as obtained primarily by participating federal agencies.
   [c] SRF: State/regional future—Estimates of present and future conditions provided primarily by participating river basin commissions, state agencies, and other sponsors.

---

responding to the 1978 census. It provides more detailed farm level information on factors such as the nature of the irrigation facilities and practices, the crops grown, and their yields. This follow-on survey was undertaken in part to ease the respondent burden of the census; the data should be available in published form sometime in 1982.

The Bureau of the Census also conducts an irrigation census of water distributors or irrigation organizations once every ten years. The most recent were done in conjunction with the 1959, 1969, and 1978 censuses of agriculture. Two factors suggest that the irrigation censuses, which consistently show more irrigation than the agricultural censuses, are not reliable estimates of acreage irrigated. First, in some cases the estimates are based on reports of the area eligible to receive water or the total area in farms receiving water, which may be considerably greater than the area irrigated during a year. Second, when two or more irrigation organizations provide water for the same area, this area may be double counted.[36]

The 1967 Conservative Needs Inventory (CNI) and the 1977 National Resources Inventory (NRI) also provide primary irrigation acreage estimates for all states. Although they are listed under different titles, these estimates represent a generally consistent effort by the Soil Conservation Service (SCS) to describe the use and conservation needs of rural land. One by-product of the 1967 and 1977 surveys is the calculation of irrigation acreages of crop groups by state and land class. Unlike the census, the CNI and NRI estimates are not dependent on farmer responses for accuracy. They are based on detailed, on-site inspection of sample points of all nonfederal rural land. The 1977 sampling rate and techniques were designed to achieve a 95 percent confidence level with a coefficient of variation of 1 to 3 percent in estimating land use such as irrigation. The sampling rate for the 1967 CNI was even higher. Both surveys relied on trained personnel to gather the basic data at the randomly selected sites. The 1977 NRI data also were subjected to a quality check by a team of agronomists who resampled random sections.

Unfortunately, the CNI and NRI irrigation data also have limitations for studying irrigation. They include an unknown (but probably small) amount of land that was not actually irrigated in the survey year. For example, the 1977 NRI irrigation estimates include land that has been irrigated at least two of the previous four years even if it was not irrigated in the survey year. The data are not reliable at the county level, and, in states with little irrigation, the small samples result in wider percentage coefficients of variation. Furthermore, these inventories do not differentiate by crops but only by broad crop groups, such as row crops and close-grown crops. Despite these shortcomings, the 1977 NRI provided the best estimates of national and regional irrigation levels.[37]

Determining the impacts of irrigation on production or alter-

---

[36] The 1959 Agricultural Census (U.S. Department of Commerce, *U.S. Census of Agriculture: 1959*, Final Report—vol. III, Irrigation of Agricultural Lands, p. xxv) mentions these problems with using the irrigation censuses to estimate irrigated acreage. Fred Ruggles indicated in a conversation with the author that these problems still persist.

[37] A detailed assessment of the irrigation data for the western states was made as part of a larger study of irrigation in the West being undertaken by the author and is available from him.

natively on the land required to produce a given level of output also requires data on the crop mix and the yields of irrigated and dryland farming. Unfortunately, the National Resources Inventory does not provide acreage, yield, or production data for specific crops. The agricultural censuses are the only sources of comprehensive acreage data for individual crops which also differentiate between irrigated and dryland crops. Crop level data are not yet available from the 1978 agricultural census. Although the acreage of the 1969 and 1974 censuses is understated, there is no reason to expect that the census data distort the relative acreage allocated to individual crops. To the contrary, 1969 and 1974 census estimates of the percentage of total irrigated land allocated to row and close-grown crops in each of the West's farm production regions are very close to the percentages projected from 1967 CNI and 1977 NRI data. For example, estimates for 1974 of the percentage of irrigated land in the seventeen western states allocated to various crop groups are 45.3 in row and 17.4 in close-grown crops according to the census and 42.5 in row and 17.5 in close-grown crops according to a projection which starts with the 1967 CNI and 1977 NRI data and assumes that the acreage of each crop group grew linearly over the decade. Row crops include all corn, all sorghum, cotton, soybeans, other field crops, vegetables, and what the census lists as other crops. Close-grown crops include wheat, other small grains, and field seed crops.

# Discussion

## Bruce R. Beattie

Casting irrigation in the context of land conservation as Frederick does is an interesting idea. How useful it is, I am not sure. It provides one possible framework for understanding the magnitude of irrigation's contribution to U.S. agriculture. This is worthwhile. However, from a policy perspective it represents a scenario or eventuality that is most unlikely. What is provided is an estimate of additional cropland acreage that would be required to produce the *same* level of agricultural output as in 1977 but with *zero* irrigation. Surely zero irrigation is an unlikely prospect. However, if this is granted, then the relevance of attaining the 1977 output level becomes troublesome. Under zero irrigation, the appropriate level of U.S. agricultural output and its composition would change, perhaps dramatically. Finally, given the assumptions of zero irrigation and no change in desired output, the most cost-effective means for making up the output shortfall is not likely to involve the addition of 31 million new cropland acres. New import-export configurations, reserve stocks for critical agricultural commodities, and induced innovation in dryland technology on existing cropland acres are among the perhaps more likely and efficient solutions (outcomes).

Again, what Frederick provides is, I believe, useful. My comments are merely suggestive of additional directions and issues that might be addressed in subsequent research. There is one matter, however, that may be substantive regarding the land-conservation estimate. It is not clear to me from the paper whether or how cropland yielding a crop only on alternate years was accounted for in the conservation estimate. Clearly, assumptions in this regard are important in assessing the baseline conservation impact as well as in identifying potential new cropland acres as further scenarios are researched.

Frederick's comments on the future viability of western irrigated agriculture involve several interrelated issues. In general, I find myself in agreement.

On the matter of competition for water from nonagricultural users, Frederick notes that a little bit of agricultural water goes a long way in satisfying most out-of-stream demands for residential and industrial purposes. He finds, and I agree, that mandated instream requirements are a more serious threat. If Frederick and I see things differently on this issue, it would only be on the extent to which we view instream uses as being justified. If I may be permitted to quote out of context, Frederick worries me (albeit only slightly) with statements like, "Although there is no consensus as to how much water should be allocated to instream uses such as fish and wildlife, this does not mean that including these uses in the total overstates water scarcity." I suspect that in some instances the cost of an additional marginal increment to fish and wildlife habitat and other environmental quality factors is quite high and not just in terms of agricultural opportunity costs. I believe there are (or at least could be) situations where the degree of water scarcity is overstated because of questionable instream reservations.

Certainly many groundwater aquifers are being overdrafted and many of these involve important irrigated regions. However, in situations like the Ogallala, which underlies much of the Great Plains, I am not so sure that the rate of overdrafting, which is clearly attributable to irrigation, should be characterized as being "well in excess of socially efficient levels." I am told that given the nature of much of the aquifer, there is no pervasive externality problem, that is, the cone of depression around wells in the region is generally very steep and the lateral movement of water in the aquifer is surprisingly limited. The groundwater has been privately developed without benefit of public subsidy (at least directly) and the development has been undertaken in most instances at market-determined interest rates. The interests of future users (generations) is being accounted for at least as well as most of the body politic is willing to require and/or pay for. Furthermore, large quantities of water will remain in storage in the Ogallala long after the point of economic exhaustion as far as agriculture is concerned. Of course, there are other aquifers where Frederick's claim is fully justified. However, mining of a stock resource[1] is not always socially inefficient and we must be careful to resist the temptation of jumping to that conclusion in every instance.

---

[1] Water in much of the Ogallala aquifer is essentially a stock resource since the recharge rate is negligible.

Frederick's discussion of the likely consequences of rising pumping costs on the production of so-called "low-valued" crops strikes one of my pet peeves. It seems everyone's solution to the problems of irrigated agriculture is to allocate relatively more water to the production of "high-valued" crops. It is an easy trap to fall into, but it is a myth. In another part of this paper Frederick tells us, as would most persons, that high-valued crops are crops such as fruits and vegetables, that is, crops that produce a high gross return per acre. Unfortunately, gross returns per acre is but one of many factors determining choice of enterprise(s) in a given locale. More often than not, high-valued crops are characterized as requiring high-level management and high cost per acre as well as being vulnerable to considerable production and, more important, market risk. Markets for high-value crops tend to be very fragile. The problem of enterprise selection in a risky world is extremely complex and economists, of all people, should avoid the low-value versus high-value crop syndrome. Irrigation farmers are not irrational economic men. There are very good reasons why they are producing what they are producing. If water becomes scarce and pumping costs continue to rise, farmers may or may not change their crop mix, depending on their options; if they do change, it *could result* in *greater* relative acreages of low-valued crops in some areas, and that would likely represent a social optimum as well.

I find little to quarrel with on the prospects of augmenting water supply. The general economic infeasibility of large-scale interbasin water transfers is quite well known and beginning, I think, to gain acceptance even among potential recipients. However, on the matter of cloud seeding (either for rainmaking or snow pack augmentation), I am even more guarded than Frederick. I think it would be a bonanza for attorneys. The institutional barriers seem nearly insurmountable.

Others are more qualified than I am to comment on salinity. Frederick concludes that the "impacts on the overall role of irrigation will not be great." I hope he is right. I believe Ken Frederick has written a well-developed and thought-provoking paper that meets the objectives of the conference very nicely, as I perceive them. Two of his conclusions are particularly important:

1. Strategies need to be developed to overcome opposition to reform of water development, allocation, and pricing policies and

practices. There is a need to look at equity implications of reform and consider possible measures for providing compensation to the losers.

2. Irrigation's important present role in contributing to U.S. agricultural output does not justify policies that attempt to preserve that role in the face of otherwise changing resource conditions.

# 6

# Future Economic and Environmental Costs of Agricultural Land

*Pierre R. Crosson*

## Introduction

This chapter addresses the question of how the economic and environmental costs of agricultural land in the United States are likely to respond to the growth in demand for production, in technology, and in the supply of land over the next several decades. This issue is important because the cost of land is a significant element in the cost of agricultural production. Rising land costs that are not offset by declining costs of other resources or growth in productivity would increase production costs and raise questions about the adequacy of agricultural land. This underscores the point that the real issue is the cost of agricultural production, and that the adequacy of agricultural land can be judged only by its contribution to changes in cost, given the contribution of other resources.

There is no definitive answer to the question of future economic and environmental costs of agricultural land. There are major uncertainties about trends in demand for agricultural production, in technology, and in the supply of land, as the preceding chapters have made abundantly clear. The range of probable outcomes is not so broad, however, as to preclude useful discussion of the question. In

The research on which this paper is based was partially funded by grants from the Rockefeller Foundation and the Environmental Protection Agency. The paper is a revision of that given at the RFF conference on the adequacy of agricultural land. I am grateful to Irving Hoch, Lawrence Libby, Paul Portney, and Philip Raup for valuable comments.

any case, it must be addressed in order to gain perspective on the nature and importance of the agricultural land issue.

My concern is with real social costs, that is, nominal social costs adjusted for changes in the general price level. From the social stand-point, the real economic cost of agricultural land is its opportunity cost. This is included in the price of land as the capitalized value of the stream of net returns to the land when it is employed in its most productive use. If all land markets were always in equilibrium and opportunity cost were the only element in the price of land, then changes in real prices of agricultural land would measure movements over time in its real opportunity costs. In the American experience, however, neither of these conditions has been consistently met. Castle and Hoch have shown that between 1921 and 1978, factors other than opportunity cost were major, sometimes even dominant, components of the price of agricultural land.[1] They argue that the acquisition of debt is economically attractive when interest rates do not fully reflect the effects of inflation on the future value of debt.

Investment in farm real estate, therefore, may occur as a way of acquiring debt, with the future agricultural productivity of the land having little bearing on the investment decision. Of course, such in-vestments tend to increase the price of land, and when undertaken on a sufficient scale, the increase will exceed the rise in the general price level. The real price of agricultural land thus rises, but not because the social opportunity cost of the land has risen.

Castle and Hoch provide annual estimates of the capitalized value of land rents earned in agriculture, and these may be a better measure of movements in the opportunity cost of agricultural land than land prices. There are some measurement problems with these estimates of rents, but as far as they go they indicate a decline in the real oppor-tunity cost of agricultural land from the late 1940s to the early 1960s, followed by a rising trend through 1978, the last year for which Castle and Hoch provide estimates. In that year the real capitalized value of land rents was more than double the average for 1960–61.

It is not my purpose here to explain the past behavior of the eco-nomic costs of agricultural land, but rather to inquire how these costs may behave in the future. As far as I know, there is no way to provide a quantitative answer to this question. I do think some reasonably

---

[1] Emery Castle and Irving Hoch, "Farm Real Estate Price Components, 1920–78," *American Journal of Agricultural Economics*, vol. 64, No. 1 (February 1982).

well-grounded statements can be made about the likelihood that opportunity costs of agricultural land will rise over the long term. Such
statements, while lacking quantitative precision, will be useful in judging whether the nation is likely to confront a problem of adequate
agricultural land.

I focus on cropland in discussing demand–supply relations for agricultural land because if there is increasing pressure on the agricultural
land base, it most likely will reflect increasing demand for crop production, primarily for export. Growth in the demand for cropland will
increase its rental value, thus raising the opportunity costs of those
lands in pasture, range, and forest that could be converted to crops
under prevailing prices and costs of conversion. The focus on cropland, therefore, will permit inferences to be drawn about the likely
effects of increasing demand on opportunity costs of all agricultural
land, as well as land in forests.

## The Demand for Cropland

In responding to rising demand for crop production, American
farmers as a group may opt to convert land now in other uses to crops,
or to increase yields on present land by applying more nonland inputs
per acre, or, of course, by some combination of these two modes of
response. I assume they select that mode or combination of modes
which permits them to meet the anticipated increase in demand at
minimum cost. In making this calculation, and given crop prices, they
will be most influenced by the prices and marginal productivities of
nonland inputs when applied to the existing land base; by the costs of
converting forestland, pasture, and range to crop production; and by
the marginal productivity of nonland inputs on the additional land.
The lower the price and higher the productivity of nonland inputs on
existing land relative to conversion costs and the productivity of those
inputs on new land, the more farmers will adopt the yield-increasing
mode, lowering the demand for additional cropland. Of course, when
these price and productivity conditions are reversed, the demand for
additional land will be higher.

Table 6-1 shows the percentage increases between 1978–79 and
2005 in domestic and export demand for U.S.-produced wheat, feedgrains, and soybeans, as projected by Martin Abel. I take these projec-

**TABLE 6-1.**   Changes in Demand for Feedgrains, Wheat, and Soybeans in the United States, 1978–79 to 2005

(percent)

| | |
|---|---:|
| Feedgrains | |
| Domestic demand | 67–86 |
| Export demand | 107 |
| Total | 79–92 |
| Wheat | |
| Domestic demand | −0.9 |
| Export demand | 97 |
| Total | 56 |
| Soybeans | |
| Domestic demand | 28–44 |
| Export demand | 12–45 |
| Total | 21–44 |

Source:   Chapter 3, this volume.

tions as a point of departure in discussing the future demand for agricultural land.

## The Importance of Yields

The mode of response to rising demand for agricultural production can make an enormous difference in the demand for agricultural land. If all of the increase in demand projected by Abel were met by bringing more land into production, the amount of land in feedgrains would rise from an average of 102.8 million acres in 1978–79 to a minimum of 184 million acres in 2005. The amount of land in wheat would rise to 93 million acres from an average of 59.8 million, and land in soybeans would rise to 81 acres, up from 66.9 million. The *increase* in land in these crops alone would be 141 million acres, one-third of the total amount of cropland in the nation in 1977, according to the National Resources Inventory (NRI) of the Soil Conservation Service, and 14 million more acres than all the land presently with high-to-medium potential for conversion to crops, according to the NRI.

If, however, farmers adopted a yield-increasing response exclusively and yields increased at the same annual rate as in the years from the end of World War II to 1972 (about 3 percent for feedgrains and wheat and 1.7 for soybeans), then the amount of land in feedgrains, wheat, and soybeans would *decline* a minimum of 39 million acres by

2005 from the average amount in 1978–79. If one or the other of the two modes of response to rising demand were followed exclusively, therefore, the difference in the demand for land in 2005 would be 180 million acres, 44 percent of the total stock of cropland in 1977. The implications of such a large difference for the economic and environmental costs of agricultural land would be substantial.

Abel's projections of demand for U.S. production of grains and soybeans imply real growth in output of these crops, as a group, of 1.8 percent annually from 1978–79 to 2005. If yields grow at the same rate, then of course the growth in output of these crops would generate no increase in demand for land. It is useful to ask, therefore, whether over the long run the prices and productivity of yield-increasing inputs are likely to produce an annual yield increase in these crops of 1.8 percent annually.

*Input Prices*

The key yield-increasing inputs considered here are agricultural chemicals, principally fertilizers and pesticides, and water for irrigation. Energy is important in two respects: (1) because of its role as an input to production of agricultural chemicals and in pumping groundwater for irrigation and (2) because of its relation to the economics of producing energy from biomass. In both respects the price of energy is positively related to the demand for agricultural land. Higher energy prices will tend to raise the cost of agricultural chemicals and water for irrigation, thus increasing the attractiveness of the land-using mode relative to the yield-increasing mode. Higher prices for fossil fuels will also make biomass more attractive as an energy source and this will tend to increase the demand for agricultural land if the biomass is obtained from crops grown for that purpose.

Martin Abel incorporates demand for crops for energy production in his chapter so I do not treat that issue. Energy is considered only in connection with the effect of its price on costs of agricultural chemicals and irrigation water.

Earl Heady assumes that real energy prices will rise, but argues that the main impact on the demand for land in the United States is more likely to be indirectly through the effect on crop production in developing countries than directly through higher costs for yield-increasing inputs to American farmers. That is to say, the main impact would be on the demand for U.S. exports. This argument has merit; however, Abel's projections of U.S. exports take account of the effect of higher energy prices on the growth of foreign production. Accordingly, I deal only with the effect on costs of yield-increasing inputs in the United States.

Improved seed varieties of main crops have contributed significantly to yield increases in the past and will do so in the future. New varieties are considered with new technologies rather than in this discussion, which deals with prices of yield-increasing inputs. Farm machinery no doubt has contributed to larger yields, but farmers invest in machinery primarily as a substitute for labor rather than land. It is true that the increasing size and cost of farm machinery most likely has been one of the factors stimulating the growth in farm size evident in American agriculture for many years. To some extent, therefore, these characteristics have stimulated the demand for cropland. However, compared with the key yield-increasing inputs— energy, agricultural chemicals, and water—the effects of size and cost of machinery on the demand for cropland seem small, and they are not treated further here.

Abel, Heady, and Frederick assume that the long-term outlook is for rising real energy prices. Heady, while noting that there is no adequate quantitative procedure for predicting future energy prices, believes that "the wise thing for the nation" is to expect real energy prices to continue to rise at rates equal to or greater than those recently experienced. Frederick adopts the assumption from a recent RFF study that real energy prices will increase at an average rate of 2 percent from 1977 to 2000.

I accept the assumption that real energy prices will rise over the long term. This implies increasing pressure on real costs of agricultural chemicals and irrigation water. Most pesticides are petroleum derivatives so rising petroleum prices will tend to increase pesticide prices. The agricultural chemical most sensitive to higher energy costs, however, is nitrogen fertilizer. Fossil fuels are the feedstock for nitrogen fertilizer, with natural gas the most widely used source. According to Dvoskin and Heady,[2] about 30 cubic feet of natural gas are used on average to produce 1 pound of nitrogen nutrient. The nutrient content of a ton of anhydrous ammonia, the most commonly used form

---

[2] D. Dvoskin and E. Heady, *U.S. Agricultural Production Under Limited Energy Supplies, High Energy Prices and Expanding Exports,* Center for Agricultural and Rural Development, Iowa State University, Ames, Iowa, CARD Report 69 (1976) p. 160.

of nitrogen fertilizer in the United States, is 82 percent.[3] There are, therefore, about 49,000 cubic feet of natural gas in a ton of anhydrous ammonia (2000 pounds × 30 cubic feet × 0.82). At 1980 prices, natural gas would account for 40–45 percent of the total cost of anhydrous ammonia fertilizer. If the real price of natural gas increases 2 percent annually to 2000, as Frederick assumes, the technology of anhydrous ammonia production remains the same, and all other costs of production other than the price of natural gas are unchanged, then a ton of anhydrous ammonia in 1980 dollars would cost $276 in 2000, an increase of 20 percent from the $229 in March 1980. For comparison, real prices of all fertilizers (not just nitrogen) declined about 40 percent in the approximately twenty years from 1950–54 to 1970–72.

This may be a conservative projection of the price of anhydrous ammonia fertilizer in 2000 because it assumes that only the real cost of natural gas rises. Unpublished studies of fertilizer costs done at the World Bank indicate that real costs of constructing new fertilizer plants are rising, and are expected to continue to rise. Should this happen, the real costs of nitrogen most likely would rise considerably more than 20 percent from 1980 to 2000.

All such speculation about the future, of course, is subject to a large discount for uncertainty. Nonetheless, the present outlook suggests a long-term increase in real prices of fertilizer, especially of nitrogen, unless there are significant improvements in the technology of fertilizer production.

Frederick concludes that because of rising energy costs and increasing competition for water in the western states, the future growth of irrigation will be significantly less than in the past (chapter 5). He notes that higher crop prices could offset some of the effect of higher energy costs on the profitability of irrigation, but argues that "almost regardless of what happens to crop prices, irrigation cannot be expected to make the contribution to agricultural expansion that it has made in the past three to four decades."

Frederick's conclusion implies that in the future the yield-increasing mode of expansion will look less attractive relative to the land-using mode than it did in the past. This statement needs to be kept in perspective, however. Frederick's analysis shows that irrigation contributed only 13 percent of the growth in national average yields of corn between 1950 and 1977, only 7 percent of the growth in wheat

[3] U.S. Department of Agriculture, *1980 Fertilizer Situation*, FS-10, December 1979, p. 2.

yields, and 16 percent of the growth in sorghum yields. Irrigation's contribution to the growth of soybean yields was negligible since it is only recently that soybeans have been produced on irrigated land, and the acreage is still small. Thus, while the less favorable conditions for irrigation expected in the future imply diminished attractiveness of yield-increasing response to increased demand, the effect should be minor at the national level.

*Trends in Productivity and Yields*

The negative effect of rising real costs of agricultural chemicals and irrigation water on the attractiveness of the yield-increasing mode would be offset if the productivity of these inputs were to rise fast enough, or if new yield-increasing technologies are developed which make less use of these inputs. The higher cost of the inputs would itself induce farmers to look for ways to use them more sparingly, without a commensurate sacrifice of yields, and there undoubtedly are opportunities to do this. Frederick, however, does not believe the opportunities for economizing on water are so great as to offset the rising cost of the resource, and Heady argues that fertilizer use per acre is now at a position on the production function such that higher prices would induce a reduction in use, with some sacrifice of yield.

The Heady and Frederick arguments suggest that the potential for additional yield and productivity gains from present yield-increasing technologies has been nearly exhausted. Heady notes, however, that despite this there is yet no quantitative evidence that annual absolute increases in crop yields in the United States are diminishing. Swanson and Nyankori reached the same conclusion about trends in corn and soybean yields on farms in Illinois.[4] The evidence on this question is indeed hard to interpret, in large part because of extraordinary increases in yields, particularly of corn, in 1978 and 1979. Excellent weather in both years in major production regions undoubtedly was an important factor in the rise of yields, but continued technological advance must have contributed also.

My reading of the evidence indicates that since 1972 the trend in yields did in fact diminish relative to the pre-1972 period. Table 6-2 shows the relevant data. In every year since 1972, actual yields were below the pre-1972 trend yields. This was true even in the record

---

[4] Earl R. Swanson and James C. Nyankori, "Influence of Weather and Technology on Corn and Soybean Yield Trends," *Agricultural Meteorology* vol. 20 (1979) pp. 327–342.

**TABLE 6-2.** Indexes of Crop Yields in the United States, Actual and Pre-1972 Trend

(1967 = 100)

| | (1) Actual | (2) Trend | (3) Col. (1) − Col. (2) |
|------|------|------|------|
| 1972 | 118 | 115 | 3 |
| 1973 | 113 | 117 | − 4 |
| 1974 | 103 | 119 | −16 |
| 1975 | 110 | 121 | −11 |
| 1976 | 110 | 124 | −14 |
| 1977 | 116 | 126 | −10 |
| 1978 | 119 | 128 | − 9 |
| 1979 | 127 | 130 | − 3 |

*Sources:* U.S. Department of Agriculture, *Changes in Farm Production and Efficiency, 1978,* Statistical Bulletin 628. 1979 harvested cropland from H. T. Frey, U.S. Department of Agriculture, in a personal communication. 1979 crop production from U.S. Department of Agriculture, *Agricultural Outlook,* April 1980.

The numbers are indexes of crop production divided by harvested cropland, converted to a 1967 base. The yield trend was calculated with a least-squares regression of yields against time in the years 1950 through 1972. The trend equation is $63.3 + 2.23t$, where $t_1 = 1950$.

years of 1978 and 1979. The behavior of yields since 1972, however, does not necessarily reflect the approaching exhaustion of the potential of yield-increasing technologies. It undoubtedly is owed at least in part to the diminished attractiveness of these technologies after 1972 because of the escalation of fertilizer and energy prices. While, as Heady shows, the real price of fertilizer declined from the peak reached in 1975, it remained well above the 1972 level in 1976–78, and rose again in 1979. Real energy prices rose continuously after 1973. These price increases would have reduced the attractiveness of yield-increasing technologies even if their marginal productivity was undiminished. The amount of harvested cropland did in fact increase after 1972, rising from 289 million acres that year to 343 million acres in 1979.[5] Since the additional land was inferior to land in production in 1972, and the quantity of nonland inputs per acre increased more slowly, the trend of yields would be expected to flatten for these reasons alone.[6]

[5] 1972 data, U.S. Department of Agriculture, *Changes in Farm Production and Efficiency, 1978.* 1979 data from H. T. Frey, USDA, personal communication.

[6] The quantity of purchased inputs per acre of harvested cropland increased 2.6 percent annually from 1950–52 to 1970–72. From 1970–72 to 1979, the annual rate was 1.0 percent. (Calculated from data in U.S. Department of Agriculture, *Economic Indicators of the Farm Section: Production and Efficiency Statistics, 1979* ESS Statistical Bulletin 657.).

Thus while the rate of yield increases does appear to have slowed after 1972, this could reflect a shift by farmers from yield-increasing to land-using technologies in response to higher prices of inputs rather than to the diminishing productivity potential of yield-increasing technologies. However, if real prices of yield-increasing inputs rise as expected, the slower rate of increase in yields most likely would continue unless, as Heady puts it, large "breakthrough" technologies are developed which permit a move to a much higher per acre production function. Such a breakthrough—something comparable to the development of hybrid corn, for example—is a distinct possibility over the next several decades. Lu, Cline, and Quance argue, however, that even if such technologies are developed—they mention enhancement of photosynthesis and bioregulators in crop production and twinning in beef cattle production—they are not likely to have much impact on total productivity or yield increase by 2000, and their full effect would not be felt until about 2025.[7] Moreover, in the Lu et al. scenario, these technologies are developed only as a result of a sharp increase in real investment in agricultural research and extension, from 3 percent, the rate over the last four decades, to 7 percent annually. There is no assurance that such an increase in R & E spending will occur.

If Lu et al. are right, then the kind of "breakthrough" technology mentioned by Heady is not likely to have much effect on crop yields over the period considered in these conference papers. Given the projected increase in real prices of yield-increasing inputs, the implication is that the slower rate of increase in yields since 1972 would continue.

Translation of this generalization into specific projections of yields for grains and soybeans involves great uncertainty. The yield trend of these crops since 1972 is obscured by extreme variations in weather and by the small number of years included. The weather effects are particularly troublesome because they severely depressed yields in 1974, raised them in 1978 and 1979, then depressed them again in 1980. Yield behavior since 1972 thus is a treacherous basis for projecting yields. I dealt with this by examining yield behavior in the ten USDA producing regions and making judgmental projections assum-

[7] Yao Chi Lu, Philip Cline, and Leroy Quance, *Prospects for Productivity Growth in U.S. Agriculture,* U.S. Department of Agriculture, Economics, Statistics and Cooperatives Service, Agricultural Economic Report No. 435, Washington, D.C., September 1979.

ing that the trend of national yields would be dominated by trends in the major regions. Yields in other regions were then projected proportionately to one another and so as to be consistent with the projections for the nation and the major regions.

As it turned out, this procedure gave projections for wheat and soybean yields in 2005—Abel's target year—almost identical to those obtained by fitting a least-squares trend equation to the yield data for 1973–80. The projection for feedgrains, however, is about 7 percent less than would be obtained with the least-squares procedure. The reason is my expectation that the price of nitrogen fertilizer in the future will behave differently relative to the price of corn than it did in 1973–79. From 1973 to 1975 the price of nitrogen fertilizer rose sharply relative to the price of corn, and the amount of nitrogen applied per acre of land in corn declined. From 1975 to 1979 the price of corn rose relative to the price of nitrogen and per acre applications rose. This pattern must have tended to depress corn yields in 1973–75 and then raise them to 1979. If the price of nitrogen rises relative to the price of corn over the next several decades, as I expect, then per-acre applications of nitrogen to corn ought to increase more slowly than from 1975 to 1979. Accordingly, I expect corn yields to rise more slowly from 1979 to 2005 than from 1973 to 1979. Since corn currently accounts for about 70 percent of the land in feedgrains, and for an even larger percentage in my projections, the slower growth in corn yields implies slower growth in yields of feedgrains.

The resulting projections of yields of wheat, soybeans, and feedgrains, when divided into Abel's projections of production, give a projection of 292 million acres in these crops in 2005, 62 million acres more than in 1977–79. Where would the additional land come from? According to the National Resources Inventory taken by the SCS, there were 413 million acres of cropland in the United States in 1977. In 1980 some 346 million acres of cropland were harvested and crops were lost on 12 million acres. Allowing for about 30 million acres of land which year in, year out, are in fallow and for roughly 20 million acres which each year are unavoidably idle for a variety of reasons, it appears that the nation's cropland is now fully utilized, or substantially so. This indicates that accommodation of the additional 62 million acres of cropland needed for grains and soybeans in 2005 would have to come from shifts of land that now is devoted to other crops, or is in fallow, or is idle; or from conversion to crops of land now in pasture, forest, or range.

I believe that most of the additional land for grains and soybeans will come from conversions of pasture, forest, and range. According to land use specialists at the USDA, the 20 million acres of idle cropland each year is about the minimum that can be expected. Most of the fallow land is in the Plains states, and if pressure on the land base in that region mounts, farmers might find ways of reducing the land in fallow without fatally compromising the economics of wheat production. Some of the additional land needed for grains and soybeans could come from land now in hay and other crops. There currently are about 60 million acres of land in hay, a relatively low-value use. If the demand for land for grains and soybeans rises as projected, there likely could be a shift to these crops of some land now in hay.

On balance, perhaps 10–15 million acres of cropland now fallow or in other crops could be shifted to grains and soybeans in 2005. The implication is that 47 to 52 million acres of land now in pasture, forest, and range would be shifted to these crops. This is the projected net increase in the demand for cropland, that is, the additional cropland farmers would demand in 2005 given real crop prices of 1978–79, higher real prices of yield-increasing inputs, and the technological conditions reflected in my projections of yields. The effect of this increase in the demand for land on the opportunity cost of agricultural land, on the amount of additional land actually brought into production, and on the costs of production will depend in large measure upon the costs of converting to crops land now in forest, pasture, and range.

## The Supply of Cropland

There are no comprehensive estimates of the supply of cropland in the United States. The closest approximations are the estimates provided in the NRI, which show that in 1977 there were 36 million acres of land with high potential for conversion to cropland and 91 million acres with medium potential (see chapter 4). High potential land was defined as that with "favorable physical characteristics" and of a sort which had been converted in the vicinity in the three years preceding the survey (1974–76). Commodity prices and development and production costs of 1976 were assumed. Medium potential land also has favorable physical characteristics, but conversion costs are estimated to be higher than for high potential land.

*Conversions to Cropland*

As noted above, Abel's projections of demand for grains and soybeans assume that their real prices in 2005 will be the same as in 1978–79. Table 6-3 indicates that 1976 prices of corn and soybeans, expressed in 1978–79 dollars, were greater than 1978–79 prices of these crops, while the 1976 price of wheat, after adjustment to 1978–79 dollars, was less than 1978–79 wheat prices. These relationships suggest that at 1978–79 prices, less land could be economically converted to soybeans and corn than the NRI estimates of potential land would indicate, but that 1978–79 prices of wheat would justify conversion of land to wheat production. These judgments are inconclusive, however, because crop prices are only one of the elements determining the supply of potential cropland. Yields, prices of inputs, and conversion costs, including opportunity costs, also are important. Yields of all three crops were higher in 1979 than in 1976, and real fertilizer prices were lower. Both changes would increase the amount of potentially convertible land in 1979 relative to 1976, at least partially offsetting the negative effect of lower real crop prices. We have no information on changes in opportunity costs and other conversion costs between 1976 and 1978–79.

Studies done at Iowa State University and the University of Arkansas provide clues to the supply of potential cropland in the Mississippi Delta and in Iowa. Table 6-4 is based on those studies. Comparison of the prices in table 6-4 with 1978–79 prices in table 6-3 indicates that with 1978–79 crop prices, land in both regions could be economically converted to wheat and soybeans, but not to corn. The supply of potentially convertible land in the Delta is completely inelastic

**TABLE 6-3.**   Prices Received by Farmers for Wheat, Corn, and Soybeans ($ per bushel)

|  | 1976 prices in dollars of 1978–79 | 1978–79 prices |
|---|---|---|
| Wheat | $3.30 | $3.40 |
| Corn | 2.60 | 2.34 |
| Soybeans | 8.24 | 6.36 |

*Sources:*   1976 prices from U.S. Department of Agriculture, *Agricultural Statistics 1978*, deflated by the increase in the CPI from 1976 to 1978–79. 1978–79 prices from *Agricultural Outlook*, May 1980.

**TABLE 6-4.**  Land in the Mississippi Delta and Iowa Potentially
Convertible to Crops Under Alternative Assumptions

|  | Crop prices in 1978–79 dollars | | | Convertible land (million acres) |
|---|---|---|---|---|
|  | Wheat | Corn | Soybeans |  |
| Iowa | $2.97 | $2.66 | $5.82 | 0.09–0.16 |
|  | $3.60 | $3.08 | $6.59 | 0.5–1.0 |
| Mississippi Delta | $2.97 | $2.66 | $5.82 | 2.6 |
|  | $3.60 | $3.08 | $6.59 | 2.6 |

*Sources:* Iowa—Orley M. Amos, Jr., *"Supply of Potential Cropland in Iowa,"* Iowa State University, 1979, unpublished study jointly sponsored by Resources for the Future and Iowa Agriculture and Home Economics Experiment Station. Real prices of purchased inputs assumed to be one-third higher than in 1978. Yields assumed to be 20 percent higher than the average for 1967–77. The low estimates of convertible land reflect an 8 percent discount rate and the high estimates reflect 4 percent.

Delta—Robert N. Shulstad, Ralph D. May, and Billy E. Herrington, Jr., "Cropland Conversion Study for the Mississippi Delta Region," University of Arkansas, 1979, a study done for Resources for the Future. Real prices of purchased inputs assumed to be one-third higher than in 1978. Yields assumed higher than average in 1978, but precise amount not given. A ten percent discount rate is assumed.

Given the above assumptions about prices of inputs, yields, discount rates, and conversion costs, the crop prices to the left would justify conversion of the amounts of land to the right.

with respect to crop prices over the range of prices considered. In Iowa the supply of land would respond to higher prices, although the prices of corn and wheat required to elicit that response are above 1978–79 levels.

The yield assumptions incorporated in the studies of Iowa and the Delta are conservative considered as projections to 2005, and the estimates of potentially convertible land are sensitive to assumptions about yields. If yields more appropriate to 2005 were used in the Iowa and Delta studies, they likely would offset much if not all of the negative effect on estimated potential of relatively low crop prices.

The NRI shows that in 1977 there were 2.2 million acres of high and medium potential land in Iowa. Given the likelihood that by 2005 rising yields would offset relatively low crop prices, Amos' study suggests that a quarter to half of this land could be profitably converted to production of grains and soybeans.[8] If these proportions hold for

---

[8] Note that Amos' estimates assume real prices of inputs to be one-third higher than in 1978.

the Corn Belt as a whole, then 3.6 million to 7.2 million acres of the
14.4 million acres of high-to-medium potential land in that region
could be converted to crops by 2005.[9]

There were 10 million acres of high-to-medium potential land in
the Mississippi Delta in 1977 according to the NRI, about four times
the amount estimated as convertible in the University of Arkansas
study. However, that study was confined to land defined as part of the
Delta, while the NRI estimate is for the three Delta states as a whole
(Arkansas, Louisiana, and Mississippi). Under the price and other
conditions specified in the University of Arkansas study, therefore, it
is likely that more than 2.6 million acres would be convertible in the
three states.

*Conversions to Nonagricultural Uses*

The Iowa and Delta studies, together with the NRI estimates of high
and medium potential land, indicate that under the price, yield, and
cost conditions projected for 2005, the potential supply of cropland
could be expanded to accommodate a substantial increase in the demand for it. It is doubtful, however, that the entire projected net
increase of 47 to 52 million acres for grains and soybeans could be
accommodated without increasing the opportunity costs of cropland
and other agricultural land. Brewer and Boxley indicate that between
1967 and 1975 about 2 million acres per year of land in crops, pasture,
range, and forest were converted to urban and other nonagricultural
uses. Some 675,000 acres were cropland, and according to another
paper by Boxley, not more than 200,000 acres were pasture, forest, or
range with cropland potential.[10] Conversion of agricultural and
forestland to nonagricultural uses will continue, but I expect the rate
of conversion to diminish. Conversions between 1967 and 1975 were
powerfully influenced by the growth of population and its spread to
rural areas, and by construction of the interstate highway system.
While population will continue to grow and to demand additional land
in rural areas for residential and other nonagricultural purposes,
current projections indicate that the absolute rate of population

---

[9] Potential cropland in the Corn Belt from the NRI.

[10] Robert Boxley, "Competing Demands for U.S. Agricultural Land in the Year
2000," Technical paper IV, prepared by the research staff of the National Agricultural
Lands Study, January 1981.

growth is expected to be less than in 1967–75. And the interstate highway system now is substantially completed.

Strip mining of coal is likely to become more important over the next several decades and will take some of the land now in crops or with potential for conversion to crops. However, Brewer and Boxley (chapter 4) cite studies indicating that the total amount of additional land turned to energy development by 2000 would be less than 2 million acres, and not all of it would come from present or potential cropland.

For these reasons I expect the future rate of conversion to nonagricultural uses of land now in crops, and of pasture, forest, and range land with cropland potential to be less than the roughly 875,000 million acres per year converted between 1967 and 1975. There is no reliable basis for estimating the rate of future conversions. For purposes of this discussion I assume it to be 750,000 acres per year. Under this assumption, nonagricultural uses would diminish the supply of present and potential cropland by 21 million acres from 1977 to 2005, a period in which farmers are projected to demand a net addition of 47 to 52 million cropland acres. It can be assumed that most of the projected conversion of 68 to 73 million acres would come from the 127 million acres now in pasture, forest, and range with high or medium potential for conversion to cropland.

It is likely that conversion on this scale would significantly increase the cost of agricultural land for two reasons. (1) Over half of the converted land would be of medium potential and, according to Brewer and Boxley, this land would have higher conversion costs than high potential land. (2) The conversion most likely would reduce the supply of land in forest, pasture, and range sufficiently to raise the price of that which remained, unless land-saving technologies were developed for those lands.

The NRI shows that in 1977 there were 923 million acres of nonfederal pasture, range, and forestland. Seven or 8 percent of that would be required to accommodate the projected demand for crops and urban uses in 2005. While the percentage reduction in supply of pasture, range, and forestland is not large, allowance must be made for the possibility that demand for land for these uses may also be increasing. For example, demand for wood as feedstock for energy production may increase significantly over the next several decades. At a meeting of the Bio-Energy World Congress and Exposition, held in Atlanta in April 1980, most speakers agreed that wood rather than grain is the most economical source of biomass for energy production.[11]

The supply of pasture land probably would be most affected by the increased demand for land for crops and urban uses. The NRI shows that in 1977 there were 133 million acres of pastureland, 51 million of which had high-to-medium potential for conversion to cropland. In their study of conversion costs in the Mississippi Delta, Shulstad et al. found that costs of converting pasture to crops generally were lower than costs of converting forests, and this is intuitively reasonable. It seems likely, therefore, that to satisfy the projected demand for cropland, the 51 million acres of pasture would be the first to go. No doubt there is range and forestland that could be converted to pasture, but this could not occur without a cost.

Over the next several decades, mounting pressure on the agricultural land base is likely to increase the real economic costs of that land. I have no basis for estimating how much this increase might be, but the fact of rising land costs would itself be significant because real costs of nonland inputs seem likely to rise also. With rising real costs of both land and nonland inputs, the average cost of agricultural production also is likely to increase unless productivity advances more rapidly than now is generally expected.

This scenario contrasts significantly with the experience of American agriculture from the end of World War II to the early 1970s. In that period average real production costs declined from the late 1940s to the early 1960s and showed no trend from the early 1960s to the early 1970s.[12] As indicated at the beginning of this paper, agricultural land costs, as measured by rents, declined from the late 1940s to the early 1960s, then increased to the early 1970s. Average real prices of purchased inputs, however, declined in the latter period and this, combined with rising productivity, was enough to offset the effect on average production costs of rising real prices of land (and of labor).

Should production costs rise, as the projected scenario suggests, then both domestic and foreign demand for grains and soybeans might grow less than Abel projected since he explicitly assumes con-

[11] *Science*, vol. 208 (May 30, 1980) p. 1018. Roger Sedjo, director of RFF's forest research program, tells me there is a consensus that real prices of forest products will rise over the long term, suggesting higher opportunity costs of converting forestland to crops.

[12] Pierre Crosson, "Long-Run Costs of Production in American Agriculture," February 1979, unpublished paper, Resources for the Future.

stant real product prices of 1978–79. The implication is that demand for land would grow less than I have projected and that upward pressure on land prices therefore would be weaker. However, it is not clear how much higher prices of agricultural commodities would depress demand. Projections by the USDA to 1990 of demand for grains and soybeans show a trend much like that projected by Abel, despite a projected increase in real prices for feedgrains and soybeans. (Up between 25 and 30 percent from 1974 to 1990.[13]) If one accepts the USDA projections, the implication is that Abel's projections are conservative, given his assumption of constant real prices of 1978–79.

Untangling the effects of higher real costs of agricultural production on the growth of demand would require a more precise estimate of those costs than I have made and a far more detailed investigation of demand elasticities than I can undertake. I take the cited USDA study, however, as evidence that demand could rise along the trend projected by Abel even if real grains and soybean prices increase. Therefore, my projected increase in the demand for cropland and its consequences for the cost of agricultural land are not inconsistent with some increase in real crop prices.

It is not clear whether the projected increase in the real economic cost of agricultural land would raise concern about the adequacy of land. Much would depend on the amount of the increase, and on how much costs of production rise. Indeed, costs of production are what really count when the issue is capacity to produce, and rising land costs would be of small concern if they were offset by declining costs of other resources. Since in the projected scenario, production costs rise, the scenario probably implies increasing concern about the adequacy of agricultural land as a factor of production.

## Environmental Costs

Rising economic costs of land and production may be accompanied by higher environmental costs. The environmental costs considered here are those resulting from erosion. Conversion to crops of land now in other uses will destroy plant and animal habitat, and expanded agricultural production may also exact higher environmental costs be-

[13] Projections by the USDA's National Interregional Agricultural Projections (NIRAP) model, done in the summer of 1980.

cause of unintended effects of pesticides and fertilizers. I believe these other environmental costs are less important than those of erosion, however, and because of space limitations I do not address them.[14]

Erosion costs are of two sorts: (1) off-farm costs resulting from siltation of reservoirs, stream beds, and other water bodies, and diminution of water quality by suspended sediment; and (2) on-farm costs resulting from reduced productivity of the land. There are no reliable estimates of either of these two sorts of erosion costs, although there is a consensus that they are not negligible. Pimentel et al. cite various sources indicating that some 450 million cubic yards of sediment are dredged annually from rivers and harbors in the United States at a cost of about $250 million, that the reduction in useful life of reservoirs caused by siltation costs about $50 million per year, and that other sediment damages bring the total annual cost to $500 million.[15] These estimates evidently relate to the 1960s, so the present dollar amounts would be substantially larger even if the amount of sediment were unchanged.

Of course, erosion from farmland is not the only source of sediment. Pimentel et al. indicate that on average there are 4 billion tons of waterborne sediment annually in the United States and that 3 billion tons originate in agriculture. Meister et al. assert that 3.6 billion tons of soil are eroded annually, 2.7 billion tons of it from agricultural and forestlands.[16] Since much of the eroded soil does not reach water bodies, being deposited instead in gullies and other low-lying places, the figure given by Meister et al. implies much less waterborne sediment from agriculture than the 3 billion tons given by Pimentel et al.

According to the NRI, water-induced erosion from agriculture and forestland in 1977 was 3.9 billion tons, substantially more than the amount estimated by Meister et al. Of the 3.9 billion tons, 3.7 billion came from agricultural land and grazed forestland.

[14] These other environmental costs, and the reasons for considering them to pose smaller long-term threats than erosion, are treated at length in Pierre Crosson and Sterling Brubaker, "Resource and Environmental Impacts of Agriculture in the United States," unpublished manuscript, 1980, Resources for the Future.

[15] D. Pimentel, E. C. Terhune, R. Dyson-Hudson, S. Rochereau, R. Samis, E. A. Smith, D. Denman, D. Reifschneider, M. Shepard, "Land Degradation: Effects on Food and Energy Resources," *Science* vol. 194 (October 8, 1976), pp. 149–155.

[16] A. D. Meister, E. O. Heady, K. J. Nichol, and R. W. Strohbehn, *U.S. Agricultural Production in Relation to Alternative Water, Environmental and Export Policies*, Iowa State University Center for Agricultural and Rural Development, CARD Report 65, Ames, Iowa 1976.

There are no reliable estimates of the loss in productivity of American agriculture because of past erosion. Sources given in Pimentel et al. assert that over the past 200 years at least a third of the topsoil on the nation's croplands has been lost to erosion, but such estimates obviously are subject to wide margins of error. And in any case, they say nothing about the productivity declines resulting from the loss of topsoil. Nonetheless, I am prepared to believe that there has been a significant loss of productivity, but it obviously was not a net loss since yields now are higher than ever before in U.S. history. Whatever the loss in productivity because of erosion, it has been more than compensated for by improvements in technology and management. This is not to downgrade the importance of the erosion-inflicted losses, but to note that in judging whether their social costs present a problem, it is necessary to consider the costs of the options for reducing erosion or offsetting its effects. It is altogether possible that from the social standpoint it may be most cost effective to accept certain erosion-induced productivity losses to gain the higher productivity of the technologies causing the erosion. However, this statement must be qualified. The fact that the technologies adopted in the United States have more than compensated for any productivity losses induced by erosion does not necessarily mean that the path of technological change was socially optimal. That path was determined by millions of decisions made by American farmers over the years, each acting to promote his own interest. A farmer's interest in maintaining the productivity of the land may extend over only a few years or at most decades, while society's interest extends over generations. Various studies in fact show that the adoption of practices that would indefinitely maintain the productivity of the land would not serve the economic interest of farmers unless their planning horizon extends over fifty years or more and they discount future earnings at a very low, or even zero rate.[17]

The social interest does not necessarily require indefinite maintenance of the productivity of the land. Conceivably, technologies could be developed which would greatly reduce or even eliminate the need for land as a source of nutrients, for example, hydroponic farming. However, such technologies are not now on even the most

[17] See, for example, Earl Swanson and David MacCallum, "Income Effects of Rainfall Erosion Control," *Journal of Soil and Water Conservation* vol. 24, no. 2 (March-April 1969) pp. 56–59. Wesley D. Seitz, C. Robert Taylor, Robert G. F. Spitze, Craig Osteen, and Mack C. Nelson, "Economic Impacts of Soil Erosion Control," *Land Economics* vol. 55, no. 1 (February 1979) pp. 28–42.

distant horizon. It is prudent, therefore, to assume that much land will be needed indefinitely to support agriculture, in which case differences are possible between the farmer's interest and society's interest in preserving the productivity of the land.

According to the NRI, 4.6 billion tons of soil were eroded by water and wind from U.S. agricultural land and grazed forestland in 1977. Erosion of cropland by water averaged 4.7 tons per acre that year and wind erosion in the ten Plains states added an additional 2.1 tons per acre to the national average. Total erosion of cropland by wind and water thus averaged 6.8 tons per acre, 1.8 tons more than the maximum set by the SCS as consistent with maintaining the productivity of the soil over the long term. Per acre erosion of grazed forestland, pasture, and rangeland averaged 3.9 tons, 2.6 tons, and 2.8 tons, respectively. These national averages conceal wide variations in erosion by region. In the Corn Belt, for example, erosion by water from cropland averaged 7.7 tons per acre, and in the three Mississippi Delta states it averaged 7.3 tons per acre. Erosion on cropland exceeded 5 tons per acre on 92.8 million acres, 22 percent of the total amount of cropland in 1977.

The USDA has made estimates of the long-term effects of present erosion on productivity of the land which suggest that these could be serious. It is important, therefore, to consider whether our projections of production and land use imply an increase or a decrease in erosion relative to the current amount.

To examine this issue, I used the results of work done for Resources for the Future at Iowa State University's Center for Agricultural and Rural Development (CARD). CARD has developed a model of U.S. agriculture which, among many other things, will predict the erosion consequences of alternative patterns and amounts of crop production and land use. As part of research at RFF on relationships between U.S. agriculture and the environment, I made projections to 2010 of crop production and harvested land. At CARD these projections were run through the model to derive corresponding projections of erosion. The results, with 1977 data on erosion and cropland, are shown in table 6-5. They show an increase of 1.6 billion tons, or 84 percent, in total erosion from cropland and of 2.7 tons per acre, or 57 percent. These increases occur primarily for two reasons: (1) a major proportion of the increase in cropland is in corn and soybeans, which are particularly erosive crops; (2) the additional 63 million acres of land are more likely to erode when converted to crops than land in crops in 1977. These two factors are reflected in the much greater per acre amount of erosion on the additional land (25.6 tons) than the per acre amount on 1977 cropland (4.7 tons).

The increase in erosion would not be net because there already is some erosion on land now in pasture, forest, and range. The per acre amount on these lands is only 2.5 to 3.0 tons per acre per year, however, so the net increase in annual per acre erosion after conversion of the land is likely to exceed 20 tons per year, judging from table 6-5.

Table 6-5 suggests that the additional 47 to 52 million acres of cropland projected in this paper to 2005 would substantially increase erosion relative to 1977. The increase probably would be less than shown since the projected increase in cropland is less. However, Abel's projections of crop production give more weight to corn than the projections underlying table 6-5. This would tend to increase per acre erosion relative to the projections here.

The projected increase in erosion from cropland in 2005 suggests that the environmental costs of erosion also could rise significantly. When the projected amount of erosion in table 6-5 was run through a sediment delivery model developed at Resources for the Future by Henry Peskin and Leonard Gianessi, a doubling of the amount of sediment delivered to the nation's rivers, lakes, and reservoirs from 1977 to 2010 was indicated. The increase in sediment delivered by 2005 probably would be less, but still significantly above 1977. The social cost of sedimentation in terms of impaired water quality doubtless would rise also.

**TABLE 6-5.**   Sheet and Rill Erosion and Cropland in the United States in 1977 and Projected to 2010

|  | 1977 | 2010 | Change, 1977 to 2010 |
|---|---|---|---|
| Cropland (million acres) | 413 | 476 | 63 |
| Sheet and rill erosion from cropland (million tons) | 1,926 | 3,537 | 1,611 |
| Sheet and rill erosion per acre (tons) | 4.7 | 7.4 | 25.6[a] |

*Note:*   Sheet and rill erosion is caused by the impact of rain and the subsequent transport of soil particles by the movement of water across the land. It thus does not include erosion by wind.

*Sources:*   1977: the NRI, Soil Conservation Service. 2010: projections done for RFF by the Center for Agricultural and Rural Development, Iowa State University.

[a] The change in erosion divided by the change in cropland.

The increase in erosion would tend also to increase costs in terms of diminished productivity of the land. The actual reduction in productivity is likely to be less than the increase in erosion would suggest since technology typically can compensate for a substantial amount of soil loss. The economic cost of doing this might be high, however. Since the impact of erosion on productivity of most soils is gradual, the full loss of productivity would not be evident by 2005, but only until well into the twenty-first century.

*Tillage Practices and Erosion*

The CARD model projections of erosion are sensitive to the kinds of tillage technologies and conservation practices the model selects as most profitable. The tillage technologies are (1) fall plowing with the moldboard plow, residue removed (here called conventional tillage); (2) spring plowing, with or without the moldboard, with residue left until then (here called low conservation tillage); (3) spring plowing with something other than the moldboard, and planting in the residue (here called high conservation tillage). The four conservation practices are straight row planting, contouring, stripcropping, and terracing, each of which may be practiced with any of the tillage technologies.

Leaving crop residue on the land reduces erosion; the greater the amount of residue and the longer it is left, the greater the reduction. Consequently, land in low conservation tillage typically is eroded less than land in conventional tillage, and the reduction with high conservation tillage is yet more pronounced. The difference in the amount of erosion between the two types of conservation tillage is considerable. This became evident when I compared the run of the CARD model underlying table 6-5 (here called run 2) with an earlier run (here called run 1). Run 1 used preliminary projections of crop production and harvested land that were higher than the final projections used in run 2. Yet run 1 yielded only 2.32 billion tons of erosion (4.7 tons per acre) compared to run 2's 3.54 billion (7.4 tons per acre). The main reason for the difference was that in run 1 the model put 35 percent of harvested land in the low form of conservation tillage, 48 percent in the high form, and 17 percent in conventional tillage. In run 2 the percentage of land in conventional tillage was about the same, but the percentage in high conservation tillage fell from 48 to 31 percent and that in the low form rose to 51 percent. The switch between the two forms of conservation tillage occurred because of constraints I placed on the model's freedom to choose between them. A study I made of tillage technologies[18] led me to conclude that by 2010 some 50 to 60 percent of cropland could be in some form of conservation tillage. Thus run 1's 83 percent appeared high.

This view was reinforced by the knowledge that the model takes account of the long-run effects of erosion on crop yields, a characteristic which favors conservation tillage, particularly the high form, over conventional tillage. I think it probable that farmers give less weight to long-term effects than the model does. I was particularly skeptical of the high percentages put in conservation tillage in run 1 in the Ohio basin (86 percent) and the Upper Mississippi basin (98 percent). My analysis of tillage technologies suggested that in much of the Ohio basin soils are too moist to support such a high percentage of land in conservation tillage; and in much of the Upper Mississippi region (which includes most of Minnesota and Wisconsin in addition to most of Iowa and Illinois) too low soil temperatures in the spring would be similarly limiting.

For these reasons, run 2 of the CARD model sets an upper limit of 60 percent on the proportion of land that can be in high conservation tillage in the Ohio basin. In the Upper Mississippi the limit was 70 percent. In all other regions the model was free to choose between the two tillage systems. The higher level of erosion with run 2, despite lower projections of production and land, indicates the power of high conservation tillage relative to low conservation tillage in reducing erosion.

The differing results of the two runs of the CARD model suggest that the erosion consequences of my projections of cropland to 2005 will be strongly conditioned by farmers' choices between conventional and conservation tillage, and between the two forms of conservation tillage. The percentage of cropland in some form of conservation tillage increased from a negligible amount in 1965 to 23 percent in 1979, almost solely in response to the economic advantages of conservation relative to conventional tillage.[19] As indicated above, I concluded from my analysis of the economics of conventional and conservation tillage that farmers most likely will continue to shift

[18] Pierre Crosson, *Conservation Tillage and Conventional Tillage: A Comparative Assessment* (Ankeny, Iowa, Soil Conservation Society of America, 1981).
[19] Acreage in conservation tillage in 1979 from *No-Till Farmer*, vol. 7, no. 3 (March 1979).

to conservation tillage, and could use the technology on 50 to 60 percent of the nation's cropland by 2010. My analysis was not sufficiently detailed to distinguish between high and low conservation tillage. The results of runs 1 and 2 suggest, however, that unless most of the projected expansion in conservation tillage is the high form, the projections of land use imply significantly higher costs of erosion by 2005. Even if all of the projected 50 to 60 percent of the land is in high conservation tillage, some increase in these costs is likely, given the projections of land use.

The prospective increase in erosion could be forestalled by development of techniques or programs which strengthen farmers' incentives to adopt conservation tillage, particularly the high form. Techniques that overcome present obstacles posed by poorly drained soils or too cool soil temperatures in spring, or development of new herbicides to deal with weeds not now adequately controlled, would make conservation tillage economically attractive on soils and in areas where it cannot now compete with conventional tillage. Such techniques or herbicides may be forthcoming precisely because they would have economic payoff. Or they may be developed as a matter of deliberate social policy if they are perceived as the most cost-effective way of dealing with the prospective erosion problem. Greatly expanded cost-sharing programs conceivably might encourage farmers to adopt conservation tillage, such programs being seen as either substitutes for or supplements to public investment in research to extend the limits of conservation tillage.

I have deliberately limited this discussion of environmental costs to erosion. I must note, however, that the lower costs of erosion resulting from the spread of conservation tillage may be partially offset by higher costs resulting from greater use of pesticides, especially herbicides. The weight of the evidence at present is that the damage to unintended targets of herbicides is small, but not all possible avenues of damage have been adequately investigated.[20] In view of the likely continued spread of conservation tillage and its great importance in holding erosion costs in check, research to more fully explore the environmental impacts of herbicides should receive high priority in the USDA and in the Environmental Protection Agency.

[20] The environmental implications of increased herbicide use with the spread of conservation tillage are discussed in Crosson, *Conservation Tillage and Conventional Tillage.*

Sterling Brubaker discusses some of the policy alternatives for dealing with the prospective increase in erosion, so they are not addressed further here. Should it appear that erosion is likely to increase as table 6-5 suggests, the prospect may trigger both private and public responses that could prevent or greatly reduce the amount.

## Conclusion

I have reached two principal conclusions: if over the long term, demand for crops and animal products grows as projected by Abel, then (1) the real economic costs of agricultural land likely will rise, and (2) the environmental costs of erosion could increase substantially. Both conclusions are strongly conditioned by my analysis of technological trends. Given the projected increases in demand for crops, my expectation that technological improvement in crop production will be slow compared with the experience since World War II is a major reason for concluding that the economic costs of land will rise. Similarly, my expectation that conservation tillage, particularly the high form, will not spread on the scale predicted by the CARD model is the basis for concluding that costs of erosion could rise significantly. These expectations may prove mistaken. I may have misread the recent performance of crop production technologies, and there may be more potential in them for productive gain than I expect. In addition, the actuality or near prospect of rising real costs of agricultural land and agricultural production may itself spur investment in new yield-increasing technologies to reduce pressure on the land. Although the work of Lu, Cline, and Quance suggests that the payoff to even a major increased effort of this sort would be long delayed, they may be mistaken. And as noted above, the prospect of greatly increased erosion may itself evoke the private and public responses needed to counter it.

From the end of World War II to the 1970s, American agriculture experienced a revolutionary transformation marked by rapid technological change, unprecedented increases in productivity, and declining real costs of production. One of the most notable characteristics of that experience was a steady decline in the demand for agricultural land. Now, at a time when demand for our agricultural product is rising faster than before, the impulse which spurred earlier technological advance seems weakened. Unless we can somehow strengthen it, the rising pressure on our land and other agricultural resources will find release in higher real costs, to the detriment of the nation and to those elsewhere who benefit from the abundance of American agriculture. Technology, an expression of human ingenuity and effort, has helped to conserve our land while yielding us bountiful harvests. We will be foolish indeed if we do not now maintain it in robust good health.

# Discussion

## Earl R. Swanson

Adequacy of agricultural land is not an all-or-none question, but rather a relative one. Crosson chooses the real economic cost of land as the indicator of adequacy and predicts that it will rise in the next quarter century. This increase represents a continuation of the upward trend of the capitalized value of annual rents from the early 1960s to the late 1970s. It is derived by combining the independent projections of (1) demand for cropland, (2) the potential supply of cropland, and (3) technical change (expressed as crop yields). In th· chapter by Martin Abel, the increase in output required is estimated to grow at the rate (annual compound) of 1.8 percent, resulting in an increase of approximately 56 percent in the next quarter century.

To gauge the additional acres needed to meet these requirements for the year 2005, the expected crop yield increases must be estimated. Crosson uses yield trends for the period 1973–79 as the starting point for these estimates and finds that 62 million additional acres above those of 1977–79 will be needed by 2005. These additional cropland requirements would, according to Crosson, result in a significant increase in the real cost of agricultural land. He notes that a major reason for this cost increase is the expectation of a relatively slow technological improvement in crop production.

It is useful to place the requirement of a 1.8 percent increase in grain production in the context of historic rates of increase in the North Central states.[1] From the period immediately preceding World War II to the mid-1970s, grain production (including soybeans) increased 2.8 percent a year. About 80 percent of the increase was attributable to higher yield, which rose 2.25 percent per year, substantially above the aggregate yield increases in Crosson's calcu-

[1]George F. Patrick and Earl R. Swanson, "Components of Growth in Grain Production in the North Central States: 1937 to 1977," *North Central Journal of Agricultural Economics* vol. 1 (July 1979) pp. 87–96.

lations for the year 2005. Land requirements are sensitive to seemingly small changes in the rate of yield increase. For example, if crop yields were to increase by 1.5 percent until 2005, the additional land required would be only 20 million acres compared with the 62 million acres under the Crosson yield assumptions.

In addition to historical experience, assessments of future crop yields should consider the presently available, but not generally adopted, stock of technology. This stock may be divided into two parts. First, there is the available technology for which the economic incentive for adoption is reasonably strong and the management requirements are only moderate. There is a second part for which there is virtually no economic incentive for adoption and for which the management requirements may be quite sophisticated, even in the presence of strong economic incentives.

To examine the first part (existence of economic incentives), we draw on some evidence obtained from comparing yields on a set of well-managed farms with those on average farms. The Allerton Farms of Piatt County, Illinois, provide such a set of data.[2] Over the twenty-eight-year period starting in 1950, corn yields on these farms have been approximately 13 percent higher than on all farms in Piatt County. The soybean yields have remained about 9 percent higher on the Allerton Farms than on farms in the remainder of the county. The rate at which new technology enters the stream and the diffusion pattern for this technology have combined in such a way that the yield gap, in percentage terms, has not changed substantially over this period.

A measure of available, but not yet necessarily economical, technology comes from a recent survey of 549 farmers and research workers in 33 states.[3] The survey included a sample of those fields which yielded over 200 bushels of corn per acre. This is approximately two times the national average of 1978 (101 bushels per acre) and 1979 (109 bushels per acre). A doubling of yields in twenty-five years implies a compound annual growth rate of slightly less than 3 percent.

In a survey of farming practices, the following were indicated as important in the achievement of these high yields: (1) hybrid selection,

[2]Earl R. Swanson and James C. Nyankori, "Influence of Weather and Technology on Corn and Soybean Yield Trends," *Agricultural Meteorology* vol. 20 (August 1979) pp. 327–342.

[3]David W. Dibb and William M. Walker, "200-Bushel Corn: How Some Did It," *Crops and Soils* vol. 32 (November 1979) pp. 6–8.

(2) precision planting (usually with higher populations than average), (3) fertilizer application, (4) moisture, (5) early planting. Note that no new technology is involved here, rather simply adjustments and fine tuning of the old system. Certainly there is interaction among the practices that are listed for achieving yields of at least 200 bushels of corn. However, some practices demand much less energy. Crosson's yield projections have appropriately taken into account increases in the real price of energy and it appears that energy price increases would have their greatest impact on fertilizer application and irrigation. Yield improvements obtained through genetic engineering are likely to increase fertilizer and water requirements.

The effect of energy price on yields can be assessed by looking at the results of a linear programming model of the Corn Belt.[4] In this experiment, the nitrogen fertilizer price was more than doubled and the impact on cropping patterns and fertilizer use assessed. Corn yield decreased only 2.5 percent, indicating that prior to the increase in nitrogen fertilizer price, farmers were operating in the flatter part of the yield response function. Further, the model treated the price of corn as an endogenous variable. As fertilizer prices more than doubled, corn prices increased moderately (about 15 percent) and output declined. This indicates that if the real price of fertilizer rises, as Crosson expects, then Abel's assumption of constant real crop prices is questionable. If crop prices in fact rise, then demand likely would be less than Abel has projected.

In discussing environmental costs, Crosson emphasizes soil erosion. Unlike grain production, which must be aggregated across regions to obtain an estimate of requirements in the year 2005, sediment damage is localized. It is not very meaningful to talk about aggregate off-site damages and soil losses for the nation or even for large regions; one must usually specify a rather small area. Crosson correctly points out the two facets of the erosion problem: the loss of productivity and the off-farm sediment damage. The relative importance of these varies dramatically from watershed to watershed and this needs to be taken into account in developing soil conservation policy. Because the productivity aspect of soil erosion is discussed in the environmental section of the chapter, subsequent to the estimates of yield increases and

[4]E. R. Swanson and C. R. Taylor, "Potential Impact of Increased Energy Costs on the Location of Crop Production in the Corn Belt," *Journal of Soil and Water Conservation* vol. 32 (May–June 1977) pp. 126–129.

land requirements, it is difficult to determine how important it will be to yields in the next twenty-five years.

In order to induce adoption of conservation tillage, it is not enough for farmers to recognize that this practice substantially reduces erosion. In my judgment, the economic incentives need to be much stronger than they are to overcome the inertia of following current systems of tillage. Many farmers remain to be convinced of the long-term benefit.

Crosson concludes that "the environmental costs of erosion could increase substantially." Public recognition of these potential cost increases is not apt to come rapidly. Although fertilizer becomes a poorer substitute for soil as the subsoil is approached, the yield impacts of soil loss are not often dramatic or widespread. The complex relationships between fertilizer, depth of topsoil, and yields need much more attention in order to improve both farmer decisions and public policy. We need to be reassured that the environmental costs of soil erosion include an assessment of consequences *beyond* the year 2005.

Predictions of the role of pesticides as they influence crop productivity are an important part of an assessment of environmental costs. It is likely that the mix of pesticides, crop rotation, biological controls, and other methods which has been labelled "integrated pest management" will receive much more emphasis during the next twenty-five years. The pattern of increasing genetic resistance to given classes of chemical pesticides is likely to continue. This, together with the regulatory actions presently underway, increases the incentive to shift to more complex pest control methods, with modified use of chemicals. My own judgment is that these methods will be developed and adopted rapidly enough that the transition period will not affect yields substantially.

A final comment deals with the method of analysis. Abel's initial demand projections were done in terms of constant real prices. Had there been an opportunity for successive iterations among the persons developing the independent projections of demand, technical change, and cropland supply, it is likely that the estimated land requirement for grain and soybeans would be somewhat less than 62 million acres. For example, the increases in real crop prices themselves would exert an influence on investments in production and adoption of yield-increasing technology, thus increasing Crosson's somewhat pessimistic crop yield projections. Further, consumption might also be slightly reduced. Nevertheless, the expectation of an increase in the real economic cost of land in the next quarter century is a conclusion consistent with the information presently available. Crosson has effectively set the stage for examining the policy alternatives relevant to a prospect of increasing cropland scarcity.

# 7

# Agricultural Land: Policy Issues and Alternatives

*Sterling Brubaker*

## Introduction

While this volume is about agricultural lands, only one chapter (that by Brewer and Boxley) deals directly with the land base. Most of the attention has been on demand for agricultural commodities and on the various combinations of resources by which that demand can be met, land being only one of those resources. Thus, the problem is seen to be not just one of preserving the agricultural land base; as always, it is one of the best use of economic resources. To what extent will other resources substitute for land in agricultural production and to what extent may demand for agricultural output be forced to adjust to competing uses of land? Is some agricultural land better employed in other pursuits? The papers in this volume remind us that there is no inflexible requirement for agricultural output and even less of one for land in agriculture. Thus, we must consider not just policies for land retention, but rather, a wider range of options affecting agricultural demand, supply, and land.

There is little doubt that the United States can supply its own basic food needs into the indefinite future and its obligation to supply the rest of the world is not unlimited. But even if there is a very high level of foreign demand, capital and technology (and perhaps even labor!) still can substitute for land; there is no fixed relationship between land and output. Nevertheless, the public still tends to see land availability

The research on which this paper is based was partially funded by grants from the Rockefeller Foundation and the Environmental Protection Agency.

as the main determinant of agricultural capacity; the scientific revolution's effects on agriculture are still relatively new.

There are uncertainties that apply to all aspects of the problem, but in view of the many possible paths for adjustment, it is difficult to justify measures that would freeze land in farming. Nonetheless, a prudent attitude toward a remote and uncertain future justifies "leaning against the wind," in the parlance of the Federal Reserve, whenever possible to encourage preservation. Measures taken to encourage retention of land in agriculture should directly serve that social purpose and should not simply provide tax relief while land is held for development.

I would like to review briefly the character of the problem as it has emerged from the discussion in the earlier chapters on demand and supply prospects and the agricultural land base and then discuss three possible dimensions for policy: those that affect yields, those that might limit demand, and those that seek directly to retain land in agriculture. Finally, I sum up the most promising lines of action as I see them.

## Factors Affecting Agricultural Land Supply

In the foreseeable future, domestic food and fiber needs will not place pressure on productive capacity, given current demographic and dietary trends and a very modest growth in yields. That conclusion emerges clearly from the preceding chapters. There would be no concern for the adequacy of agricultural lands if it were not for the role of exports in total demand. Thus, foreign demand and our response to it will play a crucial role in an assessment of land adequacy. Exports in turn depend on demographic and income trends abroad and on the relative competitiveness of American agricultural commodities on world markets, as well as upon our own trade policies.

### Crop Demand

No one can foresee accurately what these trends will look like. True to the long-range forecaster's proclivity for projecting the present but flattening out the distant future, Martin Abel (chapter 3) has given a plausible review of world demand and supply conditions for the next twenty-five years. He shows U.S. exports of grain and oilseeds maintaining or slightly increasing their share of world markets, with most of the increased domestic production (but less than one-half of the corn) going to export. With the United States currently supplying almost 60 percent of world trade in grains, surely the maintenance of that share should meet our sense of obligation to world consumers and still provide a strong market for American farmers. The results are modified if corn is used domestically on a large scale for sweeteners and fuels, but even so, the production increases called for seem within reach through yield improvements.

The world's craving for meat is reflected in the export demand for U.S. grains. That component of demand most likely will remain strong. Whether domestic meat consumption will display the same income elasticity as in the past may be somewhat more questionable. There is now widespread belief in the United States that meat eating on the present scale is either unhealthy or immoral and that belief, whether or not it is justified, could slow the growth of consumption, especially of beef. Of course, beef is the most profligate converter of grain to meat. At the same time, fibers and starches are regaining respectability and may compete for room in the diet of a health-conscious public. If this occurs, it will relieve some of the pressure that feedgrain production now places on agricultural land.

*Yield Trends*

Just as exports are crucial on the demand side, yield trends dominate the supply side. In many parts of the world, scientific agriculture is only beginning, and the prospects for high rates of yield increase seem good. Yield growth abroad would restrain demand for U.S. exports. If yield increases in the United States can be maintained at past rates, then again the problem of agricultural land adequacy fades.

There is concern that the yield potential of the technology and plant varieties currently used in the United States is nearly exhausted and that further yield increases must come from new sources. Heady (chapter 2) finds no convincing evidence that current technologies are spent, and he cites other sources indicating that agricultural productivity should respond adequately to increased spending on research. However, one past source of yield increase—the growth of irrigation—is not likely to play the same role over the next few decades, even though increases in total irrigation and supplemental irrigation in the humid East may shore up yields in some circumstances (see chapter 5).

### Land Degradation

Rather little is said in these discussions about the negative effects of modern commercial agricultural technology and high-level production on yield potential. Soil erosion, salinization, and compaction will force the withdrawal of some acreage from crops and will bleed away the productive potential of more. So far, their effects have been mitigated by the success of yield-increasing chemicals and genetic improvements, and the loss of productive potential is slow and hard to measure. This loss is not likely to assume major proportions during the next few decades and it may be diminished further as farmers adopt reduced tillage practices, or if USDA control programs now being contemplated are successful. Nonetheless, if the horizon is extended and action to conserve soil is neglected, then there are implications for land adequacy. Soil conservation programs may be seen as a substitute in some degree for retention of agricultural land.

### Land Use Shifts

While the major uses of land in the United States show surprising long-term stability, as Brewer and Boxley note (chapter 4), there has been considerable shifting of land back and forth between categories. Once-cropped lands in New England and Appalachia have returned to forest or pasture, to be replaced by midwestern grasslands. Woodland in the Mississippi Delta and elsewhere has been converted to crops. More intensive agriculture needs better soils and climate to justify its expensive imputs, so regional shifts are inevitable in an integrated national market. New England's thin, rocky soils and cool climate are not the most propitious for crops, nor are Appalachia's erosive slopes, while the exhaustion of virgin timber stands in the West and consequent development of timber farming in parts of the South and Northeast offers a productive alternative to crops.

The one inexorable shift, however, has been from all categories of land into land for urban and related use. The shift is a result both of population growth and of more liberal per capita use of land for urban purposes. It may decelerate in the years ahead, as slower population growth, energy constraints, and planning considerations favor more compact settlements, and some important use categories, such as highways, expand very little (despite the popular perception). Moreover, only about one-third of the land absorbed for urban purposes on a national basis comes from cropland, though in some regions the percentage is far higher. Two facts are at the core of concern about rural/urban land shifts: (1) unlike other shifts, this one is essentially irreversible, and (2) urban uses commonly can outbid all other uses for land, so the shift cannot be resisted at the market level.

## Land Policy Considerations

Prices can provide some measure of the opportunity costs of land in different uses and hence of the costs of blocking shifts. If we choose to prevent the development of land whose value in agriculture is far lower than in urban use, the cost of doing so must be reckoned. Market prices are a very imperfect measure of this cost at best, but their most important defect is that they overstate the value of land in agriculture.[1]

At the same time, a social component consisting of planning, zoning, transportation, and utilities plays a key role in determining the development value of raw land. That component is subject to policy and in many instances can be directed away from the best cropland onto other land without great penalty in land development costs or urban efficiency. Where that strategy cannot be applied and prime land remains a candidate for conversion, what rationale is there for slowing the shift more directly through land retention policy?

The remaining rationale is largely that the market is myopic, that even the fairly reassuring relationship of demand and supply envisioned for the next twenty-five years may be upset, that a longer range view will in any case require arresting the irreversible shift of cropland to urban use, and that prudence requires erring now on the side of preservation. Of course, myopia extends to all facets of the problem. Who would have foreseen that mechanization and the scientific revolution would lead to a decrease in the amount of farmland needed for crops? Will foreign markets be sustained two generations hence as population growth moderates and yields abroad benefit from the

---

[1] Emery Castle and Irving Hoch, "Farm Real Estate Price Components, 1920–78," *American Journal of Agricultural Economics* vol. 64, no. 1 (February 1982).

spread of advanced technology? Will synthetic foods, farming under glass, hydroponics, or other developments diminish the need for agricultural land in the remote future? Prudence carries some risk.

I am left without any strong sense that agricultural land retention is an urgent problem. A nation that exports over one-third of its grain has a large margin for adjustment if it chooses, even before considering the reserve land base. However, that comfortable margin rests on assumptions about growth in production that warrant policy attention. Furthermore, the process of converting agricultural land to urban use is disorderly and could profit from tidying up in a number of ways. It is useful to look at the areas where policy may operate.

Three broad areas that bear on agricultural land adequacy will be examined: policies for maintaining and increasing per acre yields; policies that serve to limit demand for food and fiber; and policies that intervene directly in land use to encourage retention of prime lands and the conversion of noncroplands to crops. Within each of these areas a number of approaches are possible.

### Maintaining and Increasing Yields

*Research.* Increasing domestic yields is, first of all, a matter of creating and adopting more productive technology and of preserving the productive potential of land that is already in agriculture. There is widespread belief that the adoption of new technology does not lag far behind its development when the technology is profitable; thus, more emphasis should be placed on research than on agricultural extension services. Only a few years ago, a nation troubled by farm surpluses seriously considered the desirability of reducing the agricultural research establishment on the grounds that it made no sense to increase capacity in a time of surplus. However, research is not easily turned on and off.

Agriculture is a classic instance where research, if it is to be done, becomes largely the province of government. The farm product is undifferentiated and the market is composed of small firms. Agricultural research, being heavily based on science, cannot be undertaken by farm enterprises. Therefore, it is especially susceptible to policy decisions. If the concern is with land adequacy, then research should focus on the crops that are the major users of land—grains, oilseeds, cotton, and hay. Given that energy constraints may affect future technologies, research that has energy conserving potential deserves special attention. Nitrogen-fixing varieties and pest and drought resistance all are features of plant breeding that deserve emphasis. Improved protein content also would be land conserving, since much land now is used in protein production.

Although the federal government predominates in setting agricultural research priorities through its funding operations, there are areas such as new pesticides and pest management services where private suppliers may contribute to research if they are not smothered by regulation. The potential for quick and dramatic advances in plant and animal genetics through recombinant DNA techniques has not yet been demonstrated, but this is one area where private incentives may be strong and change could be rapid.

Research and policies affecting the cost of agricultural inputs may be important to increasing agricultural yields. This area seems badly neglected. If existing inputs become expensive, their use is discouraged. The most obvious cases are fertilizers and pesticides; energy policies, trade policies, or environmental policies all may affect the cost of inputs and thereby per-acre yields. Of course, price is not the only factor that may discourage the use of chemicals. If their development and marketing is restricted by regulation, there may be an adverse effect on yields.

*Conservation and Yields.* Agricultural land is a dynamic resource whose potential yield is affected by the way it is managed. Soil can be improved through careful attention. The more common consequence of modern field agriculture, however, is damage to the soil that must be compensated for by ever more expensive treatment if yields are to be maintained. Nutrients and organic matter can be added and soil amendments made. Compaction is a problem that is not fully appreciated, but it can be countered by management techniques. The problem of tilth and its relation to yield is not well understood, but in principle it should be managable. If properly informed, the farmer can be expected to make economic decisions about soil management that will not differ from those that society would make. The possible damage to the soil or loss of its productivity appears to be reversible within a human time frame.

Excessive soil erosion is a more difficult problem, however, for several reasons. The damage may be irreversible within an economic planning horizon, the farmer may see it to his advantage to sustain the erosion rather than correct it, and the amount of damage nationwide is significant. A recent USDA study done in conformity with the Resources Conservation Act (RCA) figures that, under a middle range scenario of demand fifty years hence, about one-third of the gross erosion at that demand level is not economically justified from a social standpoint.[2] From the farmer's standpoint, however, much of it may be justified, since he does not bear the full costs or may have a different financial horizon.

Soil loss at 15 tons per acre per year in excess of the rate of soil regeneration costs an inch of topsoil in ten years. If the soil is deep enough, management may compensate to prevent severe loss of productivity. But for some thin soils, this loss rate would remove the land from production over fifty years, and for many others yields would be reduced. The RCA report finds corn yield losses of 2 to 3 bushels per acre for each inch of net soil loss. For many farmers this loss is less than the cost of arresting the erosion.

Of course, not all cropland erodes at such rates and the net loss of yield through erosion will not be dramatic. Insofar as we have numbers on erosion, they come from application of the universal soil loss equation, and for future conditions they are worked out through the Iowa State University model, with the latest version incorporated in the RCA runs.[3]

Major producing states such as Iowa, Missouri, and Mississippi are currently the most afflicted, along with Kentucky, Tennessee, and the Southeast. Over three-fourths of all cropland eroded at rates of less than 5 tons per acre from sheet and rill erosion in 1978. Most of the erosion above 5 tons per acre—about 90 percent—occurred on 10 percent of the cropland, where rates of loss per acre were 10 tons or more per year.[4] For most crops, losses of less than 10 tons per year will have a very minor effect on potential yields over the next fifty years—perhaps 1 to 3 percent at most. Above that level, but affecting only a small acreage, yields fall off sharply by 10 to 40 percent, depending on crop, area, and rate of soil loss. This same 10 percent

---

[2] U.S. Department of Agriculture, *RCA Summary of Appraisal, Parts I and II and Program Report,* Review Draft 1980, p. 15.

[3] The universal soil loss equation, developed by the USDA, relates rainfall, soil and topographic features, crop management and conservation measures to total soil loss. The Iowa State University model is a linear programming type allowing analysis of various aspects of the U.S. agricultural economy.

[4] U.S. Department of Agriculture—Soil Conservation Service, "Basic Statistics—1977 National Resources Inventory (NRI)," February 1980, Part II, p. 3-14.

of cropland, or more than 40 million acres, will have significant losses of yield potential over the period if erosion continues at past rates. The RCA study estimates that the loss of potential crop yield over the next fifty years resulting from current levels of erosion will be equivalent to the output of 23 million acres. While that figure may not be catastrophic, it is far from negligible.

*Conservation and Policy.*    Are such losses tolerable? If it were possible to see beyond open-field agriculture to some future system of controlled food production, we might view soil as minable over a century or two. Few persons have that much confidence in technology. A more common attitude among economists is that the portion of the problem for which the social benefits of control exceed the costs should be corrected now, leaving the rest to the future when different conditions may warrant a different level of control. While the public appears willing to support conservation measures,[5] it is not clear that there is a political consensus that would provide the financial and regulatory instruments to carry them out.

The RCA document stated specific numerical goals, all aimed at approaching or maintaining soil loss rates at "T" value or below.[6] It also offers seven possible strategies for soil conservation, which are not necessarily mutually exclusive. Techniques for arresting erosion are known, but farm operators do not always find it advantageous to use them. All of the proposed strategies rely on one or more of the ingredients of education, technical help, and inducements, either positive or negative.

Education and technical help, which are essential to any plan, have been provided for decades. Apart from fostering the further spread of conservation tillage, they probably hold little potential to reduce erosion much below current levels. Farmers who have torn out shelter belts and plowed grasslands in recent years have not done so out of ignorance, but rather for income, and conservation tillage has spread as it proved to be economically viable.

Positive inducements have been mostly in the form of cost sharing of conservation measures or payments for holding land out of crops.

[5] Louis Harris and Associates, Inc. in a survey done for the U.S. Department of Agriculture of public attitudes toward conservation, January 17, 1980.

[6] "T" values are defined by the Soil Conservation Service as the maximum rate of soil erosion that will permit a high level of crop productivity to be sustained economically and indefinitely.

When the cost share is a high proportion of the farmer's cost of the measures, it may appeal to him, especially if it serves to increase yield or reduce the cost of field operations.

There has been little experience with negative inducements such as soil loss taxes, pollution charges, or fines. All of the emphasis has been placed on winning the cooperation of farmers. The USDA does not like to threaten its clientele. This pattern emerged in another age when farmers were poor, numerous, and not well informed about conservation. It persevered when soil conservation programs became part of the rural income maintenance apparatus that cushioned the great post-World War II adjustment in the farm economy. Today, farmers are fewer and they are well-educated and substantial businessmen. There is little reason to treat them differently from other groups in society. However, there is some question about the legal and ethical basis for compelling soil conservation practices aimed principally at protecing the productive potential of private land.

The long record of public involvement in soil conservation bespeaks a public interest in the matter. Where the aim is to control widespread third-party costs, the public interest is clear and the police power to regulate that is granted by the Constitution applies. Even in the case of water pollution arising from agricultural land, there is a marked reluctance to require abatement, despite the fact that some authority for it exists. The most acute water pollution from agricultural land could be handled by treating a very small acreage. Abatement requirements have been imposed on industries at their own cost, even when income or output is impaired in consequence, but farmers are treated differently. Is this only a matter of administrative convenience? concern that farmers are less able than industry to support the costs? Or is it some residual proagrarian bias that views the agribusinessmen in the same way as the yeomen of yesterday?

Those consequences of erosion that affect only yield pose a more difficult problem. They most directly affect the farmer and, if they fall within his planning horizon and financial capabilities, he may be motivated to correct them. Those are two big ifs. The work of Seitz et al. suggests that a farmer might wait a very long time to realize a real return on investment in erosion control, and that time is further prolonged by the interest rates applicable today.[7]

[7] W. D. Seitz, D. M. Gardner, S. K. Gove, K. L. Gunterman, J. R. Karr, R. C. F. Spitze, E. R. Swanson, C. R. Taylor, D. L. Uchtman, and J. C. Van Es, *Alternative Policies for Controlling Nonpoint Agricultural Sources of Water Pollution* (Athens, Ga., Environmental Protection Agency, 1978).

The public has an interest in maintaining a supply of farm products that the farmer's own interest in soil conservation may not be willing or able to accommodate. If the public is to assert that interest, it might do so through negative incentives, either pecuniary or prescriptive. Imposing costs on the farmer in a competitive market may force land out of production, defeating the immediate intent. On the other hand, if positive incentives are used—if the public invests in yield-increasing measures—is it fair to surrender the gains to private holders? Obviously not, one would say, even while recognizing that our society is replete with instances, starting with education, where private parties claim the direct benefit of a social investment. Moreover, it would be difficult to distinguish what portion of a farm's capital value or income is derived from public investment. Indeed, the value of agricultural land is very much affected by public policies and investments, including research on yield-increasing technologies, which would be impossible to sort out. If we want the private holder to be the active agent of a public purpose above and beyond his own perceived interest, we must expect to use positive inducements. At the same time, having offered the inducement, it seems reasonable to require performance.

Two of the proposed RCA strategies would address this problem. One is a straightforward purchase of soil loss reduction on an annual basis. It would allow the farmer to decide on the most efficient means of achieving the reduction. (In that regard it would not differ from a soil loss tax—a form of negative inducement.) It would permit the public to determine how much conservation it considers worth paying for. It doubtless would be very expensive if pursued on a comprehensive basis and, if the contracts were of too short duration, it might favor short-term practices even when long-term ones would be preferable. However, tillage and rotation practices are among the more promising means of control and very likely would prove cost effective for dealing with much of the problem.[8] Given that three-fourths of cropland already meets "T" values and more is close to it, the contracts could be concentrated within a budgetary limit on certain vulnerable but productive lands.

The other approach consists of two variants of cross-compliance, one with a bonus for good performance and the other carrying a

[8] Douglas A. Haith and Raymond C. Loehr, eds., "Effectiveness of Soil and Water Conservation Practices for Pollution Control," draft report to EPA, Cornell University, Ithaca, 1978.

penalty for poor performance. There is political resistance to the penalty variant, though from an intellectual standpoint it has appeal. The farmer has no vested right to public programs that promote agriculture, and the public is entitled to demand responsible behavior if he accepts that which is granted. In practice, public programs have been built into the whole structure of agriculture, and farmers on some marginal land, hard pressed at present, might prefer to forgo cultivation rather than undertake improvements.

Although much of this discussion of measures to maintain and increase yields has focused on erosion control, for the next few decades the greatest payoff is more apt to come from research on new technology. The harsh fact is that soil conservation programs have not been very effective, and conservation always seems to be postponable. Public investment in other programs has greater impact on yields. That conclusion is hard to accept—I would be happy to have it disproved.

*Limiting Demand*

Land in crops is used principally to produce grain and soybeans, and they, in turn, are used mostly to feed animals or are exported. If the aim were to reduce demand for agricultural land, then we could restrict exports and/or the feeding of animals. Policy objectives are never that simple, however. The United States wishes to be responsive to foreign demand both for humanitarian reasons and to support its balance of payments, and continues the production of grainfed animals as the low-cost way of satisfying consumer preferences. Policies that restrict demand, domestic or foreign, will be very unpopular with consumers and producers. However, if there is concern that existing or prospective levels of production will invite environmental damage and destructive use of the soil, or if the transfer of agricultural lands to other uses is resisted because it leaves insufficient capacity to meet demand, why not examine ways to limit demand?

*Pricing Exports.*    Projections of export demand are premised on the competitiveness of American agriculture in world markets. While our competitive strength is real enough, it is not the result of pure competitive markets. Programs that subsidize agriculture abound, and the environmental costs of agricultural production often are not reflected in price. Those costs are paid by Americans one way or another. I have no estimate of how much the price of American farm products would rise if all subsidies were abandoned and environmental and soil loss costs were reflected in price, nor do I know what effects such steps would have on output and the demand for agricultural land. In principle, there could be no objection to policies aiming to rectify this subsidy of consumers, especially foreign consumers who bear none of the subsidy costs or domestic environmental costs. It would be a major undertaking to correct this by rooting out subsidies at the source. An export levy reflecting these elements to the extent that they can be estimated would be a far simpler approach for correcting the foreign component. The distortion caused by the failure of export price to reflect full cost reverberates back onto the domestic economy. We are trading soil for oil—underpricing a renewable resource and using it beyond sustainable capacity in exchange for current consumer gratification.

More drastic restriction of exports could be contemplated but is harder to justify. Forthright export quotas would be effective but are not needed and are anathema to both buyers and sellers. Export bans have been used ineffectively for political punishment of would-be buyers. Export limits also could be used as a domestic antiinflationary measure, but sectoral approaches usually should defer to general policies in this area.

*Promoting Foreign Output.* One effective way of limiting export demand, and one that would answer humanitarian concerns as well, would be to foster production abroad, especially in the developing world. This would involve transferring and developing technology suitable for foreign conditions and investing in the development of new land and water resources. Private foundations and international lending agencies have been very effective in assisting agricultural technologies for the developing world. However, especially in the tropics, there is a great deal still to be learned, and adaptation to local conditions needs much detailed work. Uncultivated lands can be developed in Latin America and parts of Africa in significant amounts, but the cost of doing so is high and often beyond the means of local authorities. In much of Asia, where population density is high and the food margin very thin, land is very scarce. Nonetheless, investment, particularly in water supply, could greatly enhance output in some countries, especially India.

Promoting foreign output seems infinitely superior to agonizing over whether an acre diverted to urban use here may someday deprive a Bangladeshi of food. Moreover, by creating capacity for others to help themselves, we respond to the themes of self-reliance and independence now so strongly asserted in the developing world. Long term, no country should have the obligation to feed another on other than commercial terms; that implies the right of the exporter to use its land to its own best advantage.

*Reducing Grainfed Meat Consumption.*    Limiting domestic demand without loss of nutritional adequacy would be possible by shifting the diet away from meat and by making better use of forage and other nonfood resources to feed animals.

Two forces act to restructure diet. Price is one. If demand for grain is strong enough abroad, then the cost of producing domestic grain-fed animals must rise. This has happened in recent years, though its full effect on consumption habits may not yet have worked through. Each downward fluctuation in meat prices raises anew the consumer's hope that he can maintain old patterns. This is an area where we can let price operate to control demand. The American diet is rich enough in protein and could easily substitute other protein sources for meat at less cost in grain and land.

Abstinence on the part of the American consumer out of a guilty conscience is not called for, nor are government programs to restrict meat consumption needed. A better approach is for the government to sponsor research on the relationship between health and dietary standards and to publicize the results. This occurs already. In combination with a national concern with health and exercise, it may prove important over time, assuming that the amount of conflicting advice can be reduced.

Until recently, the nation has never given very systematic attention to its forage resources. Management practices on public lands are being initiated to arrest deterioration and improve rangeland yield where consistent with other objectives. This becomes all the more important if private pasture lands are encroached on by cropland development. At the same time, much of the agricultural and forest biomass not previously used by animals is proving to be adaptable as feed. Increased availability of nongrain feeds both relieves pressure on the land and permits the production of a leaner animal more suited to present dietary wisdom.

*Summary.*   Demand-limiting measures do not have the same popular appeal as yield increases as a means of sparing agricultural lands. Nonetheless, such measures should not be ignored. In view of demographic prospects for the rest of the world, helping to promote production abroad seems a sensible long-run strategy for the United States. Export controls are not called for at present, but a modest levy on exports to recover costs unreflected in export price would deserve consideration if agricultural land supply becomes tight. The public should be allowed to make up its own mind on the composition of its diet in response to price and in the light of medical research findings. If foreign demand leaps beyond foreseeable capacity, then the country faces a different problem in which direct export limits would need to be considered, but it is not appropriate to shape agricultural land policy around such a contingency.

### Retention and Expansion of Cropland

The agricultural lands problem commonly is viewed as one of retaining existing cropland and identifying and ensuring the availability of potential cropland that can be converted if necessary. A quality dimension has been added by the recent discussion of prime land preservation. About two-thirds of all prime land presently is cropland and about half of all cropland is prime land, so the two categories overlap to a major degree. Demand is seen as pressing in inexorable Ricardian fashion against a land base that cannot be expanded and even is threatened with shrinkage through "paving over" and erosion. Thus, it is argued, agricultural land must be protected directly from these threats.

*Expansion of Cropland.*   The argument that "they aren't making any more land" seems compelling, even though the Dutch and the Mississippi River are working at it. What are the possibilities for expanding the cropland base? The identification of potential cropland is elusive. Under American conditions, lands with 40 percent slopes or a rocky river wash are not potential cropland, yet in Taiwan, for example, such unlikely prospects are being forced into crop production. The current definition of potential cropland excludes many rural lands in New England, Appalachia, and the South that once were farmed. Physical attributes of the land and associated water and climate are only one element in determining potential for crops. Equally important are economic variables, including the costs of conversion, any special operating costs of production, and commodity price developments.

SCS figures for potential cropland indicate there were 127 million acres with high and medium potential in 1977.[9] A given acre may shift between the two categories as farm prices and development costs change. One could also look at prime farmland not presently in crops. There are 115 million acres of this, all in class I–IV lands and most of it potential cropland but now in forest, pasture, or range, or used for other purposes. Such are the identifiable reserves of cropland.

The costs of converting potential cropland to crops are extremely variable. Some pastureland needs only to be put to the plow, and in other cases minor changes are all that are needed. More commonly, land must be cleared, drained, or shaped at considerable expense. Work done for Resources for the Future in Iowa and Arkansas revealed very limited amounts of land likely to be converted under plausible assumptions about farm prices and conversion costs, but compellingly high demand would shift prices upward and make conversion more attractive, at least in Iowa.[10]

Another cost of conversion should not be neglected. The reserves of potential cropland tend to be concentrated in some highly erosive parts of the country. Lands presently in pasture or woodland probably are in that use because they are more difficult to crop. If less well-adapted land is brought into crops; some increase in gross erosion can be expected over that from an equivalent amount of better land.

No special policy with regard to the conversion of potential cropland seems called for. Such land should be expected to meet the same environmental standards as other lands, however. Owners will undertake conversion if market demand for it is strong enough. Conversion implies that the land is being put to more productive use. In its existing use as forest or pasture, it is better protected against deterioration than it will be in crops, but that conversion cost is unavoidable. There may be reason to protect potential cropland as well as present cropland against development for urban use if other land with less crop

[9] USDA-SCS, "Basic Statistics—1977 National Resources Inventory (NRI)," February 1980, table 16.

[10] Orley M. Amos, "Supply of Potential Cropland in Iowa," Ph.D. dissertation, Iowa State University, 1979; and Robert Shulstad, Ralph D. May, and Billy E. Harrington, Jr., "Cropland Conversion Study for the Mississippi Delta Region," University of Arkansas, 1979, prepared for Resources for the Future.

potential is available for development. Some conversion of potential cropland to crops will be actively resisted because of the implied loss of wetland or wildlife values not found on existing cropland.

*Cropland Retention Policies.* Most states and many local jurisdictions have some provision for encouraging the retention of land in farms. The protection of prime lands is stated policy of the U.S. Department of Agriculture and that policy is endorsed by the Environmental Protection Agency. The federal policy, with its focus on prime lands, clearly is aimed at protecting the productive base. State and local policies are more of a mixed bag. In all cases they proclaim the intention of preserving land in farming and ensuring the viability of local agriculture, but the support for such measures does not come from analysis of national demand and supply relationships or from a conscious decision to act in the long-run national interest. Rather, there often is an urban interest in retaining adjacent open space (without quite paying for it), and a rural interest in less onerous terms for holding land until it is ripe for development. There also is legitimate concern that spotty development and the encroachment of urban concerns into the countryside is inefficient from the standpoint of both city and country. The social, environmental, and fiscal problems created by the process may force land out of production or into less intensive use long before it is needed for development. This can be aggravated by the disappearance of agricultural support services as farm operations thin out. Not all farmland retention programs address this latter concern, however.

The federal policy on prime lands seems rather toothless. Environmental impact statements for federal programs are expected to consider the effect of the programs on the preservation of prime lands. However, this is only one factor in determining whether a federal investment or environmental action will proceed and that action, in turn, usually is not decisive in determining whether most private lands will be developed. State and local actions are far more influential, and market factors still more so.

State and local programs for farmland retention are based, either individually or in combination, on planning, zoning, preferential tax assessments, regulatory concessions, or public acquisition of property rights. With the exception of the latter (and not even then in all cases), the programs do not ensure long-run retention of the land in agriculture. Perversely, they act now, at a time when cropland is not in short supply on a national basis, but may leave the land unprotected later at a time when the threat becomes real. Moreover, they often are not so discriminating as to protect only land threatened by conversion and, therefore, they may waste public fiscal and administrative resources to no purpose.

Agricultural zoning may have voluntary features and be combined with incentives, as in Wisconsin, or it may be mandated by local authorities, as in Oregon and Hawaii. Zoning aims to exclude nonagricultural pursuits that are inconsistent with agriculture, in particular housing and urban development. Minimum tract size may be set at a level that would make residential holding prohibitive, and environmental regulations are those appropriate for a rural setting. Property tax protection is automatic in this case, since the land is not legally available to more intensive use. There is no assurance that land zoned for agriculture will be the best farmland, but in practice this is apt to be the case. However, precisely those lands closest to existing development and therefore those most susceptible to encroachment are the ones most apt to be excluded. Zoning is more effective in preventing the spread of tiny holdings that are primarily residential in character that result in the land being withdrawn from commercial agriculture. Zoning is notoriously impermanent. It does not resist intense pressure for reclassification when development moves toward the land in question. Thus, it is not a sure long-run retention technique, but it may promote better intermediate use of the land in agriculture.

Preferential property tax assessments are the most common agricultural land retention programs.[11] Nearly all states have them in one form or another. The usual pattern is to permit the land to be taxed according to its value in agriculture rather than its value for development. Details vary by state. The privilege may be contracted for a term of years, and there may be provision for recovery of some or all of the forgone taxes if the property subsequently is converted to nonfarm use.

This device also is highly impermanent, for at the expiration of the contracted term, the farmer is free to sell to a developer and the responsibility for back taxes (if applicable) is simply a consideration in evaluating his net price. In effect, the public eases the cost to him of holding his land until it is ripe for development. It may be productive

[11] Leonhard U. Wilson, *State Agricultural Land Issues* (Lexington, Ky., Council of State Governments, 1979).

during the holding period, although some land held under this incentive is only nominally farmed. It is widely agreed that preferential assessments are not a very effective means of holding land in agriculture. More important, they do not retain land against the day when it may be needed in farming, but rather, only during the time it is not needed for development. Moreover, unlike zoning, tax preference does nothing to prevent spotty development. One farmer may contract to hold his land while a neighbor sells. Thus, the objectives of efficient development and efficient agriculture and of maintaining a viable local agricultural economy are not well protected by this device. As a means of impairing the transfer of land out of agriculture, it is ineffective.

The public acquisition of some or all of a farmer's property rights could ensure the continued availability of the land for farming. The favored variant is purchase of development rights rather than fee simple title. Appealing in principle, this usually founders in practice. The logical place to acquire development rights is on that land most threatened by development, since unthreatened land will remain in farming without public expense. But the cost on precisely those threatened acres is the highest and the farmer most aware of the value of his land for development, as New Jersey quickly discovered. In that state, a law providing for a demonstration program for the purchase of development rights was weakly funded, and no rights in fact were purchased before the law expired. It was suggested that $20 billion would be required to buy rights on one million acres of New Jersey farmland. Ample funding may permit such a program to work if it is undertaken far enough ahead of development, as on Long Island, but the more likely prospect is frustration. One cost-saving version is to purchase rights for a fixed term rather than in perpetuity, but in that case the land is not protected in the long run.

There being no compulsion to sell, a pattern of public acquisition would inevitably be spotty and subject to the same objections as all other devices except zoning. While the control becomes permanent, the cost can be enormous.

A variant known as land banking contemplates eventual development but allows public control over the timing and over subsequent capital gains; however this responds to urban rather than rural needs. Public acquisition of farmland for retention in farming means that the land must be rented and, in consequence, it does not benefit from the care and investment that an owner-operator would give it.

All of the devices for farmland retention are flawed. Only acquisition has the prospect of preserving farmland against the day when it might be needed. Only zoning gives the hope of providing an orderly separation of town and country to the benefit of each. Acquisition is prohibitively expensive and zoning is notoriously subject to political influence and corruption. None of the programs pursued at a state or local level is closely keyed to national needs. Their inspiration is open space, urban planning convenience, or tax avoidance.

How important are policies for farmland retention from a national standpoint? The demand and supply for farm products nationally and the size of the potential cropland reserve do not indicate an acute problem now or in the foreseeable future. Crosson's projections (see chapter 6) take us fairly close to the margin of availability, but even in his examples not all of the potential cropland is used. While there often are local reasons for farmland retention policies, these usually do not correspond to national concerns. Retention policies are not very effective. Even if they were, they could only affect some portion of the agricultural land that would otherwise be taken for urban use. The usual figures of 2 to 3 million acres of rural land taken annually for urban purposes grossly exaggerate the draft on cropland. Less than one-third of that goes into urban development proper and of that, only 35 to 40 percent is cropland.[12] The 2 to 3 million acres, projected indefinitely, becomes alarming; the lesser figure does not seem so.

Urban growth will be accommodated on the principle that "everyone must go somewhere," though the land requirements for this are less rigid. Moreover, if the trend toward a stable population persists, the absolute amount of additional land needed to house it, even at present ratios, is modest and would dwindle toward zero by the middle of the next century. Urban growth policies can be a far more powerful influence on the per capita land requirements of cities than land retention policies emanating from the countryside. Policies to fill in existing urban land, small lot zoning, encouragement of high rises, and more compact settlement patterns amenable to public transportation—all of these diminish urban pressure on the countryside.

The other side of the coin is the greater affluence of double earner

[12] H. Thomas Frey, *Major Uses of Land in the United States: 1974,* U.S. Department of Agriculture, Economics, Statistics and Cooperatives Service, Agricultural Economic Report no. 440, 1979, p. 18.

families with their capacity to indulge discretionary tastes, such as sitting on a few acres. This exurban threat can be significant and is one that farmland retention policies, especially agricultural zoning, could address.

Finally, the concern about land adequacy and retention has been useful in making local authorities aware of options in controlling the direction of urban growth. The planning of public services such as utilities and transportation can be shaped so as to shunt growth into areas that may be quite suitable for development but which are not used intensively in agriculture or suitable for it. Where such opportunities exist, awareness can make for wise policy. Thus, in my judgment, explicit farmland retention policies (except for the control of exurbanization through zoning) are not likely to be very effective or necessary, while current social trends, if reinforced by metropolitan planning and zoning, could have significant effects.

## Conclusion

Which dimensions for action seem most appropriate to the agricultural land problem as it appears at present? Given the national interest in high production and a high level of exports, demand-limiting strategies, though potentially effective, are too unpalatable to be relied upon. Education about diet and health, along with exposure to world prices, may temper domestic demand, but foreign demand seems likely to take up any slack. In practice, the consequences of insufficient agricultural land will be a marginal reduction of exports—hardly a national disaster.

Yield-increasing strategies are more consistent with the American tradition and hold sufficient promise to deserve pursuit. It has been suggested that the fruits of research are slow to show up in yields, but that is of little concern, since the land problem is not immediate anyway. If the country can get back on the yield track, there is no problem. There have been revolutionary advances in research in biology and genetics in recent years. Agricultural research should seek to take fuller advantage of them. Targets include the production of plants and animals that are more efficient synthesizers and are adapted to soils, climates, or feeds not presently well utilized. The preservation of the yield potential of cropland is a special aspect of a yield strategy that could be the equivalent of providing tens of millions of acres over the next half century. It also is one way of discharging our obligation to future generations.

Direct agricultural land retention policies have only very minor effects and will not be important in preventing development. However, they could prevent the idling of rural land in the hands of speculators or other owners not interested in farming it.

As an economic resource, land should be used efficiently. It would be hard to make a case that land is more valuable in agriculture than in urban uses when the market denies it several times over. Constricting the supply of land for urban use can result in onerous costs for housing and other productive uses. The case for control over the development of farmland is more convincing if it comes from the urban side as an argument about urban efficiency in the provision of services and control of externalities—that is, as an urban planning device to control sprawl. Since agricultural land is capable of yielding a stream of income that will be lost if it is not collected each year, idle agricultural land represents true inefficiency. Policies that promote productive use of land in agriculture during the time that it may be ripening for development are consistent with an efficiency standard.

Equity issues abound with regard to agricultural land policies, although, unhappily, there is no agreed-upon definition of equity. One set of issues concerns the effects of policies on present land holders. Anyone who has held land over time has seen its value affected by a host of government policies influencing credit, trade, transportation, marketing, education, conservation and environmental regulation, agricultural technologies, and production controls. On balance, such policies have enhanced land values by making other resources more readily available to farmers, so as to raise the productivity of their land, and by opening access to markets. Anyone buying land now does so with some assumptions about the continuity of the present range of policies. But our system does not guarantee against policy change; it is a risk that all must bear, subject only in the case of land to the constitutional protection against the "taking" of property.

A policy that has unequal incidence is not ordinarily viewed as inequitable as long as a public purpose is served—indeed, unequal incidence may be an objective of policy. Policies to increase farm income—acreage allotments, marketing orders, price supports, etc.—generally are not viewed by farmers as inequitable, though they may interfere with how the land is used and prevent some more enterprising farmers from taking full advantage of their capacities.

Note that the cost, or the inequity, in this case is borne by the rest of society. Some current measures for erosion and pollution control or restrictions on development threaten to impose costs on farmers and are seen by them as unfair, if not illegal. So often beneficiaries of the system, farmers may not get much support if they insist on refinements of equity when policy asks something of them.

There has been a continuing evolution toward the dilution of fee simple ownership rights, and that is having its effect on rural lands. Planning and zoning have been the most important in accelerating this trend, but environmental regulations and building codes also have been important. All rely on the police power and are subject to strictures against taking private property without compensation. They place limits on the use of agricultural lands and on their conversion, and they bring uneven losses and gains. The courts have tolerated restrictions that impose losses so long as significant use is still possible. Most restrictions on land use have been enacted in response to some fairly tangible and immediate local need.

It seems much harder to justify use of the police power to enforce restrictions on land use that are based on projections of future needs at some remote time and place. Thus, if the public truly wants to retain land in agriculture and to conserve soil resources (as distinct from defense against the offsite consequences of erosion), then it should be prepared to offer compensation. That will introduce an element of realism into the proposals. By the same token, the public should claim what it has bargained for—that is, real soil conservation and public control over when and how much land is converted from agriculture, as well as some public claim to gains over the period of control.

The main other equity issue concerns what heritage each generation leaves the next. It is recognized that we must consume depletable resources but is often felt that renewable resources should be conveyed intact. This has intuitive appeal, since preservation and proper management should allow perpetual use from renewables. However, the true legacy that we leave is capacity to produce. If that capacity is enhanced, need its form be maintained? In the case of depletables we run the technological race to gain access to lower grade resources without increased cost. When renewable yields are increased on a sustainable basis, we engage in an analogous process. Our obligation to future generations is not simply to preserve but also to progress. However, having made this bold flirtation with the temptress of technological progress, I suspect that many of us will still want to go home with Prudence as our long-term partner.

# Discussion

## Norman Berg

Brubaker is dealing with one of the most difficult areas of policy decision facing Americans today. While I agree with practically all of the technical data and many of the conclusions he has set forth, I am a conservationist and not an economist, and it would be astonishing if I did not view resource conditions and policies somewhat differently.

Brubaker examines three broad areas of policy bearing on the adequacy of agricultural lands: (1) policies for maintaining and increasing per acre yields; (2) policies that limit demand for food and fiber; and (3) policies that encourage retention of prime farmlands and conversion of noncropland to crops. I would like to comment on each area in turn.

First, I am concerned over his statement that a greater "payoff" in raising crop yields during the next few decades is more likely to come from research and technology than from control of soil erosion. We cannot afford to support one approach at the expense of the other; it is not an either/or proposition. Brubaker himself notes that yields per acre are not rising today as fast as they used to. This leveling off of gains in productivity is not limited to the United States; it is happening all over the world.

Further, many of the scientific developments already applied to American agriculture, including chemical fertilizers and pesticides, have masked physical damage to the soil resource in some parts of this country. The soil is being "mined" in many parts of the country, and it doesn't take an expert to know that such a course cannot be allowed to continue over the long run. Soil conservation, like preventive medicine, must be a continuing program.

Second, I do not believe Brubaker should dismiss forty-five years of soil conservation by saying that such programs have not been very effective. I have seen the American landscape transformed by conservation practices since the program began in the 1930s. In 1977 the Soil Conservation Service (SCS) published aerial photographs of several adjoining farms in Lancaster County, Pennsylvania, which showed clearly the difference in how they were being farmed in the late 1930s and today. There is simply no comparison. In the 1937 photo, the rolling fields were plowed in straight rows, up and down hill, with little or no concern for soil losses. In the 1977 photo, the fields are plowed on the contour and nearly all are stripcropped. There are grassed waterways to remove storm runoff safely, and the steeper slopes are planted in grass and legumes. What has happened in Lancaster County has happened all over the rural United States. Conservation farming has become a standard practice in American agriculture.

However, conservation systems keep changing, just as agriculture changes. They change as a result of research; they change in response to new and larger machinery, to new crops, to new tillage systems. The charge that farmers and ranchers have been tearing out windbreaks is an example. The Soil Conservation Service looked into that complaint and discovered that many old windbreaks were indeed being removed, some to accommodate bigger equipment and some because they had outlived their usefulness. But SCS found that even more new windbreaks were being planted. Frequently, the new ones are a single row of trees instead of multiple rows because a single row makes a better windbreak. On the whole, conservation systems have kept up very well with changes in agriculture during the last forty-five years.

Brubaker also points out that soil conservation is "postponable," and that certainly seems to be true. Frequently it is postponed, not because it isn't needed, but because the impact of soil erosion on yields is so slow and insidious and is masked by the technological gains mentioned earlier. To many people, it does not appear to matter very much whether soil conversation is undertaken today or tomorrow. It does matter, as every soil conservationist knows.

In discussing policies that limit demand for food and fiber, Brubaker makes a plea for more foreign technical assistance to help developing nations raise their farm production. "Promoting foreign output," he says, "seems infinitely superior to agonizing over whether an acre diverted to urban use here may someday deprive a Bangladeshi of food." Of course it seems superior, but foreign technical assistance, we have been reminded again and again, is not a unilateral policy decision on the part of the United States. Through the Agency for International Development, the Soil Conservation Service has sent scores of experts to many foreign nations to help increase agricultural production and teach principles of soil and water conservation. A few years ago, for example, there were twenty-five professionals in India, helping Indians solve the annual dilemma of too much water alternating with too little. They were making headway, but were asked to leave by the government of India for reasons which had nothing to do with their mission.

In 1978–80 SCS technical people were in Pakistan, Iran, and Afghanistan, but events beyond SCS control forced their withdrawal. Subsequently, a few were able to return to just one of these countries—Pakistan. The world being what it is today, I would remind Dr. Brubaker that it is one thing to want to give help and quite another to be able to deliver.

The Soil Conservation Service also is concerned about the economic well-being of the American farmer. One out of every five dollars the farmer receives today comes from the sale of U.S. farm products overseas. For ten years in a row, the value of U.S. agricultural exports has increased. The nation's economy, as well as the farm economy, relies on an agricultural trade surplus to partially offset the nation's trade deficit. In 1979 this surplus contributed about 14 billion to the balance of payments.

It does not seem likely that any other segment of the U.S. economy will rush in to fill the export breach if farm exports fall off. Certainly Detroit won't do it. This country needs a growing market for agricultural exports, and it needs conservation policies to keep the production plant healthy so that these exports can continue.

The Department of Agriculture will recommend new soil and water conservation programs to the president and Congress in response to the Soil and Water Resources Conservation Act of 1977, or the RCA. In analyzing some 65,000 responses to RCA draft documents in 1980, USDA found that most respondents favored a voluntary, locally controlled, highly subsidized, nonregulatory program. They would like more funds for on-the-ground implementation and less regulation and red tape. They are also willing to consider several new approaches to conservation, if they are convinced that they will actually result in more conservation on the land without penalizing land users. While I do not agree with Brubaker that conservation programs have been ineffective in the past, I do believe that they can be made even more effective in the future, and the RCA process offers a way to accomplish this.

In dealing with the third area in his paper, Brubaker says that the discussion of demand and supply conditions has left him "without any strong sense that agricultural land retention is an urgent problem." Many Americans disagree, as evidenced by a rash of recent articles on the subject and a growing number of public and private organizations formed to deal with some aspect of the land retention problem. "Every day 12 square miles of America's farmlands vanish forever," begins an article in the May 1980 *Saturday Review,* and dozens of similar stories appear across the nation.

What is needed for the future, as a matter of public policy, is adequate land to produce enough food, fiber, timber, and all the other agricultural commodities at reasonable cost to the consumer. When this agricultural land base is threatened, I say it is time for concern. The National Agricultural Lands Study predicts that at current rates of loss, Florida will have lost all its prime farmland to development by the year 2000. This is more than just good farmland—it is the farmland that produces much of the nation's citrus crop and other semitropical fruits. There is not too much of such land.

According to the Environmental Fund, Inc., "It has been estimated that it takes about 2.5 acres of average arable land to feed and clothe one person adequately for one year. At present, there is less than 0.8 acre for each person in the world. People may already have exceeded the long-range carrying capacity of the land. As more marginal land is farmed, desertification, deforestation, and soil erosion escalate; age-old ecological systems collapse."[1]

I believe that retention of prime farmland for farming is an urgent problem. I am not saying that every acre is needed for agriculture today, but I am saying that when good farmland is paved over, the loss is irrevocable, and that land will be needed before very many years have passed. There are many forces at work to diminish and degrade the supply of good farmland in the United States, but there are few, aside from gains in per acre yields, that have the effect of increasing supply.

Not everyone wants potential cropland brought into crops. If today's restrictions on the use of wet soils had been in effect seventy-five years ago, for instance, it would have been difficult to open up much of the Midwest to cropping. Many people today are concerned over the preservation of prairie grasses. If their concern had shaped policies fifty years ago, the country might not be able to produce the wheat it does today.

[1] Environmental Fund, Inc., "Common Sense About Population," *Wall Street Journal,* May 30, 1979.

We do not know what additional pressures will be placed on the land. The groundwater table is falling in parts of the Southwest and Great Plains, and much of the irrigated cropland there will not be irrigated forever. The production of ethanol for gasohol may put additional demands on soil and water resources. And we have seen what a single active volcano can do to local agriculture.

Many landowners in the Northeast—including many absentee owners—keep their land in trees and simply have no interest in farming. These acres are effectively "locked out" of cropland.

Large areas of land may have to be set aside as nuclear power parks, for safety's sake, or similar areas measured for disposal of toxic wastes. Surface mining, which is likely to increase with rising gas and oil prices, also will chip away at the cropland base.

When I consider all the forces, known and unknown, that threaten U.S. crop production over the next few years, I cannot be as sanguine as Brubaker about the prospects for abundant farmland in the future.

It could be, of course, that higher costs of energy, water, and sewage, and public services will slow down suburban sprawl and make it more economic to build and rebuild within the limits of our present cities. If the American suburb prices itself out of the market, state and local governments will not have to develop so many schemes for retaining rural land for agriculture and forestry.

The tax revolt may also play a part. A study by the California Office of Planning and Research looked into the fiscal impact of ten new residential developments after Proposition 13 was passed. The overwhelming conclusion of the studies is that new residential development does not pay its way under the tax limitation. Those developments that come closest to paying their way were located in "infilled" areas where major utilities were already in place. The spread of Proposition 13-type limitations on taxes should further discourage suburban sprawl.

Even though I disagree with him on some points, Brubaker has raised some important policy issues and analyzed them intelligently.

# Discussion

## Daniel W. Bromley

I have taken my task to be rather more than the provision of some reactions to Brubaker's chapter because the chapter covers a great number of issues, yet none of them is explored in any depth. We are treated to a suggestive paper, but it is cautious; too cautious for my taste. There are many places where I might have wished to quibble with the author, but the majority of the issues would not have been substantive, which is not to say that there aren't some crucial issues of substance which have been inadequately treated in other chapters. I had hoped that Brubaker would raise at least a few of these for general discussion. Hence my criticism of the paper is less concerned with what was said than it is with what was *not* said.

There are seven areas which were not treated adequately either in the conference discussions, or in the policy issues raised by Brubaker and I would like to bring them up here.

1. *Failure to Distinguish Policy Objectives from Policy Instruments.* An instrument becomes an objective when it appears in the utility function of someone involved in the decision process. Only those means *not* found in utility functions can legitimately be referred to as policy instruments. The public concern for the adequacy of agricultural lands has been voiced with a purposeful blurring of policy instruments and policy objectives. The general public can be forgiven for this, but what excuse is there for economists?

It is my hypothesis that the agricultural lands question is a smoke screen that allows discussants to avoid two essential facts. The first is that there is now some recognition that private ownership of a valuable natural resource is not always consistent with the socially optimal choices that are made. This view is held by those with a greater interest in the public goods aspects of land, particularly urban residents who enjoy the open-space attributes of land. For these people to raise the ownership issue would certainly arouse the ire of the agricultural sector, and so they address it through an avenue of known sympathy among farmers—the relentless encroachment of urban sprawl onto the nation's food-producing capacity.

The second fact is that there is resentment against a class of entrants into the land market. This view is held by agricultural interests, and the target of their enmity is none other than the "speculator" who bids up land values, brings urban problems to the quiet countryside, and drives up property taxes in the process. However, challenging the speculator/developer would be anathema to those in the agricultural sector since the developer is merely doing with land what they themselves consider essential to their freedom—buying it and selling it. One cannot be consistent about the merits of individual enterprise yet denounce speculators for doing what most farmers would love to do.

Hence, both major participants in the agricultural lands issue do not articulate their real policy objectives. It is much easier to mobilize public sentiment under the banner of a food scare than it is under the desire to get more favorable tax treatment, or to have less urban sprawl. Pluralism works best when it is possible to disguise one's greed by appeal to some higher social calling. This behavior can be excused as the norm for the general public, but I find it curious that we can fail to at least mention it at a conference on agricultural lands.

2. *Failure to Recognize that Land Is a Flow Resource and not a Stock Resource.* Our preoccupation with land area has tended to obscure its basic nature. Contrary to conventional wisdom, land is a flow (renewable) resource. The services of land—nutrients, wildlife habitat, visual aesthetics, and so on—are replenished over different time horizons. The fact that I enjoy the open rural vista today in no way diminishes that which is available for someone else tomorrow.

The essence of a stock resource is that once it is used, there is nothing left for someone else. Surely this does not apply to land, except in a very special sense. Of course, if land is in agriculture, it cannot also produce commercial space or homes. But land can be in agriculture and at the same time support wildlife, provide urban dwellers with some satisfaction, and process carbon dioxide. Most of these uses are important, and yet none of them "consumes" the land in the sense that oil used today is not available for use tomorrow.

The relevance of this distinction between stocks and flows should be obvious. If land is a flow resource, then policy can be implemented to ensure that the renewable services are maintained without impairing the ability of certain other uses—such as agriculture—to continue.

3. *Failure to Distinguish Between Positional Goods and Material Goods.* We have all seen indications of the declining economic importance of land in American agriculture, largely as a result of improved mechanization, herbicides, pesticides, irrigation, better management, and so on. But this conference has not discussed the obvious fact that this declining role as an agricultural input has come about because *externality-producing inputs* have been substituted for land. As the contribution of land to output has diminished (except for land as space), the costs of agricultural production have been borne by others, often in distant places. Smugness that the land constraint has been overcome is obviously unwarranted.

As national wealth increases in terms of material goods, our knowledge of income elasticities should warn us that aesthetic goods such as scenic landscapes will rise in value in relation to material goods. Taking pride in the material sector without noticing the impacts on the aesthetic sector is not only bad science, but socially indefensible as well.

4. *Failure to Bring a Social Science Perspective to the Question of Agricultural Lands.* While it is necessary to know how many acres are allocated to different uses, this is not sufficient information for a meaningful analysis of the question of land use and availability over the next twenty-five to fifty years. What is important is who owns the land, and how capable they are of mobilizing government in their behalf.

In a sense, merely knowing who owns the land is meaningless—what matters is social control. That is, who is able to influence social policy with respect to land in general, and to specific parcels? Brubaker states: "There is some question about the legal and ethical basis for compelling soil conservation practices aimed principally at protecting the productive potential of private land." I would suggest that when the productive potential of agricultural lands becomes problematical, it is not only the farmers (owners) who are concerned or relevant. Indeed, one need not be an agrarian fundamentalist to realize that a nation's ability to feed itself is *the* basic issue in autonomy and security. If soil productivity is not a social issue, then what is? In this line of reasoning, the only interesting ethical question at all is the continued legitimacy of private ownership of agricultural land and control over the practices applied to it. That is, if private land use practices are deemed to be at odds with long-run social welfare, then where is there an *ethical* problem in protecting soil productivity? There will be a *political* problem to be sure!

Failure to step outside of the economist's paradigm in discussing the agricultural lands question means that there is no exploration of alternative institutional arrangements for land resources which might protect long-run productivity yet give farmers a reasonable degree of managerial discretion. Of course, as economists we are trained to believe that institutions are mere constraints and beyond the scope of either our expertise or our presumed "positive" science. Not only has our education failed to prepare us to consider institutions as endogenous, but it has falsely convinced us that economics is a value-free endeavor in the same league as astronomy, topology, and chemistry. Hence, we stick close to the conventional wisdom because we believe it safe (and we are comfortable with it), and fail to explore the important social science issues inherent in the question of land use and control.

5. *Failure to Ponder the Social Significance of Both Food and Land Prices.* Our sanguinity over the price of land and food is quite without justification. As social scientists we ought to know better than to believe the politicians who brag about how little of our disposable income is spent on food. Food is cheap because two important costs are not included. The first noncounted cost arises from the many externalities generated in the production of food. Soil erosion, destruction of wildlife habitat, poisoned birds and fish, and odors are off-site costs which never become part of the price paid in dollars for agricultural products.

Ecology-minded students of economics are delighted to hear that many manufactured goods are artificially cheap because external costs are not included. They obviously favor the proposed remedy, which would be for the manufacturers to pay a tax which would be passed along to consumers—the degree depending on the elasticity of demand. This would then alter the relative prices of polluting and non-polluting goods and direct consumption patterns away from the polluting goods.

Who ever talks about the artificial cheapness of agricultural products in the same way? Only a heretic would dare raise the question, and yet the price of food is a major contributor to its overconsumption by the middle and upper classes. What is good for our pocketbook is bad for our waistline.

The second noncounted cost of agricultural products is to be found in the significant subsidies to the land-grant university system and the extension services. The United States is second to none in these categories, and that is reason enough to be proud. This aspect of underpricing of agricultural products is rarely mentioned, owing in no small part to the fact that many of those who are aware of it are also the recipients of it. Only the independently endowed seem to have the moral fiber necessary to denounce those public programs which directly benefit them.

Emery Castle and Irving Hoch at Resources for the Future are finding that land prices overstate land value in agriculture. They offer several hypotheses about why, but one important issue, mentioned above, is that the externalities from agriculture are not included in the calculus of farmers or society and this omission tends to inflate land values.

6. *Failure to be Clear About What Is Scarce.* The discussion about the adequacy of agricultural lands has usually taken place in isolation from any concern over population pressure, and on the assumption that society's present diet will remain unchanged. Of course there are reminders of the large proportion of land devoted to grains for livestock feed, but we rarely come to grips with diet composition and population pressure on the land. In the United States there are approximately 64 persons per square mile, and approximately 415 persons per square mile of cropland. Several persons at this conference have worked in countries with a population density (total land, not cropland) of over 1,000 persons per square mile. Indeed, in Bangladesh it is 1,500 per square mile, in Taiwan it is 1,200 per square mile, and in Japan it is 770 per square mile. On the island of Java in Indonesia there are rural areas with a population density of 2,500 per square mile. In short, it is very difficult to believe that land is scarce in the United States. This is not to deny that there are local areas of great concentration, but as a nation we have a long way to go before population pressure is noteworthy.

If agricultural land is not particularly scarce, what about food? Again, we cannot really become exercised over the abundance of food, although its distribution is obviously an important moral and economic issue. As indicated earlier, the adequacy of agricultural land is raised as a policy issue when in fact there are other more controversial issues actually motivating concern; a focus on land availability is a strategic ploy to avoid raising the more controversial issues.

Open space near urban areas *is* scarce; good agricultural land near markets *is* often scarce; but agricultural land in general is hardly scarce. In his paper Brubaker says; "If the concern is with land adequacy, then research should focus on the crops that are the major users of land—grains, oilseeds, cotton and hay." It seems to me that it also makes sense to focus research on those crops grown in areas of genuine conflicts over land use. For instance, what are the prospects for transportation which will mitigate the costs of carrying on certain types of agriculture further from existing markets?

7. *Failure to be Analytical About the Nature and Extent of Irreversibilities.* My final point refers to the matter of reversing actions which have been taken earlier. We need to be reminded of the important distinction between technological irreversibilities and economic irreversibilities. In one sense, I see no reason why some old subdivisions could not be leveled and the land converted back to agriculture or forestland. This could not be widespread, but I suggest that there is more flexibility in moving among some land uses than has been recognized either in casual discussions or in analysis.

In conclusion, as economists, we should all devote more of our attention to some of the central issues which underlie the recent concern for the adequacy of agricultural land. We should show more imagination in helping to define the social problem. We should remember that land is a flow resource, not a stock. We should be more careful in determining the social value of land in alternative uses. We would contribute important new insights if we could step outside of our paradigm from time to time. We could be of greater assistance if (1) we would help to identify the full social costs of agricultural products; (2) we would be more analytical about what is truly scarce, and (3) we were more careful about the nature and existence of irreversible actions.

I quite agree that we could not have spent much time at this conference on some of these issues, and consider the focus of this conference most appropriate as a starting point. But with this material now as a background, I do hope that we begin to ask these more fundamental questions about the nature of the land resource in the United States.

# 8

# Market Performance and the Adequacy of Agricultural Land

*Emery N. Castle*

The adequacy of agricultural land as a factor of production was tackled in a straightforward manner in the conference reported on in this volume. The discussion included demand for and supply of agricultural land; the role of technology, including irrigation trends; and economic and environmental costs of expanded food production, as well as public policies. The papers speak for themselves and no attempt is made in this final chapter to restate the conclusions drawn by the authors and discussants, but it may be useful to view some of the findings as well as the conference itself from a different perspective.

This chapter is in two parts. The first part briefly examines the performance of the market for agricultural land. The conditions which lead to market failure have been used to advantage in identifying and analyzing many resource and environmental issues and it can be asked why a similar approach was not used in this conference. The discussion makes it clear why this body of thought was not used as an organizing framework for the conference even though the systematic development of this line of thought identifies some relevant issues touched upon only lightly in this volume. The second part of this chapter interprets the substantive findings of the conference from the viewpoint developed in the first.

This chapter was written after the conference was held. It draws heavily upon introductory and welcoming remarks I made in opening the conference and upon some comments made at its conclusion. The conclusions drawn and the summary statements made here represent only my own judgment and do not reflect a consensus of all participants. Neither does the chapter represent a position of Resources for the Future because the organization does not take a position on such issues. Thus, I write as an agricultural and resource economist and not as an officer of RFF.

231

## Performance of the Agricultural Land Market

In order to place the discussion of land use for food and fiber production in perspective, it is useful to ask whether there are reasons to
believe the market for land will do an inadequate job of providing for
these uses. After having explored this question, it is easier to draw
conclusions as to what was and was not learned from this conference.

There is an extensive general literature on market performance.
Bator, among others, has written authoritatively on the subject.[1]
Drawing upon Bator, there appear to be two major reasons why the
agricultural land market might not function perfectly. One is the
possible production of *externalities;* the other is the existence of *public
goods.*

Externalities occur when output or consumption of one party has an
effect on the welfare of another that is not reflected in the prices and
costs associated with the first activity. Thus, if the herbicide applied by
a farmer drifts to an urban area and damages urban shrubs or gardens, a negative externality has been imposed. If dogs kept as pets by
urban residents kill sheep or other domesticated livestock owned by
farmers, a negative externality in the other direction exists. In neither
case will the prices and costs of food and fiber production in such
locations correctly reflect the social costs or benefits of such activities.

Public goods exist when one person's enjoyment of those goods does
not diminish their consumption by another and when it is not possible
or economical to exclude a second individual from using them (as in
the case of a radio transmission). A beautiful sunset is one example, a
view of a well-tended field, a herd of cattle, and a flock of sheep are
additional examples. Private property rights cannot be made to reflect
the full social costs and returns associated with the production and
consumption of public goods.

The market failure framework, as advanced by Bator[2] and followed
generally in the literature, is usually based on three major assumptions. The first is that government actions are limited to establishing
the framework within which markets can operate, which includes
providing for property rights that can be bought and sold. The second

---

[1] Francis Bator, "The Simple Analytics of Welfare Maximization," *American Economic
Review* vol. 47 (March 1957) pp. 22–59.
[2] Francis Bator, "The Anatomy of Market Failure," *Quarterly Journal of Economics* vol.
72 (August 1958) pp. 351–379.

is that the other markets in the economy, including the capital markets that link time periods, are working perfectly. The third is that information about the future is perfect and that all decision makers have perfect foresight. When it can be demonstrated that markets do fail under such assumptions, the hypothesis can be advanced that government intervention may be desirable. However, more than the existence of market failure is needed to justify intervention; such failure is a necessary but not sufficient condition for intervention because additional investigation is required to determine whether government intervention will yield results superior to the nonintervention situation.[3] The point here is that in the market failure literature, government intervention is the end point of the analysis; the role of government generally is not a variable. Before that line of thought is developed here, externalities, public goods, and imperfect knowledge as applied to agricultural land will be discussed briefly.

Suppose that agricultural land near urban areas produces a good—food—and a service—open space. The definition of property rights will have a great deal to do with the relative importance that is attached to each. Under the competitive conditions that generally exist in agriculture, and if the farmer is not held responsible for the negative externalities he inflicts on others, the price he receives for placing food on the market will be less than the full social cost of producing it. If the urban dweller, in the enjoyment of open space, tramples on crops or damages livestock and does not compensate the farmer accordingly, this enjoyment is provided at less than its full social cost.

There seems to be little question that negative externalities do indeed exist in the fringes between urban and farming areas. The question may now be asked: Does the agricultural land market recognize and properly value externalities to their full extent? My answer is probably not. A pattern of development that tends to minimize the amount of fringe area can be expected to reduce negative externalities. Thus, developments that result in a patchwork of agricultural and nonagricultural land use are undesirable because they tend to increase these negative externalities.[4]

To my knowledge, the public good aspect of agriculture production

[3] Emery N. Castle, "The Market Mechanism, Externalities and Land Economics," *Journal of Farm Economics* vol. 47 (August 1965) pp. 542–556.

[4] Marion Clawson, *Suburban Land Conversion in the United States: An Economic and Governmental Process* (Baltimore, Md., Johns Hopkins University Press for Resources for the Future, 1971) chapter 9.

near urban areas has not been investigated to any great extent, even though the utility of open space in and near urban areas is well accepted. But the use of land for urban open space competes with agricultural production unless urban access is denied. To the extent that agricultural land yields public goods, the value of those goods will not be reflected in the price of the land.

While patchwork development will tend to increase negative externalities, it will provide more open space for urban residents in close proximity to their residences. Knowledge of the way these externalities and public goods are related in particular areas is of considerable value to planners and decision makers. Both externalities and public goods may prevent the agricultural land market from working perfectly, although it is not possible to state whether the land will be overvalued or undervalued because of these imperfections. The public goods provided by agricultural land and the negative externalities of agricultural production are enjoyed and borne by those in proximity to agricultural areas. Consequently, the tendency has been to look to local or state governments rather than to the federal government to correct or adjust for market imperfections. There are many variations in the way that local areas have recognized and have attempted to cope with such matters, including zoning, taxation, and the purchase of development rights. In contrast, most federal remedies (e.g., regulation of agricultural pesticides) are applied regardless of the location of agricultural production and are designed to treat externalities on a broad geographic base.

When the government is introduced as a variable, a market-oriented analysis will not suffice. Governments build roads, locate public schools, zone lands, and otherwise influence economic activity in a number of ways. There are almost always alternatives in the location of government facilities and some choices will create more "fringe areas" between urban and agricultural area than others. Clawson has noted that at any given time many urban areas have sufficient undeveloped land to provide for their needs far into the future.[5] Some land remains undeveloped for long periods because there is little inducement to develop it. Markets usually reflect government policies quite promptly and undesirable land development often is the result of a mixture of government action and market performance. Thus, patchwork development may be as much the result of government zoning and taxing policy as market failure.

[5] Ibid.

The rate of conversion of land from rural to urban uses is also subject to myriad demand and supply forces, with numerous distortions undoubtedly on both the demand and the supply side. The reservation price of land is influenced by taxation, capital costs, risk, and the life cycle of the farm family.[6] Speculation in land as well as property tax policies contributes to the existence of considerable undeveloped land in many urban areas.

Another major assumption underlying the market performance framework is that all other markets in the economy provide appropriate price incentives except for the one being studied. This includes those markets which relate decisions between and among time periods—the capital markets with interest rates serving as the reward for waiting and as the measure by which future returns should be discounted. Since land is a durable and long-lived asset, the performance of the capital market becomes crucial to an understanding of the performance of the agricultural land market.

In the preface to this volume, reference was made to the seminal article by Theodore W. Schultz entitled "The Declining Economic Importance of Agricultural Land." In the approximately three decades since the appearance of this article, the price of agricultural land in the United States has increased more rapidly than the general price level. If the market for agricultural land, including the related markets in the economy, such as the capital markets, is working perfectly, this increased real price would signify increasing scarcity of such land. Thus, it is useful to examine the question of whether the price of agricultural land accurately reflects its scarcity in agricultural use.

Rising real prices for agricultural land may reflect influences other than a scarcity of land for the production of food and fiber. Man does not live by bread alone and agricultural land is not held for the production of food and fiber alone. Real property, of which land is a part, plays an important role in the dynamics of our society and the U.S. economy. The rational person, motivated by potential economic gain, will hold land for at least two purposes. One is the contribution it will

[6] See Allan Schmid, *Converting Land from Rural to Urban Uses* (Baltimore, Md., Johns Hopkins University Press for Resources for the Future, 1968); Earl O. Heady, *Economics of Agricultural Production and Resource Use* (Englewood Cliffs, N.J., Prentice-Hall, 1952) chapter 14; and George E. Peterson, "Federal Tax Policy and Land Conversion at the Urban Fringe," George F. Break, ed., *Metropolitan Financing and Growth Management Policies: Principles and Practice* (Madison, Wis., University of Wisconsin Press, 1978) chapter 3.

make to income and this will be reflected in its rental value or its contribution to production. The other reason is the contribution land makes to net worth if the price of land increases more rapidly than other investments. But why, one may ask, would it do this unless the price of that which is being produced, say, food, is not also increasing more rapidly than the general price level? There are at least two reasons why this might happen.

If there is a demand for agricultural land in other uses, it will influence agricultural land prices. And if that demand is increasing more rapidly than the demand for land in agricultural uses, the price of agricultural land may rise more rapidly than if its sole potential use was in producing food and fiber. No doubt this has been happening to a considerable extent and much agricultural land is held with the idea that it may someday have value in a nonagricultural use. Yet the potential for such use cannot explain the significant increases in prices that have been experienced for all agricultural land.

There is another way that net worth may be enhanced. This is through the liabilities one has rather than one's assets. If the rate of interest is less than the rate of inflation, after allowance has been made for time preference, it is to one's advantage to hold debt during times of inflation. The purchase of real property—agricultural land—is one means by which debt can be acquired. So long as interest rates do not account fully for inflation, and if inflation is probable, the demand for assets which can be used to obtain debt can be expected to grow.

Research that Irving Hoch and I have been doing is designed to relate and measure the relative importance of these motives for purchasing agricultural land. We have used data for the entire United States and utilized the period from 1921 to 1978, which includes the great Depression as well as the inflationary period since World War II.

Our findings indicate that about 50 percent of the benefits derived from holding land during this period resulted from the contribution of land to income, with the other half of the benefit coming from increases in net worth or capital appreciation. Further, about two-thirds of the increase in net worth has resulted from decreases in the value of debt. We call this the inflationary effect. While further research is needed before these numerical results are accepted, we are confident that the influences we have identified and the directional effects of these influences are valid.

This research throws some light on the issue of agricultural land scarcity. It demonstrates that the real cost of land to the owner-operator has been substantially less than would be suggested by changes in the market price of agricultural land. Our data indicate that the real cost of land, relative to the cost of other items used in agricultural production, decreased from 1949 to 1960, increased from 1960 to 1972, and has declined from 1972 to 1978. While one cannot be confident of trends since 1972 because of the extreme volatility in prices of several items, the attractiveness of land as a farming investment since 1972 probably has not provided significant incentive for land-saving practices and technology to be adopted during that time period.

The third assumption, which underlies the market failure framework, that of perfect knowledge and perfect foresight, is especially troublesome to many in the case of agricultural land. The fear exists that the high incomes and government policies of the present generation will result in decisions which are land-using. Future generations may be more concerned with the adequacy of their food supply than they are with single-family residences with large lots, or superhighways. Thus, the price signals which exist may be myopic and give undue weight to present as contrasted with future needs.

It is not possible to address such a question adequately in principle or on the basis of reasoning alone. We know the future is uncertain, and, by definition, it is impossible to say what policies should be followed to optimize future welfare. There are some guidelines which can be suggested and such evidence as is available can be evaluated from that point of view.

One reason there is greater concern about the invalidity of the assumption of perfect knowledge in the case of agricultural land is that the future cost might be quite high if agricultural land does prove to be in short supply in the future. To the extent that land removed from agricultural production cannot be reclaimed except at a very high cost, such concerns are indeed valid. As will be detailed subsequently, it is not clear that the amount of agricultural land that has been lost or is likely to be lost for the remainder of this century is enough to affect significantly the capacity of the United States to produce food. Further, it is not clear that the cost of reclaiming all land "lost" to agricultural production would be high. For example, the production of vegetables in urban gardens has become significant in the United States and if the need arose could be expanded greatly.

Nevertheless, the fact remains that we do not have perfect foresight and the markets cannot be relied upon to predict the long-run future with precision. That is why conferences of the type reported on in this volume are important. They provide experts with an opportunity to evaluate market performance in the light of the best information that can be assembled. On the basis of such assessment, judgments can be reached as to whether government intervention is necessary to correct for market inadequacies, including inadequate or imperfect foresight. The preceding chapters need to be studied in that light.

The foregoing paragraphs on market performance and agricultural land make several points. First, there are numerous imperfections in the market for agricultural land. Local land markets may be affected by the existence of externalities and public goods. To the extent that such imperfections exist, and it is my observation and belief that they do, they constitute a significant and important policy problem at the state and local level. But the impact of local government policies— zoning, taxation, and the location of public facilities, including highways—makes it quite difficult to judge how markets would perform in the absence of such influences.

Distortions in the capital markets also have a most profound effect on the agricultural land market. As noted, interest rates have tended to underestimate inflation, which has made the holding of debt desirable. The purchase of agricultural land has been a means of acquiring debt; agricultural land has been a desirable asset and as a result the demand for agricultural land has increased over what it would otherwise have been.

## The Adequacy of Agricultural Land: Some Reflections on Public Policy

The papers presented at the conference were designed to illuminate the supply and demand conditions for agricultural land into the first decade of the next century. To do justice to this subject, it was necessary to consider the demand for food both domestically and internationally, and also assess the land base in the United States as well as the technology used in agricultural production.

It is probable that both the domestic and international demand for food will increase. The recent growth in agricultural exports is consistent with such a prediction and it is government policy to further expand such exports. Not only does this make farming and agribusiness more profitable, it also enhances the U.S. balance of payments and, to the extent such trade reflects comparative advantage, the welfare of importing countries may be increased. Except for short-lived exceptions, it has been the policy of recent administrations, as it is of the current one, to encourage agricultural exports. This encouragement is manifested in numerous ways, including promotion activities abroad by the U.S. Department of Agriculture.

What, then, are the factors that may influence the cost of agricultural production in the United States if exports continue to expand? The increased output will result from expansion at the extensive margin as well as from greater intensity on the land that is farmed. Cropland acreage increased during the 1970s and is probably as high at present as it has been at any time in this century. Even so, the use of other inputs has been increasing and productivity (the relation of total outputs to total inputs) has also improved.

As the papers in this volume indicate, there is uncertainty as to whether the rate of productivity increases that have been enjoyed in recent decades can be sustained. No doubt this will be much influenced by the level of public investment in research to improve agricultural productivity.

Recognition of the above variables and the uncertainty associated with each makes understandable the wide variation in current projections of cropland that is expected to be used during the remainder of this century. Because of these variations, it is prudent to reflect on the consequences if some of the more extreme projections should turn out to be correct. Those of the National Agricultural Lands Study call for a greater acreage of cropland than any others that have been made. As noted by Crosson in chapter 1, much land highly subject to erosion would be cropped under such assumptions. Such a development would undoubtedly be associated with significantly higher real costs for the production of food at the farm level, only part of which would be reflected in its price. Policy makers in the United States would then be faced with the consequences of the expanded exports, and the focus of the policy discussion would shift from the adequacy of agricultural land to (1) the possibility of increasing real cost of food production with higher food prices to the consumer, or (2) the extent to which the export price of agricultural foodstuffs fails to reflect the full real social costs of production.

Both of these questions are of national importance whether the extreme projections of the National Agricultural Lands Study are realized or not. The first question calls attention once again to the need to make social investment in agricultural research an integral part of national agricultural policy. With respect to the second, there is little doubt that the market fails to reflect the full environmental costs of agricultural production. This has long been recognized in the literature, but the policies proposed and adopted have not been successful in internalizing these environmental costs so that they will be fully reflected in the cost of foodstuffs. There is substantial renewed interest in this most difficult problem. Additional attention by policy makers and researchers is fully justified; this problem should command a high priority, especially since it is official policy to expand agricultural exports and because of the growing magnitude of the problem.

One possible development that could have a most significant effect on agricultural land use and the cost of production of foodstuffs at the farm level was not explored in depth in the conference. This is the use of agricultural crops for the production of alcohol fuels. The programs and goals now provided for in the law, with enormous government subsidy, call for production of 10 billion gallons of ethanol by 1990. If corn is the feedstock, as presently indicated, this level of ethanol production would require 100 million metric tons of corn, one-half of the record crop of 1979 and almost 60 percent of 1980's lower production. Use of corn for ethanol production on this scale would greatly increase pressure on the nation's land and other agricultural resources. Indeed, the requirement for additional land would dwarf the likely loss of land to nonagricultural uses in the 1980s. Those who are concerned about the pressures being placed on our agricultural land resources would do well to ponder the implications of the presently legislated ethanol program. It is important, however, to contrast the resource impact of the full development called for in this program and that assumed by Abel in chapter 3; the former is substantially greater than the latter.

With the above as background, the issue of the adequacy of agricultural land can be discussed more fruitfully. There is considerable discrepancy among the projections as to the amount of agricultural land that will be converted to nonagricultural uses in the future, but it is possible to say some things about the probable impact of the loss on agricultural output. If exports are increased so much as to require the cropland acreage assumed by the National Agricultural Lands Study, it is unlikely that slowing the rate of conversion by any amount would be significant when evaluated against the social costs of policies that would be required. (Brubaker's pessimistic evaluation of the effectiveness of past policies is relevant here.)

The following data may be helpful in reaching a judgment as to whether reducing the rate of conversion of cropland to nonagricultural uses can be a means of increasing agricultural output. It is estimated that the annual loss of cropland to nonagricultural uses amounted, at a maximum, to 675,000 acres per year from 1967 to 1975 (Brewer and Boxley, chapter 4). If this annual loss were reduced by one-half over, say, 1977 to 2005, and were added to the cropland base in 1977, it would amount to less than 3 percent of the cropland base in 1977, which was 413 million acres. A 50 percent reduction in the rate of conversion would amount to 337,500 acres annually, which is about one-tenth of 1 percent of the 1977 cropland base. Projections of annual yield increases for the coming decades are in the 1 percent to 2 percent range (see Crosson, chapter 1). It follows that only a very small change in yields per acre is needed to equal in significance a very large change in the rate of conversion of cropland to nonagricultural uses. Thus, I am not persuaded that the loss of agricultural land to nonagricultural uses is a matter of major national concern. Nevertheless, as noted above, analysis of the problem does make explicit issues which deserve the most serious consideration.

It is also clear that agricultural land use is of major importance in many communities. Land use control is one of the principal means many local jurisdictions have of directing their destiny. The provision of open space, the kind and location of development desired, as well as numerous problems of public finance are all related to land use considerations. Perhaps one of the major contributions of this volume will be to permit these problems to be addressed without the added complication of great concern for the adequacy of agricultural land as a factor in meeting long-term domestic and foreign demands for food and fiber.

The Johns Hopkins University Press
Baltimore, Maryland 21218

# Index